Al-Qaida in Afghanistan

Since 9/11, al-Qaida has become one of the most infamous and widely discussed terrorist organizations in the world, with affiliates spread across the globe. However, little known are the group's activities within Afghanistan itself, something that Anne Stenersen examines in this book. Using an array of unique primary sources, she presents an alternative narrative of al-Qaida's goals and strategies prior to 9/11. She argues that al-Qaida's actions were not just an ideological expression of religious fanaticism and violent anti-Americanism, but that they were actually far more practical and organized, with a more revolutionary and Middle Eastern–focused agenda than previously thought. Through Stenersen's analysis, we see how al-Qaida employed a dual strategy: with a small section focused on staging international terrorist attacks, but at the same time with a larger part dedicated to building a resilient and cohesive organization that would ultimately serve as a vanguard for future Islamist revolutions.

Anne Stenersen (M.Phil., PhD) is a Senior Research Fellow at the Norwegian Defence Research Establishment (FFI) in Norway. With an academic background rooted in history, Arabic and Middle Eastern studies, she has conducted research on militant Islamism, with a focus on CBRN (chemical, biological, radiological, and nuclear) terrorism, al-Qaida and the Taliban.

Al-Qaida in Afghanistan

ANNE STENERSEN
Norwegian Defence Research Establishment

CAMBRIDGE
UNIVERSITY PRESS

CAMBRIDGE
UNIVERSITY PRESS

University Printing House, Cambridge CB2 8BS, United Kingdom

One Liberty Plaza, 20th Floor, New York, NY 10006, USA

477 Williamstown Road, Port Melbourne, VIC 3207, Australia

4843/24, 2nd Floor, Ansari Road, Daryaganj, Delhi – 110002, India

79 Anson Road, #06-04/06, Singapore 079906

Cambridge University Press is part of the University of Cambridge.

It furthers the University's mission by disseminating knowledge in the pursuit of education, learning, and research at the highest international levels of excellence.

www.cambridge.org
Information on this title: www.cambridge.org/9781107427761
DOI: 10.1017/9781139871501

First published 2017

Printed in the United Kingdom by Clays, St Ives plc

A catalogue record for this publication is available from the British Library.

Library of Congress Cataloging-in-Publication Data
Names: Stenersen, Anne, author.
Title: Al-Qaida in Afghanistan / Anne Stenersen, Norwegian
Defence Research Establishment.
Description: Cambridge, United Kingdom; New York, NY:
Cambridge University Press, 2017. |
Includes bibliographical references and index.
Identifiers: LCCN 2016059491 | ISBN 9781107075139 (hardback) |
ISBN 9781107427761 (paperback)
Subjects: LCSH: Qaida (Organization) | Taliban. | Terrorists – Afghanistan. |
Terrorism – Afghanistan. | Terrorism – Religious aspects – Islam.
Classification: LCC HV6433.A32.Q2 S74 2017 | DDC 363.32509581–dc23
LC record available at https://lccn.loc.gov/2016059491

ISBN 978-1-107-07513-9 Hardback
ISBN 978-1-107-42776-1 Paperback

Contents

Maps and Tables

Acknowledgments

There are a number of people and institutions who deserve thanks. Let me start with the institutions. The book project would not have been possible without the support of my employer, the Norwegian Defence Research Establishment (FFI). In particular, I thank the Director of FFI's Analysis Division, Espen Skjelland, and research director Espen Berg-Knutsen for their support and encouragement.

A huge thanks also to institutions that assisted me during fieldwork in Afghanistan, Pakistan, and the United States during the period of 2009–2015. I express my sincere gratitude to the Centre for Conflict and Peace Studies (CAPS), and its former director Mr. Hekmat Karzai, who hosted me during fieldwork in Kabul in 2009. Thanks also to the kind staff at the Afghanistan Center at Kabul University (ACKU) who helped me locate a number of rare historical sources from the 1980s and 1990s. In Pakistan, I am indebted to Mr. Saifullah Mehsud at the Federally Administered Tribal Areas (FATA) Research Center (FRC), who generously hosted me during research in Islamabad in 2015, Mr. Mohammed Amir Rana at the Pakistan Institute for Peace Studies (PIPS), The National Library of Pakistan, and the *Dawn* Newspaper archives in Karachi. In the United States, a huge thanks goes to the Conflict Records Resource Center (CRRC) at National Defense University in Washington, DC and its director, Mrs. Lorry C. Fenner, for hosting me several times during the period of 2011–2015. The CRRC's collection of internal al-Qaida documents is truly unique and this book would not have been possible without it.

Furthermore, I cannot express how thankful I am to the Afghans and Pakistanis I met and interviewed during my fieldwork, who showed me immense hospitality and who generously shared their unique local insights and knowledge with me. Due to the political sensitivity of the topics treated in this book, and the controversies my arguments might create in some circles – although I only aspire to present the truth – I have decided to not mention your names. Just know that I am extremely grateful for your contributions.

Finally, I am indebted to research colleagues inside and outside Norway who contributed to the project with their huge knowledge and insights on al-Qaida, jihadism, terrorism, Afghanistan, Pakistan, and the Middle East. I am most of all indebted to my long-time colleagues and friends at the FFI's Terrorism Research Project: Brynjar Lia, Thomas Hegghammer, Petter Nesser, and Truls Hallberg Tønnessen, who encouraged and inspired me on a daily basis. Special thanks also go to Jacob Ravndal and Erik Skare for fruitful comments and discussions and Henrik Gråtrud for his meticulous work reading and summarizing Arabic primary sources. There are many others I should thank who contributed in various ways: Noman Benotman, Bette Dam, Leah Farrall, Will McCants and Prakhar Sharma, in addition to those of you who requested to stay anonymous. Last but not least, I thank my friends and family for their encouragement and moral support. A special thanks to Thomas G. S., for everything.

Any errors of analysis or fact are, of course, my responsibility.

Note on Transliteration

The transliteration of Arabic words into English has been simplified by making no distinction between emphatic and nonemphatic consonants, and between long and short vowels. When *ayn* and *hamza* appear at the beginning of a word, they have been omitted. In other positions they are represented by the signs ' and '. Arabic names follow the same transliteration rules, except for names that already have a widely used spelling in English (e.g., Osama bin Laden). English names and words occurring in Arabic texts have been transliterated back to their original form (e.g., land cruiser not land kruzar).

Note on Sources

The main sources used for this study are internal documents from the al-Qaida network. These documents were found in Arab camps and safe houses in Afghanistan after the fall of the Taliban regime in November 2001. Most of the documents were captured by the US military and transferred to the US Department of Defense, where they were stored in a classified database known as Harmony. Since 2005, a selection of the documents have been de-classified and made available to academic researchers through the Combating Terrorism Center (CTC) at West Point, New York, and the Conflict Records Research Center (CRRC) at the National Defense University in Washington, DC. Another collection of internal al-Qaida documents were retrieved by journalists who were present in Afghanistan to cover the US-led invasion in late 2001. A small number of these documents were later paraphrased or published in full in Western newspapers.[1] A third collection of al-Qaida documents have been made available to the public after being presented as evidence in court cases against suspected terrorists in the United States.[2] In sum, these collections amount to several thousand pages of internal al-Qaida correspondence and other written material affiliated with al-Qaida including diaries, battlefield reports, camp schedules, lists of al-Qaida members, meeting notes, and personal letters.

A second, important source used in this study are memoirs by Arab, Afghan, and Pakistani individuals close to the events. They include

---

[1] Alan Cullison, "Inside al-Qaeda's hard drive: Budget squabbles, baby pictures, office rivalries – and the path to 9/11," *The Atlantic Monthly*, September 2004.

[2] In particular, the trials against Khalid al-Fawwaz in Southern District of New York (2015); *United States v. Babar Ahmad* (2014), and *United States v. Arnaout* (2002).

jihadists, former Taliban officials, journalists, and Pakistani officials.[3] Some of these memoirs have only been used by researchers to a limited degree before – including Fadil Harun's *War on Islam: The Story of Fadil Harun* and Abu al-Shukara al-Hindukushi's *My Memoirs from Kabul to Baghdad*.[4] The former is written by an al-Qaida veteran who served as al-Qaida's secretary from 1998. The latter is written by an Egyptian jihadist who served on various frontlines with Arabs in Afghanistan, and who eventually joined al-Qaida in 1999 or 2000. Other memoirs have also been consulted including Vahid Mojdeh's *Five Years Under Taliban Sovereignty,* Mustafa Hamid's book series *Chatter on the World's Rooftop,* and Ayman al-Zawahiri's memoir, *Knights under the Prophet's Banner*.[5]

A third, and arguably controversial source used in this study is a collection of classified memoranda from the US prison at Guantánamo Bay, Cuba known as *The Guantánamo Files*. They were leaked to the public in 2011 by *Wikileaks*.[6] The memoranda summarize US intelligence about each of the prisoners detained at Guantánamo in order to recommend continued detention or release. Part of the intelligence is based on information extracted from Guantánamo prisoners under duress, and in some

---

[3] Including, but not limited to, Abu Zubaydah, *The Abu Zubaydah Diaries, vol. 1–6,* translated to English by the Federal Bureau of Investigation, U.S. Department of Justice, published by *Al-Jazeera,* December 3, 2013; Malika El Aroud, *Les soldats de lumière [Soldiers of light],* Dépôt légal: D/2003/9625/2, Imprimé en Belgique; Mustafa Hamid, *tharthara fi saqaf al-alam* vol. 1–12 (Place and publisher unknown, year unknown); Jamal Isma'il, *bin ladin wa al-jazira wa ... ana* (Place unknown: Dar al-Huriya, 2001); Vahid Mojdeh, *Afghanistan wa panj sal sultah taliban [Afghanistan and five years under Taliban sovereignty],* 2nd ed. (Tehran: Nashreney, 1382 H. [2003]); Wakil Ahmad Mutawakil, *Afghanistan aw Taliban [Afghanistan and the Taliban]* (place and publisher unknown, 1384 h. [2005]); S. Iftikhar Murshed, *Afghanistan: The Taliban years* (London: Bennett and Bloom, 2006); Jean Sasson, N. bin Laden and O. bin Laden, *Growing up Bin Laden: Osama's wife and son take us inside their secret world* (Oxford: Oneworld, 2009); Abu Mus'ab al-Suri, "*muqabala ma'a sahifat al-ra'i al-amm al-kuwaytiyya,*" [transcript of Abu Mus'ab al-Suri's interview with journalist Majid al-Ali in Kabul, Afghanistan, 18 March 1999], unpublished, courtesy Brynjar Lia; Abdul Salam Zaeef, *My life with the Taliban* (London: Hurst, 2010).

[4] With the notable exception of Nelly Lahoud's excellent study of Fadil Harun's memoir. Nelly Lahoud, *Beware of Imitators: al-Qa`ida through the lens of its confidential secretary* (West Point, NY: Combating Terrorism Center, 2012); Fadil Harun [Fadil Abdallah Muhammad], *al-harb ala al-islam: qissat fadil harun,* vol. 1 (Place and publisher unknown, 2009); Abu al-Shukara al-Hindukushi, *mudhakkarati min kabul ila baghdad,* part 1–9 (Place and publisher unknown, 2007), accessed February 5, 2016. https://archive.org/details/@alhindkoshi.

[5] Ayman al-Zawahiri, *fursan taht rayat al-nabi* (Place unknown: Minbar al-tawhid waljihad, 2001).

[6] "WikiLeaks reveals secret files on all Guantánamo prisoners," *Wikileaks,* accessed July 31, 2012,. http://wikileaks.ch/gitmo/

cases, by use of what former US President George W. Bush Jr. termed "enhanced interrogation techniques."[7] However, *The Guantánamo Files* are not raw interrogation reports, but intelligence products based on multiple sources of information including, but not limited to, prisoner interrogations. In spite of the moral and legal predicaments, *The Guantánamo Files* can hardly be ignored when studying the history of al-Qaida in Afghanistan. I have used them here to cross-check other information, to pinpoint locations of Arab training camps and guesthouses, and to fill in certain gaps in the history of al-Qaida in Afghanistan that were not covered in other sources, but that were extensively covered in *The Guantánamo Files* – for example, details about al-Qaida's recruitment procedures in the Gulf in 1999–2001.

A fourth source are declassified US documents maintained by the *National Security Archive* at George Washington University. The archive includes a large collection of diplomatic cables, primarily between the US Embassy in Islamabad and the US Department of State in the period 1994–2001, as well as other documents concerning the relationship between the United States and the Taliban.[8]

A fifth type of source used for this study is interviews with Afghan, Pakistani, and Arab individuals close to the events. Most of the interviews were conducted during the author's fieldwork in Kabul in 2009. Many of the interviewees were former Taliban officials, but representatives of other parties were also included. I have decided to anonymize all interviewees, because some of them still reside in volatile areas of the world and may or may not wish to be associated with the topics discussed in this book.

The sixth, major type of source used for this book is journalistic sources from the Middle East and Pakistan. Two archives in particular were consulted – the electronic archives of the Arabic daily *al-Hayat*, and the English-language archives of *Dawn Newspaper Group* in Karachi, Pakistan. *Al-Hayat* is a Saudi-owned international daily newspaper based in London and Beirut, and it is one of the largest circulated newspapers in the Middle East. *Al-Hayat* was selected because it covered the Taliban

---

[7] Several Human Rights organizations have condemned the use of "Enhanced interrogation techniques," arguing that the techniques are equal to torture. United States President Obama in 2009 supported the notion that techniques such as waterboarding amount to torture. "Obama: 'I believe waterboarding was torture, and it was a mistake'," *The Guardian*, April 30, 2009.

[8] "The September 11th Sourcebooks," *The National Security Archive*, accessed February 24, 2011, www.gwu.edu/~nsarchiv/NSAEBB/sept11/

regime period in Afghanistan and the role of Arab fighters in some detail, and because its journalists had relatively good access to insider sources, including sources close to or familiar with al-Qaida and Taliban's leadership. At the time, *al-Hayat* conducted several phone interviews with Mullah Omar and other Taliban representatives, as opposed to Western media that tended to rely more heavily on information from US government officials and other secondary sources. The *Dawn* archive contained articles written by Pakistani journalists with direct access to Taliban officials and other Afghan sources, in addition to invaluable information about the regional context in which al-Qaida and the Taliban were operating.

In sum, these primary sources represent a wide variety of perspectives. They represent al-Qaida's official and unofficial communications. They represent the personal accounts of militants from inside and outside al-Qaida. They also represent the perspectives of the US intelligence and diplomatic communities, and of Middle Eastern and Pakistani politicians, security officials, and observers. Each source tells the story through the lens of his or her own worldview, and since I sometimes rely on one or a few sources only, my empirical chapters are bound to contain mistakes and inaccuracies. However, I believe that the story of al-Qaida in Afghanistan is still a story worth telling, and that my overall analysis – which is the synthesis of information from a wide range of sources – is a valuable contribution to the existing literature on al-Qaida.

Maps

MAP 1. Afghanistan.

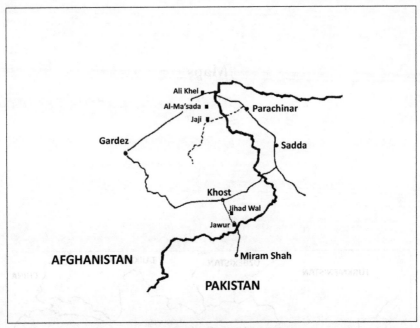

MAP 2. Jaji base and surroundings.

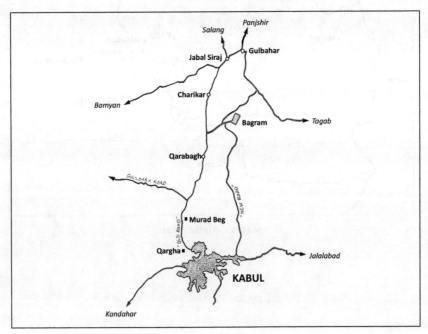

MAP 3. The Kabul front, 1996–2001.

Introduction

Al-Qaida's first recruitment video was issued in early 2001.[1] It showed footage from al-Qaida's training camps in Afghanistan. It showed groups of masked men marching in the desert, raising the black banner of the Prophet. It showed the men running obstacle courses in the day and jumping through rings of fire at night. It told the story of how two of these men, armed with nothing but a glassfiber boat and a pack of explosives, had destroyed one of the mightiest warships in the world, the USS Cole. Joining al-Qaida sure looked exciting, at least judging from the content of their propaganda.

In reality it was a rather tedious process. All recruits arriving in Kandahar from mid-2000 had to register at the Office of Mujahidin Affairs. They had to fill out a five-page form stating their nickname, country, hometown, date of birth, and mother tongue. There were questions about education, occupation, and level of religious knowledge. Recruits had to detail the circumstances of their leaving for Afghanistan, previous militant training, and their goals for the future. They had to sign the form accepting a list of "regulations and requirements" for attending training.[2] Then, they had to move to the guesthouse and wait for an appropriate training course to start. The initial process could take days or weeks.

Literally thousands of books have been written about al-Qaida since September 11, 2001, when the group carried out one of the deadliest

---

[1] *The Destruction of the American Destroyer USS Cole*, al-Sahab, 2001, accessed via *FFI's Jihadi Video Database*, Kjeller, Norway, videos no. 647 and 648.

[2] AQ-PMPR-D-001-837, "Al-Qa'eda recruitment and new personnel forms," April 25, 2001, Conflict Records Resource Center, Washington, DC.

terrorist attacks in history of the United States. Yet, there is one particular aspect of al-Qaida that remains understudied – namely, the history of al-Qaida in Afghanistan. New primary sources suggest that al-Qaida was involved in a range of activities in Afghanistan not immediately connected to international terrorism. It organized the influx of foreign volunteers to Afghanistan. It facilitated training for other militant groups. It sent some of its most senior commanders to the frontline north of Kabul to fight for the Taliban. This does not add up with the standard image of al-Qaida as an international terrorist network bent on destroying the United States, or at least forcing it to change its policies toward the Middle East. It appears there are still gaps in our knowledge about al-Qaida, and subsequently, about the broader phenomenon of militant Islamism of which al-Qaida is a part.

This book explores the following paradox: If al-Qaida was an international terrorist network bent on destroying the United States, why did it spend so many resources on training and fighting in Afghanistan? The answer is that al-Qaida in 1996–2001 followed a dual strategy. Although a small part of al-Qaida carried out international terrorist attacks, the larger part was involved in building a resilient organization. Having a strong organization would be helpful if the United States decided to invade Afghanistan, but this was not the main goal. Rather, bin Laden envisioned that the organization he was building in Afghanistan would play a crucial part in the next stage of al-Qaida's battle, which was to oust Arab dictators in the Middle East and install Islamic regimes in their place. Al-Qaida did not believe that revolution in the Arab world would happen by itself. Al-Qaida saw itself, from the beginning of its existence, as a revolutionary vanguard whose main task was to train and educate cadre for the Islamic world.

In other words, I argue that al-Qaida was more bureaucratic and had a more revolutionary, Middle Eastern-focused agenda than previously assumed. I argue that al-Qaida's goal was to establish Islamic rule across the Muslim world, but with the Middle East as its main priority. I derive these findings from a detailed case-study of al-Qaida's actions and priorities in Afghanistan over a period of thirteen years – from 1988 to 2001, using al-Qaida's internal documents as a main source. This book differs from previous studies of al-Qaida, that tend to interpret al-Qaida's goals and strategies based on a few, select primary sources – such as bin Laden's public statements and interviews – or a few, select actions – such as the 9/11 attacks.

The findings presented here have three main implications. First, it has implications on how we understand al-Qaida's strategy. Today there are two dominant and irreconcilable interpretations of the strategic rationale behind 9/11. One camp argues that the purpose of 9/11 was to drag the United States into war in Afghanistan. The other camp argues that the purpose of 9/11 was to make the United States crumble and collapse. Both these views represent thoughts and desires of bin Laden at the time of 9/11 but none of them accurately describes al-Qaida's pre-9/11 strategy. Al-Qaida's strategies were never fixed. They were constantly adjusted to make use of opportunities that arose. I argue that at the time of 9/11, bin Laden did not know how the United States would react. He envisioned a range of scenarios, from US collapse to a full-scale US invasion of Afghanistan. He was hoping for the first, but he did not rule out the second. When the United States decided to invade Afghanistan and destroy the Taliban regime, al-Qaida had to adjust its strategy accordingly. When the United States made the ill-advised decision to invade Iraq in 2003, al-Qaida again adjusted its strategy. The ability to adapt, to pursue short- and long-term goals, and to pursue multiple strategies at the same time are core characteristics of al-Qaida's strategic behavior.

Second, the findings presented in this book have implications for how we understand al-Qaida. This book takes a clear, and perhaps controversial, stance in that ubiquitous debate about what al-Qaida actually *is*: Is it an organization, a network, or an ideology? Does it have a fixed membership or not? I argue that al-Qaida was not only an organization with a clearly defined hierarchy and membership. It saw organization building as a central part of its strategy – at least prior to 9/11.

Third, the findings have implications for how we theorize jihadism and militant Islamism. The findings suggest that international terrorism against Western targets is a temporary strategy subject to change. I, therefore, question the usefulness of labels such as "global jihadism" to describe al-Qaida's ideology and rationale for fighting. I believe a different categorization is needed, at least if the purpose is to understand the strategic behavior of militant Islamist actors. I will not present a new theoretical model of militant Islamism in this book, but I believe my case study can serve as a starting point for such a theorizing in the future.

Some readers might wonder why I wrote a book about al-Qaida pre-2001, if the purpose is to understand modern militant Islamism. Why not write a book about the Islamic State in Iraq and Syria (ISIS) instead? ISIS is a more contemporary phenomenon and is certainly viewed as a more urgent threat to the West. The answer is simple. At the time of finishing this book, ISIS had existed for three years. Al-Qaida had existed for almost thirty years. By studying the history of al-Qaida over time and in a confined geographical area, I aim to identify and explain changes in al-Qaida's strategic behavior and, ultimately, lay the groundwork for theorizing on when and why militant Islamists change their strategic priorities over time.

There are several things that his book is not. This is not a book about the Taliban or about Afghanistan in general. It looks at Afghanistan and Taliban through the eyes of the Arab militants who spent time there in the 1980s and 1990s. It sheds light on some of the decision-making processes of the Taliban, but it is not a complete analysis of the Taliban's political behavior. Thus I will not answer questions such as: "Why did the Taliban refuse to expel bin Laden?" or "To what extent was the Taliban regime complicit in the 9/11 attacks?" However, I will discuss certain aspects of the relationship between al-Qaida and the Taliban.[3] I will argue that the Taliban regime actively supported al-Qaida's training camps in Afghanistan and allowed for Arabs to volunteer fighting on the Taliban's frontlines, because this is amply documented in the primary sources reviewed in this study. Moreover, I will argue that the Taliban had a *laissez-faire* attitude toward bin Laden's suspected involvement in terrorism, because this is also fairly well documented. However, I stop short of concluding that the Taliban was somehow complicit in bin Laden's international crimes. This would be beyond the purpose of this book, which is to tell the history of al-Qaida in Afghanistan and to theorize on al-Qaida's strategies pre-9/11.

Moreover, this is not a book about al-Qaida's development after 2001. I limit myself here to studying al-Qaida's strategies prior to 9/11, both due to space limitations and because the US-led invasion of Afghanistan brought about a fundamental change in al-Qaida's strategic behavior. After 2001, al-Qaida abandoned the strategy of building strong bases on the periphery of the Muslim world – in countries like Sudan and Afghanistan. Instead, al-Qaida established "franchises" in the center. These franchises were not statelike entities with large territorial control, but insurgent groups that were fighting a central government for control

[3] For a more thorough discussion of the al-Qaida–Taliban relationship, and in particular the question of why the Taliban refused to expel bin Laden from Afghanistan, even when faced with an existensial threat, please consult author's PhD dissertation from 2012. The main argument is that the Taliban protected bin Laden because they believed the domestic controversies caused by his expulsion would be more harmful to the Taliban than the international pressure. Anne Stenersen, *Brothers in Jihad: Explaining the relationship between al-Qaida and the Taliban, 1996–2001* (PhD dissertation, University of Oslo, 2012).

over population and territory. In the epilogue, I briefly discuss these post-2001 developments, which may serve as a starting point for further study. Al-Qaida's strategic behavior post-2001 merits separate treatment beyond the scope of this book.

EXISTING LITERATURE

Existing literature on al-Qaida in Afghanistan can roughly be divided in two categories: Literature on al-Qaida,[4] and literature on Afghanistan and the Taliban.[5] The two topics have traditionally been studied within different academic disciplines. Al-Qaida has been treated within Middle Eastern and terrorism studies, whereas the Taliban has been dealt with within history and Asian studies. After the US-led invasion of Afghanistan

---

[4] Michael Scheuer [Anonymous], *Through our enemies' eyes: Osama bin Laden, radical Islam, and the future of America* (Washington DC: Brassey's, 2003); Peter Bergen, *Holy War, Inc.: Inside the secret world of Osama bin Laden*, 4th ed. (London: Phoenix, 2003); Rohan Gunaratna, *Inside al Qaeda: Global network of terror* (New York: Berkley, 2003); Jason Burke, *Al Qaeda: The true story of radical Islam* (London: Penguin, 2004); Steve Coll, *Ghost wars: The secret history of the CIA, Afghanistan, and bin Laden, from the Soviet invasion to September 10, 2001* (New York: Penguin Press, 2004); Thomas Hegghammer, *Jihad in Saudi Arabia: Violence and pan-Islamism since 1979* (Cambridge: Cambridge University Press, 2010); Peter Bergen, *The Osama bin Laden I know: An oral history of al-Qaeda's leader* (New York: Simon & Schuster, 2006); Abdel Bari Atwan, *The secret history of al-Qa'ida* (London: Saqi Books, 2006); Lawrence Wright, *The looming tower: Al-Qaeda and the road to 9/11* (New York: Knopf, 2006); Brynjar Lia, *Architect of global jihad: The life of al-Qaida strategist Abu Mus'ab al-Suri* (New York: Columbia University Press, 2008); Camille Tawil, *Brothers in arms: The story of al-Qa'ida and the Arab jihadists* (London: Saqi Books, 2010); Michael Scheuer, *Osama bin Laden* (New York: Oxford, 2011).

[5] Peter Marsden, *The Taliban: War, religion and the new order in Afghanistan* (London: Zed Books, 1998); William Maley, ed., *Fundamentalism reborn? Afghanistan and the Taliban* (London: Hurst, 1998); Michael Griffin, *Reaping the whirlwind: The Taliban movement in Afghanistan* (London: Pluto Press, 2001); M. J. Gohari, *The Taliban: Ascent to power* (Karachi: Oxford University Press, 2001); Ahmed Rashid, *Taliban: Islam, oil and the new great game in central Asia* (London: Tauris, 2002); Neamatollah Nojumi, *The rise of the Taliban in Afghanistan: Mass mobilization, civil war, and the future of the region* (New York: Palgrave, 2002); Barnett R. Rubin, *The Fragmentation of Afghanistan: State formation and collapse in the international system*, 2nd ed. (New Haven: Yale University Press, 2002); Gilles Dorronsoro, *Revolution unending: Afghanistan 1979 to the present* (London: Hurst, 2005); Antonio Giustozzi, *Koran, Kalashnikov and laptop: The neo-Taliban insurgency in Afghanistan* (London: Hurst, 2007); Robert D. Crews and Amin Tarzi, *The Taliban and the crisis of Afghanistan* (Cambridge, MA: Harvard University Press, 2008); James Fergusson, *Taliban: The unknown enemy* (Cambridge, MA: Da Capo Press, 2010); Alex Strick van Linschoten and Felix Kuehn, *An enemy we created: The myth of the Taliban/Al Qaeda merger in Afghanistan, 1970–2010* (London: Hurst, 2012); Vahid Brown and Don Rassler, *Fountainhead of jihad: The Haqqani nexus, 1973–2012* (London: Hurst, 2013).

in 2001, al-Qaida and Taliban have also been studied within the insurgency and counterinsurgency literature, but these books rarely cover the period prior to 2001.[6]

Studies of the Taliban regime in the period of 1996–2001 have tended to focus on macro- and mesolevel dynamics. For example, Ahmed Rashid's account of the Taliban from 2000 continued to pursue the classical paradigm of the "Great Game" – that Afghanistan's history is shaped by external actors and that the Taliban, to some extent at least, was a product of the Pakistani Inter-Services Intelligence (ISI).[7] Newer studies, for example, Dorronsoro's book on the modern history of Afghanistan from 2004, point to domestic factors, such as tribes, culture, and ethnicities as drivers for the rise of the Taliban.[8] These studies are supplemented by literature that analyzes the impact of Taliban rule on the microlevel (i.e., village and personal).[9]

Common to most Taliban-focused literature is the omission or simplification of the impact of Arab militants in Afghanistan. This may be justified by the fact that the Arabs played a marginal role in Afghan society. The Arabs were small in number and largely kept to themselves. They had their own housing complexes, training camps and fighting units, with relatively sparse interaction with the local population. However, it is beyond doubt that the presence of Osama bin Laden and al-Qaida in Afghanistan played a direct role in shaping the history of the region. Bin Laden's presence in Afghanistan was the main justification for the US-led invasion of the country and the toppling of the Taliban regime in 2001. The Taliban's decision to host bin Laden in Afghanistan prior to 2001 continues to haunt the movement today – the fear that al-Qaida might return to a Taliban-controlled Afghanistan is, arguably, the *raison d'être* for continued international military presence in the country. The Afghanistan-focused literature acknowledges that the Taliban's decision to protect bin Laden in 1996–2001 was a fatal one. And yet,

---

[6] See, for example, Seth G. Jones, *Counterinsurgency in Afghanistan* (Santa Monica, CA: RAND Corporation, 2008); David Kilcullen, *The accidental guerrilla: Fighting small wars in the midst of a big one* (London: Hurst, 2009).

[7] Ahmed Rashid, *Taliban: Militant Islam, oil and fundamentalism in Central Asia* (New Haven: Yale University Press, 2000). For a classical account of the "great game," see Peter Hopkirk, *The great game: The struggle for empire in central Asia* (New York: Kodansha, 1992).

[8] Dorronsoro, *Revolution unending*; see also Crews and Tarzi, *The Taliban and the crisis of Afghanistan*, 59–89.

[9] See, for example, Kristian Berg Harpviken, *Social networks and migration in wartime Afghanistan* (Basingstoke, UK: Palgrave Macmillan, 2009).

the background for the decision has rarely been subjected to close scrutiny, the main reason probably being the lack of insider sources to the decision-making processes within the Taliban. A dominant narrative is thus that bin Laden was protected by a group of "hardliners" within the Taliban.

Al-Qaida-focused literature contains several rich and detailed accounts of al-Qaida's history in Afghanistan. However, most of the literature sees al-Qaida as an international terrorist network bent on attacking the United States. There has been a tendency to look on all of al-Qaida's activities in Afghanistan in this light. For example, the literature describes al-Qaida's killing of Ahmed Shah Massoud on September 9, 2001 as a "preparation" for the 9/11 attacks, rather than seeing it in its proper local context.[10] A different interpretation, which will be presented in Chapter 7 of this book, is that Massoud's assassination was a special operation behind enemy lines, designed to give the Taliban a strategic advantage in the war. Moreover, the literature gives disproportionate attention to al-Qaida's anti-American ideology and activities related to international terrorism – failing to see the broader aspects of its ideology and activities in Afghanistan. While the Taliban-focused literature rarely consults Arabic primary sources, al-Qaida-focused literature often fails to see al-Qaida as part of a local, Afghan context.

As a result, the existing literature represents a simplified understanding of al-Qaida's history in Afghanistan. With a few notable exceptions, discussions of al-Qaida in Afghanistan are seldom based on systematic use of Arabic, Pashto, and Persian primary sources.[11] In contrast, this book uses a range of primary sources that were previously not accessible to researchers, including a collection of thousands of internal al-Qaida documents. It contributes to existing perspectives on al-Qaida in Afghanistan by explaining the history from al-Qaida's point of view, as opposed to previous books that see history through the eyes of al-Qaida outsiders – the Taliban, other Arabs in Afghanistan, the Pakistanis, or Western observers. This book analyzes al-Qaida's goals and strategies on al-Qaida's own terms, using al-Qaida's own definitions as a starting point.

---

[10] See, for example, Tawil, *Brothers in arms*, 172; van Linschoten and Kuehn, *An enemy we created*, 209.

[11] There are some exceptions such as: Lia, *Architect of global jihad;* Tawil, *Brothers in arms;* van Linschoten and Kuehn, *An enemy we created;* Brown and Rassler, *Fountainhead of jihad;* Mustafa Hamid and Leah Farrall, *The Arabs at war in Afghanistan* (London: Hurst, 2015).

AL-QAIDA'S GOALS

There is no consensus in the literature on what al-Qaida's goals and strategies are. Al-Qaida's goals have been described broadly – to establish a worldwide Islamic caliphate – and narrowly – expelling American military troops from Saudi Arabia. On a different level, al-Qaida's goals have been described as political and rational – make the United States disengage from the Middle East – to irrational – that mass-violence framed as holy war or *jihad* is somehow a goal in itself.

This study aims to analyze al-Qaida on its own terms. Thus I use al-Qaida's own internal documents as a starting point, in order to see how they perceive their own goals and strategies. Al-Qaida's foundation charter from 1988 stated that al-Qaida's general goals are "to establish truth, get rid of evil and establish an Islamic nation" and the methods are fourfold:

1. Spread the sentiment of jihad in the Islamic nation.
2. Prepare the cadre through training and participating in fighting.
3. Back and support the jihad movements in the world, according to ability.
4. Coordinate between jihad movements in the world, according to ability.[12]

The charter contains important clues to understanding al-Qaida's strategic thinking. It indicates how al-Qaida should prioritize its resources by differing between obligatory and voluntary activities. Activities in direct support of al-Qaida's aims, such as "spreading the sentiment of *jihad*" and building a strong organization, are obligatory. Activities that indirectly support al-Qaida's aims, such as assisting other jihadist movements, should be carried out "according to ability." This suggests that al-Qaida may at times engage in activities that do not have a direct strategic purpose, such as training and supporting others. Frontline fighting may thus have an idealistic purpose (helping Muslims) and a strategic purpose (test and train new cadre). Al-Qaida differs from a regular army where every action should serve a strategic or tactical purpose.

Al-Qaida most certainly developed its strategic thinking over time. The 1988 charter stated that al-Qaida's strategies should be to spread the sentiment of *jihad* and educate the cadre. In 1996, al-Qaida adopted a strategy of international terrorism. Al-Qaida's strategy of international

---

[12] J. M. Berger (ed.), *Benevolence International: Court documents concerning an al Qaeda-linked charity front based in Chicago, Ill.* (N.p.: Intelwire Press, 2006): 345.

terrorism was known as the "far enemy" doctrine. Al-Qaida believed that the "far enemy," the United States, should be removed before the Muslims could succeed in their struggle against the "near enemies" – the Arab regimes. In June 2001, bin Laden himself provided an outline of this strategy:

[Our] intention is to expel (*ikhraj*) the infidels from the lands of Islam, and to expel their agents (*al-umala'*) and on their ruins and on the ruins of their agents, establish the truth, and establish Islam, and establish the religion.[13]

The quote clarifies three important points. First, bin Laden specifies a time frame for al-Qaida's fight. Al-Qaida does not want to fight until the end of time, as they have sometimes claimed in propaganda and official interviews. Al-Qaida wants to oust local rulers who do not rule according to Islam, and install Islamic government instead. Al-Qaida is fighting toward a goal; it does not see fighting as a goal in itself.

Second, bin Laden narrowed the geographical area of al-Qaida's fight. Al-Qaida did not want to establish a worldwide caliphate. Al-Qaida cared about "lands of Islam" – territories inhabited primarily by Muslims, and that, in al-Qaida's view, should be run according to Sharia law. I believe "lands of Islam" refers to the modern Muslim world rather than a historic caliphate because al-Qaida in 1996–2001 supported Islamist movements in East Asia – areas that were not part of the traditional caliphate. I also do not believe that al-Qaida saw it as a priority to conquer the Andalusian part of Spain. I believe however, that al-Qaida's strategic priority was the Middle East, not the whole Muslim world.

The third point is that bin Laden described al-Qaida's struggle as a three-phased process. Each phase should be completed before the next is begun. First, the Americans had to be expelled from the Middle East. Then, the local regimes must be removed. Then, Islamic rule can be established. Al-Qaida was against the idea of declaring an Islamic state before the territory was won, such as al-Qaida in Iraq did in 2006. It was also against the idea of establishing a state before ousting the local rulers, such as the Islamic State did when they declared a caliphate in parts of Iraq and Syria in 2014.

The three points illustrated in the Bin Laden quote – that al-Qaida is fighting towards a goal; that al-Qaida's goal has geographic limits (or at least priorities); and that al-Qaida sees its fight as a multi-phased

---

[13] Osama bin Laden, *bushrayat lil-shaykh usama,* al-Sahab, undated [ca. June 19, 2001], accessed via *FFI's Jihadi Video Database,* video no. 855.

process, are fundamental assumptions that guide the analysis conducted in this book.

The book is divided into nine chapters. Chapter 1 covers the circumstances of al-Qaida's foundation in 1988 and activities during the first years of its existence from 1988–1992. Al-Qaida was initially founded to be an elite Muslim combat unit that would serve as an example and inspiration to Afghan guerrillas. Contrary to common belief, al-Qaida did not withdraw from Afghanistan in 1989, but continued being deeply engaged on the frontlines until the fall of the Afghan communist regime to the mujahidin in 1992. Al-Qaida in this period formulated their training philosophy, which was improved and expanded under the Taliban regime.

Chapter 2 examines relations between al-Qaida, other Arabs, and Afghan factions during the Afghan civil war from 1992–1996. In this period, al-Qaida gradually disengaged from Afghanistan. It planned initially to continue using Afghanistan for training. Over time, political developments in Afghanistan and Pakistan made it difficult for al-Qaida to run systematic training courses. Only a handful of al-Qaida cadre stayed in Afghanistan throughout the civil war, overseeing al-Qaida's possessions and supporting other militant groups. Al-Qaida was a marginal actor in Afghanistan in this period, dwarfed by the networks of other, enterprising individuals hailing from the larger Afghan-Arab community.

Chapter 3 sheds light on bin Laden's return to Afghanistan in 1996 and the start of the al-Qaida-Taliban relationship. When bin Laden returned to Afghanistan in May 1996, he was initially looking for a refuge from where he could continue his proselytizing campaign against the Saudi regime. He found refuge in Eastern Afghanistan with old allies from the Afghan-Soviet war. When Taliban came to power a few months later and invited bin Laden to stay under their protection, bin Laden saw an opportunity to continue the state-building project he had failed to finish in Sudan. An internal al-Qaida document from 1997 outlines the first contours of al-Qaida's Afghanistan strategy: Taliban-run Afghanistan would be an exemplary Islamic state and a base from where to spread the Islamic revolution. Like Sudan, Afghanistan was situated on the fringes of the Muslim world, far from the US influence that prevented al-Qaida from establishing a base in the Middle East.

Chapter 4 explores the political relationship between al-Qaida and the Taliban. Bin Laden managed to secure a sanctuary in Afghanistan, even if his presence there harmed the Taliban regime's interests. This led to friction in their relationship, but in late 1998 or early 1999, bin Laden and Mullah Omar reached some sort of compromise. From then on, bin Laden would not give any media interviews or statements without the Taliban's permission. In return, al-Qaida was allowed to expand their training camp infrastructure in Afghanistan. Al-Qaida's political support to Taliban was not merely tailored to secure their sanctuary. It was part of a larger strategy of recruitment and organization building.

Chapter 5 is about al-Qaida's training camps under the Taliban. The content of al-Qaida's training in 1999–2001 suggests that the nature of al-Qaida had not changed significantly since its foundation in 1988. Al-Qaida was still an organization whose mission was to support, enable, and inspire other Islamist guerrillas. Yet, at this stage, al-Qaida had adopted a new military strategy that included international terrorism. The camps offered three types of courses: Basic training to prepare recruits for frontline fighting, specialized courses teaching a range of skills including urban terrorism, and a cadre course for building al-Qaida's own organization. Al-Qaida's primary aim in this period was organization building, while functioning as a services office for incoming recruits.

Chapter 6 is about the larger Arab community in Afghanistan and the Taliban regime's policies toward this community. Although al-Qaida achieved a dominant position among the Arab militants in Afghanistan in this period, Taliban's internal policies toward the Arabs ensured that the foreign fighter community kept multiple centers of gravity. In the end, the Taliban's policies toward the Arabs benefited al-Qaida's project to build a resilient organization.

Chapter 7 describes al-Qaida's contributions on the Taliban's frontlines. It argues that al-Qaida participated with some of the best of its cadre on the Taliban's frontlines to help the Taliban consolidate their power in Afghanistan. In 2001, al-Qaida became part of the Taliban's foreign contingent, which was numerically dominated by Uzbeks and Pakistanis. In general, al-Qaida was militarily insignificant but was able to contribute in key areas such as mine clearing and assassination operations. Al-Qaida used the frontlines systematically to educate the cadre for their own organization.

Chapter 8 discusses al-Qaida's international terrorist campaign, how it was implemented from Afghanistan, and who implemented it. The chapter argues that only a small elite within al-Qaida was involved in international terrorist planning and execution. The terrorist campaign was organized separately from al-Qaida's cadre education program. This strengthens the impression that al-Qaida followed a dual strategy in Afghanistan, comprised of both international terrorism and organization building.

Chapter 9 summarizes how al-Qaida's dual strategy in Afghanistan developed and why. The chapter concludes with a discussion of al-Qaida's strategic reasoning prior to the 9/11 attacks.

I

Vanguards

Al-Qaida was formed in Peshawar, Pakistan, in August 1988, just as Soviet military forces had started their withdrawal from Afghanistan. The goal of al-Qaida was to be an organization for Afghan-Arab veterans who would continue the struggle for the plight of Muslims elsewhere in the world after the Afghan war was over. But it is a misconception that al-Qaida gave up Afghanistan after the Soviet withdrawal. Al-Qaida's military engagement on the frontline in Afghanistan increased from 1989 and continued until 1992, when Kabul finally fell to the Afghan mujahidin. At the time of its foundation, al-Qaida was not an international terrorist organization, but aspired to be a Muslim "vanguard" that would inspire and incite the Muslims to fight. Its method – at least initially – was to establish bases on Afghan territory to participate in guerrilla fighting in Afghanistan. The history of Osama bin Laden's early activities in Afghanistan provides new insight into why al-Qaida was established and what it represented in Afghanistan at the time.

THE LION'S DEN

"It was the happiest days of my life," said Bin Laden about those October days in 1986 when he started work on a remote construction site in the Jaji region of Khost, Afghanistan.[1] The site had been discovered by

---

[1] Bin Laden's words are recounted in two different sources: Isam Diraz, *usama bin ladin yarwi ma'arik ma'sadat al-ansar al-arab bi-afghanistan* (Cairo: Al-Manar al-Jadid, 1991): 7; and Basil Muhammad, *al-ansar al-arab fi afghanistan*, 2nd. ed. (Riyadh: Lajnat al-Birr al-Islamiyya, 1991): 215.

Azmarai, one of Bin Laden's associates, on a reconnaissance trip he had taken with a group of Afghans the month before. The most amazing thing about the place was that it had a direct line of vision to the Soviet fort at Ali Khel,[2] situated next to the strategically important Parchinar-Gardez highway. And no one was there – neither the Soviets, nor the Afghan mujahidin.[3]

The place later become known as *al-Ma'sada* – the Lion's Den – and would play a central part in al-Qaida's mythology. But at the time of its founding, there was little to suggest that this would be the birthplace of the world's most dangerous terrorist organization. Bin Laden's construction team consisted of four men and a bulldozer, a tent, and three reluctant Afghan guards. The original purpose of the project was to build a forward base for the Afghan mujahidin stationed at "Jaji base" some five hours drive to the south.[4]

The Jaji base was controlled by Abdul Rasul Sayyaf and was an important base for training, supply, and staging of operations for mujahidin in the area. For many of the Arab volunteers who had never seen combat, Jaji represented a "frontline" of sorts, but it was more suitable for war tourism than real participation in fighting. The base had been expanded and fortified in 1985–1986 on the advice of Brigadier Yousaf, the Pakistani ISI's representative to the Afghan mujahidin. The same order had gone out to Jalaluddin Haqqani, who controlled a similar supply point in the southern part of Khost at Jawur (See Map 3). According to Brigadier Yousaf, "up to 60 per cent" of the ISI's supplies to the Afghan mujahidin were passing through these two bases only.[5] Needless to say, the protection of Jaji and Jawur was of high strategic importance.

In 1986, Bin Laden's construction company was involved with the work on the Jaji base. His team consisted of a handful of young Saudi men, some of whom were eager to participate in battles. According to Bin Laden's own account, he allowed two of the men, Azmarai and Shafiq, to go on missions with the Afghans and this is how the site of al-Ma'sada was discovered. In spite of its seemingly perfect location it was not used by the Afghans because it was remote and had no road in the winter. Bin Laden wrote to Sayyaf and offered to build the road. According to Bin Laden, Sayyaf agreed because he saw the "military value" of the Ma'sada

[2] Ali Khel was also known as the "Chawnay" fort.
[3] Diraz, *usama bin ladin yarwi*, 6–7.
[4] Muhammad, *al-ansar al-arab*, 211–216.
[5] Mohammad Yousaf and Mark Adkin, *The bear trap: Afghanistan's untold story* (London: Leo Cooper, 1992): 164–166.

base. Other say he agreed only reluctantly. The Afghans had several res-ervations about the spot, but Sayyaf could not leave the Arabs alone, as they were guests and sponsors of the Afghan mujahidin. He ended up supporting Bin Laden with a guard force and later, with weapons and fighters.[6]

The idea that Arabs should man the place, does not appear to have been part of the initial agreement. Bin Laden was quoted in 1991 as saying,

At that time, there was no such idea as building an independent place for Arabs. The idea was only to build a base for the mujahidin. Although I was planning for myself that when we finished the camp, and the caves and the trenches and the roads, and we did a good job, we would ask them for permission to use a cave that would hold seven of our brothers. So if the mujahidin carried out an oper-ation or there was a clash with the enemy, we would be allowed to be part of it.[7]

Other eyewitnesses from the time tell the same story.[8] Bin Laden thought the Afghans would be in charge of the place while the Arabs would keep a small element there that would go on operations with the Afghans. This is essentially how Bin Laden's men were already operating out of the Jaji base, and it is how Arabs were operating elsewhere in Afghanistan.

But Bin Laden had overestimated the Afghans – or lacked funda-mental understanding of their combat culture. They were not interested in manning the Ma'sada position, because it was too isolated and too exposed to the enemy. The Afghans were convinced the base could fall into enemy hands at any moment – so why spend resources on develop-ing it? The problem was not that the Afghans lacked fighting spirit, but that the whole concept of al-Ma'sada broke fundamentally with the prin-ciples of guerrilla warfare. The Afghans preferred to hit and run – not to defend static positions. Brigadier Yousaf met similar attitudes among the Afghans in 1985 when he ordered them to fortify the Jawur and Jaji posi-tions. The work went extremely slowly, due to the Afghans' "antipathy towards digging and reluctance to defend static positions," as he put it.[9]

Until late December 1986, the Arabs working on the base did not carry any guns. There are eyewitness statements saying that Bin Laden relied on an Afghan guard team to protect the construction work on the base. The first time Bin Laden ordered to buy weapons for the base was in the end of December, 1986. They bought rifles, rocket-propelled grenades

[6] Muhammad, *al-ansar al-arab*, 213.
[7] Ibid., 214.
[8] Ibid.
[9] Yousaf and Adkin, *The bear trap*, 166.

(RPGs), and mortars from a weapons market in Pakistan and obtained heavy weapons, including a 75mm cannon and a "Zikuyak" anti-aircraft gun, from Sayyaf.[10] The acquisition of heavy weapons indicates that Bin Laden wanted the base to be permanently manned and defendable against Soviet tank and air attacks. It was an ambitious plan, drafted by a man with no military experience on his own.

That is why, around January 1987, he asked Abu Ubaydah al-Banshiri, an experienced Egyptian fighter, to be the Emir of the base. Al-Banshiri gathered a group of Egyptian associates he had fought with in Khost – among them was Muhammad Atif, who would rise to become Military Chief of al-Qaida at the time of the 9/11 attacks – to discuss the feasibility of Bin Laden's plan. By now, it seems Bin Laden had decided that Arabs would man the base permanently.

The idea that Arabs were going to defend a static position inside Afghanistan against the Russians, was a radical idea in the Arab environment in Peshawar. Bin Laden's initiative was met by a wave of criticism, not only by the Afghans but also from within his own organization, the Services Office for Mujahidin (*maktab al-khidamat lil-mujahidin*). The Services Office had been established by the Palestinian ideologue Abdullah Azzam, in Peshawar in 1984 to assist and coordinate Arab volunteers who came to the region to support the Afghan mujahidin.

There are several versions of what exactly the criticism was about, and who was on the forefront of it. It has been argued that the establishment of al-Ma'sada eventually led to a split between Bin Laden and Abdullah Azzam.[11] This is perhaps an exaggeration. There were others in the Services Office that were far more critical than Azzam, and who actively tried to stop Bin Laden's project. Azzam did not like the project either, but he sought compromise – he said at the time, that "it would be un-Islamic and cowardly to leave our brother alone."[12] He agreed to send recruits from the Sada training camp (a training camp operated by the Services Office in Khurram Agency, Pakistan) to Ma'sada, and tried to make Bin Laden keep the Ma'sada group small. He realized it was to no avail. Somewhat resigned, he said, "... the truth is that the zeal of Abu Abdullah [Bin Laden], with the presence of money between his hands, enables him to carry out whatever he wants."[13]

---

[10] Muhammad, *al-ansar al-arab*, 227–228; 242.
[11] For example, Bergen, *The Osama*, 74.
[12] Muhammad, *al-ansar al-arab*, 233.
[13] Ibid., 234.

The primary concern from the Service Office's point of view was security. Gathering a large group of Arabs in an isolated and exposed position was simply a reckless thing to do. The Soviets could wipe them out all in one stroke, or worse – it could land a helicopter there, snatch Bin Laden and take him to Kabul! It would be an international scandal for one thing, and put the Afghan mujahidin in an awkward position. To comply with his critics, Bin Laden had to leave al-Ma'sada at times and during operations, he kept in radio contact with his men from the rear base at Jaji.[14]

Another point of criticism was of a more principal character. Should the Arabs form their own battle units separate from the Afghans, or should they spread out and fight alongside the Afghans, in order to lift their morals? Abdullah Azzam was against the idea of separate battle units.[15] Bin Laden also appears to have been against it when he started work on al-Ma'sada. He envisioned that Arabs would occupy a small section of the base and carry out operations alongside the Afghans. However, in reality this was not possible. The Afghans did not want to come forward, so what should the Arabs do? Leave the base they had been building for two months, or man it themselves, and hope that the Afghans would follow later?

To Bin Laden, the answer was obvious. It was not a sound decision from a military point of view, but Bin Laden was not a military man. He was a man of deep religious conviction. His ideal type of warfare would be modeled not on Sun Tzu but on the Prophet Muhammad. When the Afghans failed to show up at the base, Bin Laden saw the problem as a lack of resolve and courage on the part of the Afghans – a problem that he felt he had a duty and the ability to rectify. Bin Laden wanted to inspire and incite the Afghans to war in the same way that the Prophet Muhammad had done it: by leading by example. When discussing the difficulties of defending al-Ma'sada, Abu Ubaydah recalled,

... [Bin Laden] was not dissuaded by military arguments. He talked on the grounds that he wanted to gather the Arab brothers, and to lift the moral spirit of the Afghans, and that we would be at the very front of the fighting ranks.[16]

In the larger context of the Afghan-Soviet war, al-Ma'sada played a modest role. Al-Ma'sada was one in a series of frontline positions dotting

---

[14] Ibid., 235.
[15] Wright, *The looming tower*, 113.
[16] Muhammad, *al-ansar al-arab*, 237.

the mountains of Khost and Paktiya in 1986–1987, overlooking the main cities of Khost and Gardez and the roads between them. The purpose of these positions was to carry out reconnaissance of the enemy and serve as launch points for skirmishes, ambushes, and mortar attacks.

Arabs at al-Ma'sada were mainly involved in combat activity in April and May 1987. The hardest battle took place at the end of May 1987, which corresponded with the last days of Ramadan. The battle is not listed in any of the standard works on the Soviet military campaign in Afghanistan, although it is probably listed in lesser-known Russian sources, which have not been examined here.[17] The Soviet attacks on al-Ma'sada have been thoroughly described by Arab eyewitnesses to the event. The larger campaign they were part of, the three-week "Battle of Jaji" offensive, is referred in Arab and English press sources from the time.

The American mercenary magazine *Soldier of Fortune,* which actually carried one of the few available military analyses of the "Battle of Jaji" found in the Western press, described the battle as "the most important battle of 1987 – perhaps of the entire war."[18] It is beyond the scope of this book to evaluate the truth in this statement. To be sure, the Battle of Jaji was certainly no game-changer: The Soviets had already decided to withdraw from Afghanistan by the time the battle took place. The Ali Khel Garrison – the Soviet fort that the battle was designed to relieve – was abandoned less than a year later as part of the Soviet withdrawal plan.

From a military point of view, the most striking thing about the Battle of Jaji was the large number *Spetsnaz* (Russian special forces) killed and wounded, and the number of aircraft downed. An article in the *Washington Post* suggested 120 Spetsnaz were killed around Ali Khel in the end of May, and another 250–300 were killed or wounded in the first half of

---

[17] The Soviets carried out several large campaigns in Khost, which are chronicled in the standard English-language books on Soviet military operations in Afghanistan – the Zhawar I and Zhawar II operations in September 1985 and April 1986, respectively; and "Operation Magistral" in November 1987. None of these operations were directed at al-Ma'sada. The purpose of the Zhawar operations was to disrupt Jalaluddin Haqqani's logistics base and forces at Zhawar, whereas Operation Magistral aimed to open the Satukandav Pass on the road between Gardez and Khost. Lester W. Grau, *The bear went over the mountain: Soviet combat tactics in Afghanistan* (Washington DC: National Defense University Press, 1996); and Ali Ahmad Jalali and Lester W. Grau, *The other side of the mountain: Mujahideen tactics in the Soviet-Afghan war* (Fort Leavenworth, KA: Foreign Military Studies Office, 1995); Mohammad Yousaf and Mark Adkin, *The bear trap: Afghanistan's untold story* (London: Leo Cooper, 1992).

[18] David C. Isby, "Four battles in Afghanistan," *Soldier of Fortune,* April 1988, 32–34. For another account of the battle of Jaji, and especially events around al-Ma'sada, see Wright, *The looming tower,* 116–120.

June. In the same period, some 15 enemy aircraft were shot down. This was popular news to the American administration at the time, which had recently started supplying the mujahidin with Stingers.[19]

We do not know if Stingers were used in the Jaji battle. The Arabs at Ma'sada certainly did not have any. If they had, they would probably have boasted about it in contemporary sources because the Stinger was a prestigious weapon to have. The Arabs did indeed claim to have it later – in the battle of Gardez in the summer of 1991, a fighter from Bin Laden's group said they had two Stingers that they had bought from Hekmatyar.[20] But at Jaji, the Arabs said they shot at Soviet helicopters with machine guns and RPGs. This was a feasible tactic at the time because the Soviet pilots were flying at low altitudes due to the fear of Stingers.[21]

The Arabs at Jaji claimed they single-handedly killed 25 Spetsnaz who attacked the base at the end of May, 1987.[22] The numbers are not possible to confirm, but the importance here is not so much the numbers – it is the massive propaganda effect that these stories came to have on the status of Bin Laden in Afghanistan. The contribution of the Arabs at al-Ma'sada consolidated Bin Laden's status as military leader of the Arabs and paved the way for the establishment of al-Qaida as an organization independent from the Services Office.

The Arabs at al-Ma'sada may have been heroic, but they put their Afghan hosts in a difficult situation. At the height of the Soviet attack in May 1987, Bin Laden ordered al-Ma'sada to be evacuated. However, a handful of Arabs refused to leave the base, even after most of the defensive weaponry had been removed. This is the group that, according to legend, killed twenty-five Spetsnaz with their own hands. In another version of the story, Sayyaf had to send a group of Afghan mujahidin back to al-Ma'sada because it would not look good if the Afghans abandoned their guests. But in any case the result was the same. The story about the small group of Arabs at al-Ma'sada who had withstood a massive Soviet attack morphed into heroic stories about self-sacrifice and divine intervention. From here, the legend of al-Qaida was born.

[19] "Afghan rebel gains against Soviets reported by U.S. aide," *Washington Post*, July 6, 1987.

[20] Fadil Harun [Fadil Abdallah Muhammad], *al-harb ala al-islam: qissat fadil harun*, vol. 1 (Place and publisher unknown, 2009), 98. Al-Qaida's possession of Stingers is partly confirmed by Mustafa Hamid, who wrote that al-Qaida possessed four old Stingers in 1998. Hamid, *mashru' tajikistan*, 60.

[21] Isby, "Four battles in Afghanistan."

[22] Muhammad, *al-ansar al-arab*, 339.

After the Battle of Jaji in May 1987, there is sparse information of what happened at al-Ma'sada. Saudi journalist Basil Muhammad wrote that after the battle, Sayyaf ordered the Arabs to evacuate the base and to return control of al-Ma'sada to the Afghans. Bin Laden complied with the handover, but in the following months continued to send teams of Arab fighters into battles in the Jaji region. According to Basil this was done "neither with the permission of Sayyaf, nor Azzam."[23] The event may be seen as an act of rebellion on the part of Bin Laden, but should not be overinterpreted. As far as we know, Sayyaf never denied Bin Laden's men access to al-Ma'sada, he simply argued that Afghans should be in charge of it.[24] Bin Laden could probably continue to send Arabs into battle with Afghan field commanders in Jaji, so long as the commanders themselves agreed to this. This was the praxis that had existed ever since the start of the Afghan-Soviet war.

In April 1988, the Soviet forces abandoned the Ali Khel fort in Jaji as part of their withdrawal from Khost province.[25] This means that al-Ma'sada lost its tactical importance and at some point it was likely abandoned as well. But for Bin Laden and those around him, the military work in Afghanistan had just started.

THE BIRTH OF AL-QAIDA

It was July 1989, and the Arabs at Jalalabad were in a dire situation. They were constantly bombarded from the air, and on their right flank, twenty-seven Soviet tanks were rolling toward them. To defend themselves they only had a few RPGs, which would only be effective at short distance, and a 75 mm cannon. The latter was operated by a young Saudi named Shafiq, who was killed in the attack. The rest of the Arabs were forced to withdraw to the mountains to the East, where tanks could not reach them. The four-month Battle of Jalalabad was over, and it was a disaster by all standards. Around 3,000 Afghan mujahidin had been killed and wounded in the battle, including some hundred Arabs.[26]

[23] Ibid., 348–349.
[24] Ibid.
[25] "Tareekh Al Musadat 86, 87, 88 – 51.35," quoted in J. M. Berger (ed.), *Beatings and bureaucracy: The founding memos of Al Qaeda* (N.p.: Intelwire Press, 2012).
[26] Yousaf and Adkin, 231; Mustafa Hamid, *al-hamaqa al-kubra* (Place and publisher unknown, date unknown). Downloaded from Jihadi Document Repository, University of Oslo on February 12, 2016, 39. www.hf.uio.no/ikos/english/research/jihadi-document-repository/

"I was greatly affected by the news of Shafiq's martyrdom," said Bin Laden a few years later.[27] Shafiq was one of the two Saudis who had discovered the site for al-Ma'sada for Bin Laden back in 1986. In 1989 he was still fighting for Bin Laden, this time as part of a more formalized military faction, which had been established in Peshawar in August 1988. The faction would later become known as al-Qaida – "the Base".[28]

The nature of al-Qaida cannot be understood without considering historical events surrounding its formation. The most important of these events was not the Soviet withdrawal from Afghanistan, but Bin Laden's personal experiences at al-Ma'sada, which created an ambition to form an elite Muslim combat unit that would be an example to other Muslims worldwide. The foundation documents of al-Qaida note that "within six months of *Al Qaida*, 314 brothers will be trained and ready."[29] The number 314 is hardly random. It is the exact size of Prophet Muhammad's Army at the Battle of Badr in 624 CE (313 soldiers is the standard figure, 314 including the Prophet himself). We do not know if the al-Qaida founders literally meant to educate an army of 314 soldiers – but the statement underlines how religious symbolism was important to al-Qaida's self-perception.

The foundation documents indicate that al-Qaida was founded as an international organization and its operations were not limited to a specific national territory. Al-Qaida's area of operations was the Muslim world, its goal was simply to fight for Islam, or to "lift the word of God, to make His religion victorious."[30] The struggle had no end state, except to "overcome their opponents till the last of them fights with the Antichrist."[31] But the method of al-Qaida – at least initially – was to participate in frontline fighting in Afghanistan. This is a fact which has been rather under-appreciated in existing literature, because we tend to see al-Qaida as an international terrorist network instead of seeing it for what it was at the time: An elite Muslim combat unit which would spread "the sentiment of *jihad*" by participating directly at the frontlines, and by promoting a culture of martyrdom and self-sacrifice. This is why Bin Laden's first project as al-Qaida leader was to find a new location for al-Ma'sada.

[27] Diraz, *usama bin ladin yarwi*, 15.
[28] Alternative accounts on al-Qaida's establishment include: Bergen, *The Osama bin Laden I know*, 74–107; Wright, *The looming tower*, 121–144; R. Kim Cragin, "Early history of al-Qa'ida," *The Historical Journal* 51, no. 4 (2008): 1047–1067.
[29] J. M. Berger (ed.), *Benevolence International: Court documents concerning an al Qaeda-linked charity front based in Chicago, Ill.* (N.p.: Intelwire Press, 2006), 163.
[30] "Tareekh Osama 127–127a," quoted in J. M. Berger (ed.), *Beatings and bureaucracy.*
[31] The quote is originally from a hadith collection by the 9th-century scholar Abu Dawud. Berger, *Benevolence International*, 345.

In late 1988 or early 1989, Bin Laden sent a small group of fighters
to the Nangarhar province in Eastern Afghanistan. The group was led
by a Yemeni veteran of the Ma'sada battle, who went by the *nom de
guerre* Abu Tariq al-Ma'rabi. According to an eyewitness, their task was
to research new positions for al-Ma'sada. Abu Tariq gathered a handful of
fighters and set up a small base in the eastern part of Nangarhar, in one of
the many side valleys that run from the Kabul-Torkham highway into the
massive Spin Ghar mountain range on the Afghanistan-Pakistan border.[32]

At the same time a large battle was coming up. The Battle of Jalalabad,
which started on March 6, 1989, would be the mujahidin's first attempt
to seize a major city from the Afghan Communist regime. The purpose
was to seize Jalalabad, the province capital of Nangarhar in Eastern
Afghanistan. This in turn would pave the way for the mujahidin to
enter Kabul and oust President Najibullah. The battle was orchestrated
by the Pakistani Inter-Services Intelligence (ISI) in cooperation with the
Afghan mujahidin, and involved around 5,000–7,000 fighters including
eight senior commanders. The mood at the time was optimistic. It was
expected that the Battle of Jalalabad would go into history as the major
turning point in the war.[33]

According to some sources, al-Qaida's shura council was divided on
whether to participate in the battle. The battle was seen as "politically
dubious" (due to the involvement of the ISI) and the Arabs did not have
the "adequate skills" to contribute on the ground. They could perhaps
support the Afghan mujahidin with artillery, but nothing more.[34] These
were all valid arguments. Only six months had passed since the formal
establishment of al-Qaida. Al-Qaida had not yet had time to set up a
well-trained and organized combat unit – especially not for a conventional type of battle that the Jalalabad operation represented. Jalalabad
was a city situated on a large plain. The guerrilla tactics that Bin Laden's
fighters had used to attack isolated Soviet posts in the mountains of Jaji,
would not work here. Nevertheless, Bin Laden insisted that the Arabs
should participate in the battle. After all, frontline participation was raison d'être for al-Qaida. How could they be an example to the Afghans, if
they failed to turn up at what was perceived as the most important battle
of the war?

Bin Laden initially sent a group of Arabs to join Abu Tariq in
Nangarhar. After the mujahidin advanced and captured Samarkhel, a

---

[32] Diraz, *usama bin ladin yarwi*, 15–17.
[33] Yousaf and Adkin, *The bear trap*, 227–30.
[34] Hamid, *al-hamaqa al-kubra*, 62.

village only twenty kilometers east of Jalalabad, the Arabs were able to set up a series of positions close to the enemy for heavy artillery, mortars and observation. Bin Laden continued to refer to this group as al-Ma'sada. As he told journalist Isam Diraz: "[In 1989], the Arabs of Ma'sadat al-Ansar had around 18 military centers around Jalalabad."[35] In addition to static positions, the Arabs participated with at least two ambush groups that fought alongside the Afghans. Abu Tariq led one of these groups. A Saudi named Azmarai, who was one of the original founders of al-Ma'sada, led the other. They carried out operations with two Afghans in particular: Commander Khalid, who worked for Yunus Khalis, and Commander Sazenoor, who worked for Sayyaf.[36] After the initial success of the mujahidin in March 1989 with the capture of Samarkhel and a number of important positions around Jalalabad city, the battle turned into a stalemate.

According to Afghan-Arab historian Mustafa Hamid, the Arabs continued fighting "as the fronts became half-empty" when Afghan groups deserted due to the large number of casualties.[37] The Arabs were finally forced to withdraw in July 1989 when the Afghan regime re-captured Samarkhel village. Most of the Arabs withdrew to the Arab rear base at "Farm Two" situated in Batikot some 40 kilometers east of Jalalabad.[38]

We only have fragmented information about the role played by the Arabs in the battle. They were relatively small in number and it is safe to assume they played a modest military role. But they had money to buy their own personal weapons, ammunition, and transportation vehicles, which probably made them more welcome among the Afghans. They occupied important frontline positions and worked with some of the most influential Afghan commanders in the region. There is little reason to believe that Bin Laden's men were marginalized by the Afghans during the battle. The Arabs were just too few to make a real impact, and they did not possess the skills or experience needed to fight a conventional battle.[39]

The Arabs may have had another, less tangible impact on the Afghans, and on the wider Muslim world. The Arabs stayed longer on the frontlines than the Afghans, and they produced a higher number of casualties. In

---

[35] Diraz, *usama bin ladin yarwi*, 13.
[36] Masood Farivar, *Confessions of a Mullah warrior* (New York: Atlantic, 2009): 153.
[37] Hamid, *al-hamaqa al-kubra*, 32.
[38] Diraz, *usama bin ladin yarwi*, 16; Hamid, *al-hamaqa al-kubra*, 44.
[39] Mustafa Hamid wrote an analysis of the role of the Arabs in the Battle of Jalalabad. Consult Hamid, *al-hamaqa al-kubra*, 85–87.

the years following 1989, *al-Jihad* magazine – a glossy, Arabic-language propaganda magazine issued by the Services Office in Peshawar – continued to present biographies of the Arab "martyrs" who had died in the battles around Jalalabad.[40] *Al-Jihad* contributed to strengthening the narrative of martyrdom and self-sacrifice that would later become a crucial component in al-Qaida's strategy of suicide terrorism.

After the Battle of Jalalabad was over, Bin Laden received heavy criticism from certain parts of the Afghan-Arab community in Pakistan. There was one particular leaflet being circulated in Peshawar. It argued that the Arab fighters had died in vain due to the lack of proper leadership and coordination. It called for an immediate pull-out of Arabs from the Jalalabad area. The Arabs should halt further operations until a proper organization had been established that could make sound decisions regarding when and how they should contribute to future military campaigns. Apparently, the author saw neither the Services Office nor al-Qaida as qualified to fulfill that role at the time.[41]

The author was Mustafa Hamid, and it was not the last time he would criticize Bin Laden. Mustafa Hamid went on to become one of the most prolific Afghan-Arabs, and he stayed in the region as an activist throughout the 1990s but never formally joined al-Qaida. He wrote an astounding twelve-volume account of the Afghan-Arabs which is an invaluable source of information for researchers to this day.[42]

It is hard to judge how impactful Mustafa Hamid's leaflet was at the time. The Afghan-Arab environment in Peshawar was filled with internal disagreements and personal feuds. The leaflet must be seen as part of the general criticism against Bin Laden for wanting to establish his own organization separate from the Services Office, and implicitly, take over leadership of the Afghan-Arab movement.

Bin Laden was used to such criticism by now and it can hardly have made a difference, because after 1989 the Arabs retained a military infrastructure in Nangarhar. Over the course of the next two years, al-Qaida would build up a chain of bases, camps, and observation posts in the area stretching from Torkham Gate on the Eastern border with Pakistan until

---

[40] See, for example, "*ma'a al-shuhada'*," *al-Jihad* 77 (April/May 1991): 46–47.
[41] Hamid, *al-hamaqa al-kubra*, 75–77.
[42] Mustafa Hamid's 12-volume account can be accessed via *The Jihadi Document Repository* at the University of Oslo, www.hf.uio.no/ikos/english/research/jihadi-document-repository/biographies-and-memoirs/memoirs/mustafa-hamid/index.html. For an account of Mustafa Hamid's experiences in English, see Mustafa Hamid and Leah Farrall, *The Arabs at war in Afghanistan* (London: Hurst, 2015).

the Samarkhel mountain, situated only some twenty kilometers from Jalalabad. In this way, the Jalalabad frontline effectively became a new military base for Bin Laden.

THE 90'S GENERATION

"We were the nineties generation," wrote Fadil Harun in his memoirs – referring to the volunteers who came to Peshawar to join the mujahidin after the Soviet withdrawal in 1989.[43] They had missed the rigid training courses at the Sada camp. They had missed the fierce battles of Jaji in 1987 and Jalalabad in 1989. They had missed the era of Abdullah Azzam. This is probably what al-Qaida veterans told the young, black African who had postponed his studies in Karachi to come up to Peshawar to join the *jihad*.

Fadil Harun would rise to become one of the most central members in al-Qaida. But when he came to Peshawar in the early 1990s, he had barely heard of the group. And once he did, he was skeptical. "It is strange," he wrote, "that when you join al-Qaida you can no longer take specialized weapons courses ... you are put to work in the administration."[44] Harun set out to take as many specialized training courses as he could find before swearing the *bay'a*.

Fadil Harun was born on the Comoros Islands, off the East coast of Africa, in 1972. In 1990 he moved to Karachi to pursue a university degree, and it was after this that he got involved with al-Qaida in Peshawar. He rose in the ranks of the organization and in 1998 he became al-Qaida's "confidential secretary" (*al-amin al-sirr*). He survived the bombing of Afghanistan in late 2001 and continued to work for al-Qaida until he was killed in a clash with Somali security forces outside Mogadishu, Somalia, in 2011. Before that in 2009, he published his autobiography online.[45] Apart from al-Qaida's own, administrative documents, Harun's 1,156-page narrative is probably the best source available today about the history and inner workings of al-Qaida. It has been referred throughout this book, sometimes as the only source of information, because it is widely regarded as authentic by Western security analysts as well as al-Qaida's own supporters.[46]

---

[43] Harun, *al-harb ala al-islam*, 76.
[44] Ibid., 90.
[45] For a more detailed account of how Harun's manuscript was published online, see Lahoud, *Beware of imitators*, 11.
[46] For discussion of reliability and authenticity, see Lahoud, *Beware of imitators*, 3; 15–18.

The "nineties generation" as Harun called it, would play a crucial role in al-Qaida's consolidation and expansion in the early 1990s. Contrary to popular belief, it was not the Soviet occupation of Afghanistan in itself that attracted recruits to al-Qaida. It was only after 1989 that large numbers of Arab volunteers started coming to Peshawar. Some of them came to join training camps or frontlines, others to flee persecution in their home countries. The lack of a central authority in war-torn Afghanistan and the border areas in Pakistan created a competitive environment, where anyone with access to recruits and money could operate their own training camps and frontline sections. Ibn Khattab, who later became a famous Arab commander in Chechnya, commanded a group of fighters in Nangarhar. The same did Azmarai, the Saudi who had discovered the site for al-Ma'sada for Bin Laden in 1986.[47] But it was al-Qaida that emerged as the most dominant actor in this environment – probably owing to its long experience in the region and Bin Laden's personal charisma, administrative skills and access to independent sources of funding.

When Fadil Harun eventually decided to join al-Qaida in 1991, it was a rather tedious process. The al-Qaida administrators in Peshawar told Harun that he first had to complete al-Qaida's Basic Course (see Table 1.1) and get a letter of recommendation from the camp instructor. Harun had already taken basic training courses earlier in the year, as preparation for going to the Jalalabad front, and had gotten months of additional training in Khost and Nangarhar. He asked the al-Qaida instructors if he could skip part of the eight-week program and go to the front instead, but to no avail.[48]

Harun's experiences illustrate the bureaucratic nature of al-Qaida but also, a degree of professionalism. Al-Qaida was operating in a war zone full of adventure-seekers, spies, and competing militant organizations. Al-Qaida required that to work in one of al-Qaida's military units, all recruits had to go through the same standardized training. Furthermore, they had to put recruits through a tough training program as a way of rooting out spies and other unwanted elements from its ranks.

By 1991, al-Qaida had established a cluster of training camps in Southern Khost province in an area known as Jihad Wal. Jihad Wal was situated halfway between Khost city and Jalaluddin Haqqani's base at Jawur, close to the border with Pakistan (See Map 3). Jihad Wal itself was not controlled by Haqqani but by a local commander named Fayiz

---

[47] Harun, *al-harb ala al-islam*, 77, 84.
[48] Ibid., 91.

Muhammad, who belonged to Gulbuddin Hekmatyar's Hizb-e-Islami.[49] Some sources said that al-Qaida paid an annual "fee" to Fayiz Muhammed for having the training camps there. Others say that if al-Qaida had problems with the locals, they would contact Hizb-e-Islami who intervened.[50] This indicates that in the early 1990s it was Hizb-e-Islami who was al-Qaida's main protector in Khost.

It is unclear when al-Qaida established camps in Jihad Wal, but it may have been around 1989.[51] In 1991, the Jihad Wal camps appear to have been fully operational. The camp complex consisted of at least three separate camps: Jihad Wal itself, al-Faruq and al-Siddiq. Jihad Wal was used as an administrative center for al-Qaida; al-Faruq was the main training camp; and al-Siddiq appears to have been an auxiliary camp for certain types of recruits – such as "short-term" recruits who would train for a few weeks during their holiday, and then go home.[52] Fadil Harun, who trained at al-Faruq in March 1991, gave a detailed description of al-Faruq's basic course, which lasted eight weeks and comprised the following three parts (see Table 1.1).[53]

A contentious question regarding these camps, is whether they were actually "terrorist training camps." As far as is known, none of the training offered in al-Qaida's eight-week Basic Course at al-Faruq was relevant for conducting terrorist attacks in urban areas. The "introduction to explosives" part of the course was not about how to make homemade explosives, but how to use military explosives, such as landmines, in a guerrilla war setting. Other sources indicate that there were training camps in Afghanistan in the early 1990s that taught skills

---

[49] Gulbuddin Hekmatyar's Hizb-e-Islami is also known as HIG (Hizb-e-Islami Gulbuddin) to distinguish it from Yunus Khalis' Hizb-e-Islami, which is also referred to as HIK (Hizb-e-Islami Khalis).

[50] Hamid, *mashru' tajikistan*, 21.

[51] According to Mustafa Hamid, al-Qaida first started training recruits in Jaji in 1987, after the Battle of Jaji. Then they established a camp in Jalaluddin Haqqani's Jawur base. Then, they established a base in a place referred to as "Lijah" but moved it after a number of Arabs were killed in an un-named operation. After that, they established a base in Jihad Wal in cooperation with Hekmatyar. Mustafa Hamid, *khiyana ala al-tariq* (Place and publisher unknown, date unknown). Downloaded from Jihadi Document Repository, University of Oslo on February 12, 2016. www.hf.uio,no/ikos/english/research/jihadi-document-repository/, 69; Khalid al-Hammadi, "Al-Qa'ida from within, as narrated by Abu-Jandal (Nasir al-Bahri)," part 9, *al-Quds al-Arabi*, March 31, 2005, transl. by FBIS.

[52] J. M. Berger (ed.), *Ali Mohamed: Documents, transcripts and analysis regarding al Qaeda's most dangerous sleeper agent* (N.p.: Intelwire Press, 2006): 240; Harun, *al-harb ala al-islam*, 60.

[53] Harun, *al-harb ala al-islam*, 64; see also al-Hammadi, "Al-Qa'ida from within," part 4.

TABLE 1.1 *Content of al-Qaida's eight-week Basic Course, ca. 1991*

Course part	Arabic name	Content	Duration
Fundamentals	*ta'sisi*	Weapons theory, small arms firing, introduction to explosives, map reading, first aid	4 weeks
College	*kulliya*	Infantry tactics	2 weeks
Mountain	*jabal*	Heavy weapons firing with mortars, rockets and anti-aircraft guns	2 weeks

relevant for carrying out surveillance and assassinations.[54] These camps were not mainly run by al-Qaida, but by other groups such as Egyptian Islamic Jihad (EIJ) and al-Jama'a al-Islamiyya (JI). These groups had already carried out terrorist attacks against the Egyptian regime – most famously the killing of President Anwar Sadat in Cairo in 1981. Al-Qaida members may have taken specialist courses in surveillance, assassination and other types of operations in this period. But the overall picture is that al-Qaida's training camps in Khost were set up to support what was al-Qaida's main activity at the time: Frontline fighting in Afghanistan.

In the spring of 1991, al-Qaida was mainly engaged on the frontline in Nangarhar. Another large battle took place during this period: The Battle of Khost in Southeastern Afghanistan. The Battle of Khost in April 1991 did what the Battle of Jalalabad in 1989 had failed to do – namely, to capture a major Afghan city from the Communist regime. Khost was not so strategically important as Jalalabad and the battle took place in more guerrilla-friendly terrain. Nevertheless, the victory gave a much-needed moral boost to the Afghan mujahidin, who now felt they were one step closer to liberating Kabul.[55]

Al-Qaida's participation in the Battle of Khost appears to have been minimal. Mustafa Hamid remarked bluntly that "al-Qaida sent only one man to participate in that battle." He was supposed to act as part of the

---

[54] See, for example, "Testimony of L'Houssaine Kherchtou regarding his training with Ali Mohamed," from *US v. Usama bin Laden et al,* quoted in Berger, *Ali Mohamed,* 237–257.

[55] Anne Stenersen, "*Al-Qaeda* versus Najibullah: Revisiting the role of foreign fighters in the battles of Jalalabad and Khost, 1989–92," in Scott Gates and Kaushik Roy (eds.), *War and state-Building in Afghanistan: Historical and modern perspectives* (London: Bloomsbury, 2014): 131–146.

rockets supply chain for the Arabs at Khost.[56] It is unclear why Bin Laden did not send any more al-Qaida fighters to the Battle of Khost, which became a watershed event in the war between the Afghan mujahidin and the Najibullah regime.

But after experiencing some serious setbacks on the Nangarhar front in the summer of 1991, al-Qaida decided to create a new military unit that would participate at the Gardez front. Gardez was the next city to be conquered by the mujahidin after the liberation of Khost. Fadil Harun explains about al-Qaida's decision to open a front at Gardez,

The al-Qaida administration wanted to establish this frontline as a test of the new recruits and an attempt to put into practice the skills they had learned in the camps, far from the violent anarchy of the Arabs present in the other fronts such as Jalalabad. Here, the Arab fronts multiplied with their commanders that are half-disassociated from the orders of al-Qaida, and there were difficulties coordinating with them. So after the fall of Khost, the al-Qaida administration decided to establish a special front for them in Gardez.[57]

According to Fadil Harun, who is the only known source to this story, the recruits for the "Gardez company" (*sariyat gardez*) were taken from graduates of al-Qaida's tactics course. The tactics course was an advanced course in infantry tactics for recruits who had completed the eight-week Basic Course (see Table 1.1). It appears that al-Faruq started to offer this course in 1991 – which again seems to have motivated al-Qaida to opening a "special front" for the recruits at Gardez to test their skills and give them battlefield experience. Harun suggests that al-Qaida did not want to send the recruits to the Jalalabad front, which by now was mired in "the violent anarchy of the Arabs."[58] One can only speculate about the real motivations of al-Qaida: Did they see the tactics course graduates as future members of al-Qaida's secret organization, thus wanting to keep them away from competing organizations, spies, and foreign agents? Or did al-Qaida simply want the recruits to have a true and sound battlefield experience without having to deal with internal squabbles among independent-minded Arab commanders? The decision probably had elements of both.

What we know with some degree of certainty, is that al-Qaida put great effort into the "Gardez company" and that they wanted the recruits to

[56] Mustafa Hamid, *fatah khost* (Place and publisher unknown, date unknown). Downloaded from Jihadi Document Repository, University of Oslo on February 12, 2016, 11–12. www.hf.uio.no/ikos/english/research/jihadi-document-repository/
[57] Harun, *al-harb ala al-islam*, 94.
[58] Ibid.

be a meaningful part of the battle to conquer Gardez in 1991. Moreover, al-Qaida assigned some of their more senior cadre at the time to lead the company, including an individual named Abu Islam al-Masri who, at the time, was in charge of al-Qaida's training camps in Khost. The group comprised over 60 men, according to Fadil Harun, which makes it somewhat smaller than a regular infantry company. They were assigned a section of the frontline west of Gardez that belonged to Hizb-e-Islami Hekmatyar. The overall commander of the frontline was Hekmatyar's deputy Fayz Ahmed, but the Arabs were able to operate independently.[59]

In late 1991, al-Qaida's group withdrew from Gardez as the winter was approaching. The group was transferred to Nangarhar and took up new positions in an area that would forever be associated with al-Qaida: Tora Bora. The Afghan commander in charge at the time was Engineer Mahmood, who was a member of Yunus Khalis' party. Engineer Mahmood would be instrumental in ensuring Bin Laden's return to Afghanistan in 1996. None of this was known at the time. Sayf al-Adl, an Egyptian former police officer who would later become a senior member of al-Qaida, was leading the Arab group at Tora Bora. They carried out reconnaissance, drew maps of the area, and manned a site with a modified BM-12 rocket launcher. "We felt we were useful," said Fadil Harun. As far as we know, al-Qaida's fighters participated on the frontlines in Nangarhar until the province fell to the mujahidin in April 1992.[60]

During the first four years of its existence from 1988–1992, al-Qaida was involved in two main activities: training, and frontline fighting in Afghanistan. Al-Qaida's training camps in Khost were seen as tougher and more professional than the other camps offering training to Arabs. Bin Laden's targeted recruitment of former Egyptian military officers into al-Qaida probably played a direct role in shaping al-Qaida's training doctrines.

Frontline service inside Afghanistan was an integrated part of al-Qaida's training programs. But frontline fighting also served al-Qaida's more general aim of "spreading the sentiment of *jihad*" among the Muslims. Al-Qaida saw itself as an elite Muslim combat unit that would lead others by example through direct participation in fighting and promotion of a culture of martyrdom and self-sacrifice.

The professionalism of al-Qaida's training camps stand in contrast to the reckless military decisions sometimes taken by Osama bin Laden.

---

[59] Ibid., 94–95.
[60] Ibid., 100–102; Berger, *Ali Mohamed*, 140–141.

This discrepancy was caused by the peculiar mix of people that made up al-Qaida's leadership at the time: Osama bin Laden, a man with no military experience of his own, but with a strong commitment to following the ideals of the Prophet Muhammed; and Abu Ubaydah and Abu Hafs al-Masri, former officers in the Egyptian Army.

Bin Laden insisted that Arabs should step up to man al-Ma'sada base in 1987, and insisted that they should take part in the battle of Jalalabad in 1989. In both cases, Bin Laden's Egyptian military advisors had reservations about the plan, but ended up following Bin Laden's directives. The notion that Bin Laden was a gullible Saudi boy who was led astray by a group of "hardline Egyptians" should therefore be put firmly to rest. It was Bin Laden who pushed for military action in cases when no one else dared to.

2

Training under Pressure

After the start of the Afghan civil war in 1992, al-Qaida gradually disengaged from Afghanistan. Bin Laden established a new headquarters in Sudan, and al-Qaida's military committee started training guerrillas in Somalia. But al-Qaida never left Afghanistan completely. A handful of people stayed behind in the Jihad Wal camp in Khost to oversee al-Qaida's activities there. They had a policy to stay out of the Afghan civil war, something which proved almost impossible. What did al-Qaida do in Afghanistan in this period and how did they cope with the many challenges caused by the civil war?

INTO CIVIL WAR

In the winter of 1992–1993, al-Qaida's training camp complex at Jihad Wal was bustling with activity. The tin sheds that had served as housing were replaced with concrete buildings. The mosque was expanded. A new residential house was built for Osama bin Laden. "We changed the whole map of the area," recalled Fadil Harun, who was taking part in the construction work.[1] His account is a stark contradiction to most existing narratives of al-Qaida, which claim that al-Qaida abandoned Afghanistan and relocated to Sudan in this period. If this is true, why would al-Qaida spend time fortifying and improving Jihad Wal?

Although the details of Harun's account cannot be independently confirmed, it is fairly certain that al-Qaida planned to continue having a presence in Afghanistan after the war against Soviet occupation and the

[1] Harun, *al-harb ala al-islam*, 122.

Afghan Communist regime was over. Eyewitnesses confirm that al-Qaida continued to run training courses in the Jihad Wal complex in late 1992 and early 1993.[2] When the Afghan mujahidin took over Kabul in April 1992, Khost had already developed into a sprawling training ground for foreign jihadists. Pakistani jihadists had moved into the province and were training for Kashmir. Arabs were training for classical *jihad* or for revolution in their home countries.[3] There seemed to be no reason why al-Qaida should leave just yet. Instead, al-Qaida re-defined its mission in Afghanistan – from frontline fighting to training.

Bin Laden's decision to withdraw from frontline fighting in Afghanistan was in line with the majority view of the Afghan-Arabs at the time. The Afghan civil war was viewed as *fitna* (civil strife) in which it was illegitimate for Arabs to participate. Most independent commanders at the time either left the area, or started running training camps for their own purposes. Khattab, the Saudi commander who had fought in Nangarhar, opened up a front in Tajikistan. Azmarai, who had also led a group in Nangarhar, went to South East Asia to work with Islamist groups there. A Jordanian commander named Abu Harith al-Urduni, who had fought with Haqqani in Khost, left fighting altogether and settled in Khost.[4] Others went to Bosnia to fight with the Bosnian Muslims against the Serbs, or started preparing for revolution in their home countries. The goals of the Afghan-Arabs were discordant – yet the majority agreed that the Afghan civil war should be avoided.

The Afghan civil war is too complex to be treated in any detail here. Suffice to say that for the Islamists in Afghanistan and Pakistan, the most contentious issue was the conflict between the Pashtun Gulbuddin Hekmatyar on one hand, and the Tajik Burhanuddin Rabbani and his commander Ahmed Shah Massoud on the other. After mujahidin conquered Kabul in April 1992, Hekmatyar started battling Massoud's forces for control over the city. Massoud's forces occupied central positions in Kabul while Hekmatyar was left on the southern outskirts of the city in an area called Chahar Asyab. From here, he infamously started bombarding Kabul with rockets, a devastating affair that by 1996 had left most of southern Kabul in ruins.

---

[2] Abu Zubaydah, *The Abu Zubaydah Diaries, vol. 2*, 91; AQ-TBGD-D-001-153, "Report on camps," date unknown, Conflict Records Resource Center, Washington, DC.

[3] Brown and Rassler, *The Fountainhead*, 94; al-Hindukushi, *mudhakkarati min kabul ila baghdad*, part 2, 1–10.

[4] al-Hindukushi, *mudhakkarati min kabul ila baghdad*, part 3; Harun, *al-harb ala al-islam*, 116; Hamid, *mashru' tajikistan*, 24.

There was one notable exception to the general attitude among Afghan-Arabs to avoid the civil war. A fringe group of some 50 fighters fought with Hekmatyar during the war. The most prominent commanders among them were a Syrian named Abu Rawda al-Suri, who formed the "Yarmuq Battalion" to fight with Hekmatyar, and a young Palestinian commander named Abu Mu'az al-Khosti. Both of them had fought on Haqqani's frontline in Khost and Gardez prior to the fall of Kabul. Abu Rawda had previously fought alongside Massoud's forces in Northern Afghanistan.[5] However, toward the end of the 1980s, Abu Rawda became part of an anti-Massoud current in Peshawar. The current formed after allegations started to circulate among Arabs that Massoud's fighters were killing other mujahidin and that Massoud himself was an agent of foreign powers.[6] Hekmatyar's party contributed to exaggerating the rumors. Building on the anti-Massoud sentiment that had been simmering since the 1980s, Hekmatyar framed his participation in the civil war after 1992 as a continuation of the *jihad*, and saw himself as the only mujahidin leader who was truly interested in establishing an Islamic State.[7]

The war had a deep divisionary effect on the Islamist current in Pakistan. Two broad ideological camps emerged, which we may term the "Deobandi" camp and the "Ikhwani" camps. The Deobandis did not support one particular party but saw reconciliation between the mujahidin leaders as the only viable solution to end the war. Proponents of this view included scholars and students from the prominent Deobandi institutions in Karachi and at Akhora Khattak. In Afghanistan, supporters of the Deobandi view included Sheikh Yunus Khalis and his commander Jalaluddin Haqqani. They both had their education from Dar ul-Ulum Haqqania at Akhora Khattak, and they were both conspicuously absent from the war.

The other, principal stance taken by some Islamists in Pakistan is what we may call the "Ikhwani camp." The word *Ikhwanis* in this context

5 Hamid, *mashru' tajikistan*, 14, 28–29; Harun, *al-harb ala al-islam*, 98; Salih al-Hami Abu Qadama, *fursan al-farida al-gha'iba* (Place and publisher unknown, 2007): 598; "*al-amil al-mazduj "ramzi" li-"al-hayat": rattabna liqa' lil-zawahiri ma'a khattab fa-i'taqalatu al-shurta al-daghestaniyya … wa-rashwa bi-40 alf dular a'adatahu ila afghanistan*, al-Hayat," March 9, 2014.

6 This "anti-Massoud opposition" was also highly critical of Abdullah Azzam, who supported Massoud. "*Akhtar min ra'i: mustaqbal al-afghan al-arab ba'd hazimat taliban*," *al-Jazeera*, November 23, 2001.

7 Gulbuddin Hikmatyar, *Secret plans, open faces: From the withdrawal of Russians to the fall of the coalition government*, transl. by Sher Zaman Taizi (Peshawar: Area Study Centre, 2004): 1–12.

refers to ideological adherents of the Muslim Brotherhood movement (*al-ikhwan al-muslimun*) which originated in Egypt in the late 1920s. The Ikhwanis viewed Gulbuddin Hekmatyar as the only Afghan leader who sincerely wanted an Islamic revolution in Afghanistan and they viewed his main adversaries – Burhanuddin Rabbani and Ahmed Shah Massoud – as hypocrites. A main proponent of this view was Qazi Hussain Ahmad, leader of the Pakistani Islamist political party *Jamaat-e-Islami*.[8] Among the Afghans, the only proponent of the Ikhwani view was Hekmatyar himself, who was generally regarded as a spoiler by the other mujahidin parties. Hekmatyar also had support of the Pakistani Inter-Services Intelligence (ISI), who did not support Hekmatyar for ideological reasons like the Ikhwanis, but who treated Afghan politics as an extension of their own national security agenda. ISI saw Hekmatyar at the time as the best bulwark against Indian and other foreign influences in Pakistan's backyard.

Al-Qaida's relationship with Hekmatyar needs mention, because the relationship is treated only superficially in existing literature. After 1989, al-Qaida established a close, cooperative relationship with Hekmatyar's Hizb-e-Islami that appears to have been more elaborate than with the other mujahidin parties. In this period, al-Qaida built a training camp infrastructure in the Jihad Wal area and rented land from Hekmatyar for the purpose. In 1991, al-Qaida's basic course recruits were taught heavy weapons in a Hekmatyar-run training camp, which the Arabs referred to as "al-Jabal" (the Mountain). Moreover, the Bin Laden-affiliated charity Benevolence International Foundation (BIF) gave direct military support to Hekmatyar's fighters – including uniforms and blankets, rockets and other ammunition.[9]

However, after the mujahidin's conquest of Kabul in April 1992, al-Qaida stopped supporting Hekmatyar on an operational level. Al-Qaida at this time withdrew all their frontline units and weapons to Jihad Wal to concentrate on training. For this purpose, al-Qaida continued to rent land from Hekmatyar's commander Fayz Muhammad, but this appears to have been mere formality. Bin Laden's decision to abandon his old comrade-in-arms at Chahar Asyab is but one example of a situation in which al-Qaida let a theological principle (the duty to avoid *fitna*) guide their strategic decisions (to withdraw from the frontlines, and concentrate on training).

---

[8] Allama Arshad Hassan Saqib, "Delightful facts," translated from Urdu by Noshad Mehsud (*al-Irshad*, vol. and year unknown): 50–57. Accessed via *PIPS Compendium 1*.

[9] Harun, *al-harb ala al-islam*, 71; Berger, *Benevolence International*, 168–174.

Bin Laden's decision to avoid the Afghan civil war places him ideologically within the "Deobandi camp" who favored neutrality or reconciliation between Hekmatyar and Rabbani. It is possible that Bin Laden was involved in reconciliation talks between the two leaders, but probably not in any decisive capacity.[10] In any case, al-Qaida's main activity from now on was to train their own cadre for taking part in *jihad* elsewhere, and to support other groups and individuals who did the same.

Al-Qaida's decision corresponded well with the wishes of the Afghan proponents of the Deobandi current, Yunus Khalis and Jalaluddin Haqqani. Khalis said about the Arabs in 1992, "I want them to restrain themselves from forming a separate group, and they must be neutral in the discussions between the jihadi parties."[11] Haqqani's sentiments were similar. In an interview published in August 1992, Haqqani put forward three demands to the Arabs who stayed in Afghanistan:

- That they do not abandon military training.
- That they do not allow corrupt elements to enter their organization, who will instigate factionalism among them and create problems between them and the Afghans.
- That they do not form parties or groups to compete with the Afghan parties and become involved in their problems – or that they enter internal struggles that will make it hard for them to remain in the country. "They should be a peace-negotiator between parties who are quarrelling," he concluded.[12]

Haqqani at the time did not participate in the Afghan civil war, but acted as a national-level peace negotiator among the various mujahidin factions. Haqqani's demand that Arabs "should not abandon military training" likely refers to the training activities taking place in Khost at that time, designed to support jihadists fighting in Kashmir and elsewhere. Haqqani was an outspoken supporter of such activity. From the end of the 1980s he had also started expressing anti-American sentiment and support for both classical and revolutionary jihadism.[13] However, this does not mean that his ideas somehow served as inspiration for Bin Laden's global jihadi ideology as it evolved in the 1990s.[14]

---

[10] See, for example, Coll, *Ghost wars*, 236.

[11] Wazir Ahmad Munib, "*al-shaykh yunus khalis li-manba' al-jihad*," *Manba' al-Jihad* 2, no. 18 (August 1992): 24.

[12] Abu al-Harith Munib, "*al-shaykh haqqani fi hadith ma'a manba' al-jihad*," *Manba' al-Jihad* 2, no. 18 (August 1992): 20.

[13] Brown and Rassler, *Fountainhead of jihad*, 93.

[14] As argued in Brown and Rassler, *Fountainhead of jihad*, 100–101.

Anti-American and pro-jihadist ideas were both widespread among Islamists in Afghanistan and Pakistan at the time. The failure of the Afghan mujahidin to create an Islamic state in Afghanistan was hard to swallow for those who had put their hopes on the mujahidin – so conspiracy theories about the involvement of "foreign hands" naturally started to flourish. The Americans, who were widely seen as having abandoned Afghanistan once the Soviets left, were a convenient scapegoat. Pro-jihadist ideas were also widespread. One of the reasons being the conflict in Kashmir, which was widely regarded as Indian occupation of Muslim territory. However, the conflict in Palestine and Saddam's invasion of Kuwait were also topics of interest to Afghan mujahidin at the time. As a curiosity, in a speech in Mecca on September 10, 1990, Hekmatyar proposed to send Afghan mujahidin to Saudi Arabia to protect the country's two holy sanctuaries, "to replace the foreign army" as he said.[15] It was around the same time that Osama bin Laden went to the Saudi Defense minister with a similar proposal.[16]

Anyway, the gist of Haqqani's message was that Arabs should stay out of the civil war and not act as spoilers. As long as they followed these rules they were welcome to use Afghanistan to train for classical *jihad* in occupied Muslim lands such as Kashmir or Bosnia, or revolutionary *jihad* in the Middle East. When the Taliban came to power in 1995–1996, the attitude was much the same. Here lies some of the key to understanding the al-Qaida–Taliban relationship. The 'Deobandi camp' of which both Haqqani and, later, the Taliban were a part saw the various training projects of the Arabs as a commendable activity that involved risking one's own life for the defense of Islam. The activities were not at the time associated with terrorism.

Against this backdrop, al-Qaida continued with three types of training activities in Khost. First, they continued to offer basic and specialized training courses in al-Faruq and the auxiliary camp al-Siddiq. These courses were sometimes open to non-al-Qaida members. This is evident because Abu Zubaydah, a Palestinian jihadist who we shall meet later in this chapter, trained at al-Siddiq in December 1992. At the time, he was contemplating whether to go to Bosnia to fight – a common motivation

[15] "Eng. Hekmatyar proposes a united Islamic force for the Muslim world," *The Mujahideen* [English-language propaganda magazine of Hizb-e-Islami Hekmatyar] 4, no. 3 (September/October 1990): 8.

[16] Bin Laden met with the Saudi Defense Ministry to discuss his proposal in "Autumn 1990" according to Coll. See Coll, *Ghost wars*, 222–223; and Steve Coll, *The bin Ladens: Oil, money, terrorism and the secret Saudi world*. (London: Penguin, 2009), 375–376.

among Arabs in Peshawar at the time. Abu Zubaydah noted in his diary in late 1992 that he went to Khost for training "with al-Qaida, in the camps run by bin Laden."[17] This is a curious detail. It is perhaps the earliest example of a non-al-Qaida member using the name "al-Qaida" to refer to Bin Laden's organization. It shows that the name "al-Qaida" was in use among the Afghan-Arabs long before 2001 – it was not a name invented by the FBI, as suggested by some al-Qaida historians.[18]

In addition to offering basic and specialized training courses in Khost, al-Qaida allowed other jihadist groups to use their camp complex for training. Al-Qaida supported these groups with logistics and sometimes trainers. In late 1992 al-Qaida offered assistance to Ayman al-Zawahiri's Egyptian Islamic Jihad (EIJ), whose goals and philosophy at the time were different from al-Qaida's. EIJ's goal at the time was to fight the Egyptian regime, whereas al-Qaida did not want to limit the struggle to one specific territory. EIJ and al-Qaida later merged into one organization, but this did not happen until years later, in 2001.[19] At that point, al-Zawahiri had abandoned the strategy of staging revolution in Egypt and endorsed Bin Laden's global agenda.

Fadil Harun, who worked as a secretary in Jihad Wal at the time, wrote that in late 1992 the EIJ was using a section of Jihad Wal called "Khalid bin Walid" to train their members. An al-Qaida trainer gave them a course on "arming and disarming mines," and an Egyptian nicknamed "Haydara" gave training in close protection. Al-Qaida later hired "Haydara" to teach a course in close protection for al-Qaida's own members.[20] "Haydara," as it turns out, is the infamous Ali Mohamed,

---

[17] Abu Zubaydah, *The Abu Zubaydah Diaries, vol. 2,* 91. The Abu Zubaydah diaries (vol. 1-6) were translated to English by the Federal Bureau of Investigation, US Department of Justice, and published by al-Jazeera on December 3, 2013. Accessed May 21, 2015, http://america.aljazeera.com/multimedia/2013/11/original-documentstheabuzubaydahdiaries.html.

[18] Burke, *Al Qaeda,* 6.

[19] It is often assumed that the "merger" between al-Qaida and EIJ happened in 1998, when al-Zawahiri joined Bin Laden's Global Islamic Front. In this author's view, this was an agreement to cooperate on attacking US targets worldwide, but not an organizational merger *per se.* Several independent sources including Bin Laden himself, media, and US intelligence, suggest that the official merger took place in June 2001. At this point, al-Qaida and Jama'at al-Jihad merged their names to Qa'idat al-Jihad. Bin Laden, *bush-rayat lil-shaykh usama*; Anwar Iqbal, "Bin Laden forms a new Jihadi group," *United Press International,* June 26, 2001; SA-000063, "Recommendation for Continued Detention Under DoD Control (CD) for Guantanamo Detainee, ISN US9SA-000063DP [Maad al-Qahtani]," Department of Defense (Joint Task Force Guantánamo), February 15, 2008.

[20] Harun, *al-harb ala al-islam,* 120–121.

the naturalized US citizen and former instructor at the US Army's Special Warfare Center at Fort Bragg. His presence in Khost at the time was most opportune for al-Qaida, which was in a period of expansion and in need of skilled trainers to raise the competence of their own members.

This brings us to the third type of training activity run by al-Qaida in Khost – their internal courses or "cadre courses." These were advanced training courses for al-Qaida members only. The purpose was to create a pool of qualified personnel that in the future would be able to fill various positions in the organization. Fadil Harun attended such a course in late 1992, or early 1993. The contents of the course indicate that al-Qaida was still very much an organization focused on guerrilla warfare: The recruits trained on guerrilla tactics and regular warfare, and learned how to organize battles "covering everything from a squadron up to a brigade". But there was also a section on "how to form cells in cities," teaching a variety of skills associated with urban terrorism, and a "special course on pistols," which taught skills associated with assassination.[21]

In another course held by Ali Mohamed in Hayatabad in early 1993, a group of al-Qaida and EIJ members were taught urban reconnaissance techniques. As part of the course, the trainees were given practical tasks like drawing a sketch of the Iranian consulate in Peshawar, and stalking an Egyptian embassy employee throughout the city.[22] By now, it seems clear that al-Qaida's cadre were learning skills relevant for staging terrorist attacks and assassinations – as opposed to previously, when their training focused solely on guerrilla warfare. However, at the time it did not signify a strategic shift. Although al-Qaida affiliated militants staged attacks on American targets in Yemen as early as 1992, I argue that al-Qaida did not make the strategic shift to international terrorism until August 1996, when Bin Laden declared *jihad* on US forces in Saudi Arabia. Up until then, al-Qaida's military activities centered on guerrilla warfare and cadre education.

Fadil Harun claims that al-Qaida's military committee was divided into two in 1992: The East Africa section, which was tasked with training Islamist guerrillas in Somalia; and the Afghanistan section, which would continue to oversee al-Qaida's training activity in Jihad Wal. The leader of the Military Committee, Abu Ubaydah al-Banshiri, went to Kenya to establish a new headquarters there. His deputy, Abu Hafs, remained in Peshawar to be the point of contact for the Afghanistan section.[23]

---

[21] Harun, *al-harb ala al-islam*, 123–126.
[22] Berger, *Ali Mohamed*, 247–255.
[23] Harun, *al-harb ala al-islam*, 127.

However, by mid- or late 1993, Abu Hafs left Peshawar and moved to East Africa as well. The reasons for his move are unclear, but it was likely related to Pakistani police crackdowns on Arabs residing in Peshawar, which are discussed later in this chapter. Abu Hafs left for Somalia to visit the al-Qaida's training project there, and settled eventually with Bin Laden in Khartoum.

After Abu Hafs left Peshawar, the Afghanistan section of al-Qaida's Military Committee dwindled in importance. From now on, al-Qaida's presence at Jihad Wal was reduced to a group of between five and ten people, led by a US citizen of Tunisian origin – Abu Ata' al-Sharqi. Abu Ata' was known as a skilled weapons engineer but was not among the most high-ranking members of the military committee. They had all left for East Africa by this time. The Arabs who remained were given the rather dull task of overseeing al-Qaida's possessions in the area, until the al-Qaida leadership decided whether to close down completely.[24] But, thanks to a few enterprising individuals, a new mission was created: the Tajikistan project. It ensured that al-Qaida stayed in Afghanistan throughout the civil war, if only with a handful of members that were largely left to fend for themselves.

THE TAJIKISTAN PROJECT

When al-Qaida decided to move to Sudan in 1992–1993 there was a logistical problem to be solved. What to do with the weapons? At the time, al-Qaida owned several truckloads of weapons and military equipment that had been bought over the years to arm Bin Laden's guerrillas. Some of the heavy weapons were probably borrowed or leased from the Afghans; they could be returned. But what about the rest? Suppose they could be sold in one of the sprawling weapon bazaars along the Afghanistan-Pakistan border. The problem was, these weapons markets were feeding the unholy business of Afghan civil war. Besides, the prices were terrible and transporting the weapons from Khost, where they were stored, and down to Miram Shah would hardly be worth the effort.

We do not know how the al-Qaida leadership reasoned at the time. But these were some of the arguments used by Mustafa Hamid in meetings with al-Qaida's leaders.[25] Hamid had, of course, the perfect solution

---

[24] AQ-TBGD-D-001-153, "Report on camps."
[25] Hamid, *mashru' tajikistan*, 7.

to al-Qaida's logistical dilemma: Donate the weapons to the Islamist opposition in Tajikistan. The Tajik Nahda Party, led by Mohammed al-Nuri, was preparing to launch a guerrilla campaign against the Tajik Communist regime. Al-Nuri had already reached out to Islamist groups in Peshawar to get military support for their rebellion. Some of the Arabs in Peshawar thought Tajikistan could be their next Afghanistan; a continuation of their *jihad* against an ungodly Communist regime.

The "Tajikistan project" was originally Mustafa Hamid's idea, or so he describes it in his memoirs.[26] The project had at least two goals: One was to train Tajik commandos in a form of "train the trainers" program in Khost. The other goal was to supply the Tajik opposition with weapons. Hamid convinced al-Qaida to donate their weapons caches in Khost to the Tajik cause. Hamid was also able to borrow the al-Faruq training camp – which al-Qaida anyway had planned to shut down – for training Tajik recruits.[27] Over time, al-Qaida also contributed to the project with trainers. This appears to have been at the personal initiative of al-Qaida's representative in Khost, Abu Ata' al-Sharqi – and not something that was planned from the beginning.

The Tajikistan Project, which was carried out in 1993 and 1994, involved a number of famous Afghan-Arabs: Mustafa Hamid was there, Abu Zubaydah was there. Abu Ata' al-Sharqi who was al-Qaida's representative in Jihad Wal, was there. Abd al-Hadi al-Iraqi, who later joined al-Qaida and became the most high-ranking al-Qaida commander on the Taliban's frontlines, was there. Khattab, who had been fighting in Nangarhar, was not part of Hamid's project but went to Tajikistan and opened his own frontline there, just as he had done previously at the Jalalabad front. All these individuals were motivated to participation in classical *jihad* as it had been promoted by Abdullah Azzam, with the aim to fight occupation of Muslim lands or alternatively, support Muslim insurgents or separatists, such as those in Chechnya and Tajikistan. The Tajikistan project illustrates how al-Qaida was only one among several actors in Afghanistan carrying these ambitions at the time.

When Mustafa Hamid initially sought to gain support for the project, he encountered one of the major fault lines in the Afghan-Arab community

---

[26] Hamid, *mashru' tajikistan*, 7; for other accounts of the "Tajikistan project," see also Hamid and Farrall, *The Arabs at war in Afghanistan;* and Hegghammer, *Jihad in Saudi Arabia,* 54–55.

[27] Hamid, *mashru' tajikistan*, 7–8.

in Peshawar – namely, how should the Arab islamists continue their struggle after the Afghan-Soviet war was over?[28] Many of the "Afghan-Arabs" simply returned to their home countries to their normal lives. For some nationalities, like the Egyptians, it was difficult to return because they risked facing legal prosecution in their home countries. For those why stayed, some continued to be engaged in nonviolent activism such as preaching or charity work. Then, there were those who were inclined to continue with some kind of militant activity. They could roughly be divided into two groups: Those who wanted to take up arms against the Arab regime in their home country, and those who wished to take part in classical *jihad* – wars to fight occupation of Muslim lands. The Afghan-Soviet war had been the prototype of the classical *jihad* but it had also attracted men like Ayman al-Zawahiri, who at the time viewed Afghanistan as preparation for the revolutionary struggle in Egypt. This is why groups like Egyptian Islamic Jihad and Al-Jama'a al-Islamiyya ran training camps in Afghanistan, but did not send fighters to the mujahidin's frontlines – the coming Egyptian struggle was the only struggle that mattered to them.

It was to be expected, therefore, that Mustafa Hamid's project was met by resistance from other Arab groups in Peshawar. He recalls a meeting he had with an Arab faction called the Khilafat Group, in their headquarters in Peshawar:

I sat down with the Deputy leader, ten of his assistants, and a number of ordinary members. I soon realized I was subject to some kind of public inquisition. The Deputy asked me: "Why do you want to impede the jihad against the Arab Tyrants and open a project to mislead the youth?" I said that there were those who did not want, or could not, return to their home countries and it was better for them to join a useful project instead of perishing on the streets of Pakistan or in battle against a madman in Kabul.[29]

Hamid tells that, in principle, his arguments were supported, but none of the Arab groups wanted to allocate resources to his project, because they believed in prioritizing revolutionary struggles in their home countries. It did not make sense for members of Egyptian Islamic Jihad to send their men to Tajikistan, when they were fighting to establish an Islamic State in Egypt. Hamid noted, however, that Egyptians including EIJ members participated in Tajikistan on individual initiative.[30]

---

[28] For a thorough study of fault lines in the jihadi movement, see Vahid Brown, *Cracks in the foundation: Leadership schisms in al-Qa'ida from 1989–2006* (West Point, NY: Combating Terrorism Center, 2007).
[29] Hamid, *mashru' tajikistan*, 8–9.
[30] Ibid., 9.

The reason that Hamid had asked the Egyptians for support, was that he needed qualified trainers to run training courses for the Tajiks. In the end, he managed to reach an agreement with some of Sayyaf's Afghan trainers but they only stayed for one course – a rather disastrous affair, as the first batch of Tajiks were poorly motivated and lacked proper qualifications. According to Hamid the dropout rate in the first course was close to 90 percent. Although 150 recruits arrived, only 15 completed the course. Abu Zubaydah's and Abu Ata's estimates for the time are somewhat better, with 250 recruits arriving and around 50 completing the course.[31] Still, the dropout rate was a staggering 80 percent. But things improved over time.

After Sayyaf's trainers had left, al-Qaida got involved in training the Tajiks. This appears to have been the private initiative of Abu Ata' al-Sharqi, who was an old friend of Mustafa Hamid. Abu Ata' wrote to the al-Qaida leadership in Sudan and informed them about the situation, but since the communication was so slow, he had already started supporting Hamid by the time he got the approval.[32]

After al-Qaida joined the project, the training of the Tajiks became more organized. The Arabs found that the Tajiks had almost no knowledge of their own religion, so they hired some religious teachers from Haqqani's base to teach the "fundamentals of Islam." Hamid made a point of hiring Afghans to do the religious classes for the Tajiks, because the Afghans were from Hanafi Islam which was similar to the form of Islam practiced in Tajikistan. It was important not to teach the Tajik recruits Salafism, or any other foreign Islamic practices, because they would risk being alienated from their home communities.[33]

This kind of religious pragmatism was shared by Abdullah Azzam, Osama bin Laden, and others. It was despised by certain other Arab groups in Afghanistan – the so-called "Wahhabis" comprised of conservative Gulf Arabs who wanted to eradicate certain Afghan customs, such as worshipping graves and saints, on the grounds that they were un-Islamic. After the Taliban came to power, Bin Laden similarly defended Mullah Omar from attacks from Wahhabi circles in his home country.

---

[31] Hamid, *mashru' tajikistan*, 18: Abu Zubaydah, *The Abu Zubaydah Diaries, vol. 3*, 8, 141; and AQ-TRED-D-000-924, "Report by Abu 'Ataa' Al-Sharqi evaluating training trograms between Al-Qaida and Tajik mujahideen with recommendations for improvements," January 13, 1994, Conflict Records Resource Center, Washington, DC.

[32] AQ-MCOP-D-001-159, "The third report to Sudan," March 21, 1994, Conflict Records Resource Center, Washington, DC.

[33] Hamid, *mashru' tajikistan*, 16.

The official training program ended in June 1994. By this time, around eighty Tajiks had completed training in al-Faruq and were ready to go back to Tajikistan. Mustafa Hamid and a delegation of Arabs traveled with the Tajiks to al-Nahda's headquarters in Northern Afghanistan. The Arabs planned to enter the Tajik civil war alongside the Tajik trainees. But in the end, Hamid abandoned the plan due to "safety issues" as he wrote.[34]

Meanwhile, individual Arabs fought in the Tajik civil war. The most organized group was probably led by Khattab. He established a rear base on Tajik territory, just across the river Oxus which marked the border between Afghanistan and Tajikistan. From here, Khattab's fighters carried out skirmishes and mortar attacks on Tajik government forces. Militarily speaking, their contribution was not very effective and when the Tajik opposition fell into discord, Khattab left and made a name for himself in Chechnya.[35]

The formal cooperation between the Arabs and the Nahda ended in mid-1994 when Nahda entered into peace negotiations with the Tajik government. But Hamid and Abu Ata' continued to train individual Tajiks in Jihad Wal. In the autumn of 1994 they got a formal request from the Uzbek commander Tahir Yuldashev to train a group of Uzbeks as well – and so the "Tajikistan project" continued in an informal manner.[36] Tahir Yuldashev and his group, the Islamic Movement of Uzbekistan (IMU) would later play an important role fighting on the Taliban's frontlines in Afghanistan alongside al-Qaida and other foreign militants.

The other component of the "Tajikistan project," apart from the training, was to transport weapons from Khost to Taloqan in Northern Afghanistan to aid the Tajik rebels. It was not a straightforward task. If transported by land, the weapons would have to cross several frontlines of the civil war, and would almost certainly be looted by rogue commanders. So the plan initially was to transport the weapons by air.

In the winter of 1992–1993, Mustafa Hamid's group organized for the Khost airstrip to be repaired. In April 1993, the first planeload of weapons was flown to Taloqan and another plane was sent about a month later. Then there were no more planes available – but there

---

34 Hamid, *mashru' tajikistan*, 35–38.
35 Hamid, *mashru' tajikistan*, 38; al-Hindukushi, *mudhakkarati min kabul ila baghdad*, part 3–4.
36 AQ-SHPD-D-000-089, "A letter sent from the leader of a military group called Abou Atta el Charki to his training chief Abou Hafsse," September 4, 1994, Conflict Records Resource Center, Washington, DC.

were still plenty of weapons left. So the Arabs decided in the end to send a truckload of weapons by land. They obtained permission from various parties to cross through their territories, but were nevertheless stopped twice – once by the Hekmatyar commander south of Kabul, and once by a commander aligned with the Uzbek warlord Abdul Rashid Dostum.[37]

As far as we know, it was not Hekmatyar's policy to interfere with al-Qaida or the Tajikistan project. But some of Hekmatyar's commanders feared the weapons would fall into the hand of their archenemy Ahmed Shah Massoud. The suspicion was not unfounded, because Massoud was a close ally of the Tajik Nahda party at the time. So they confiscated the truck, but the issue was solved fairly quickly through negotiations. Mustafa Hamid was able to use some of Hekmatyar's Arab commanders as intermediaries to negotiate the release of the truck. It illustrates a common phenomenon among the Afghan-Arabs – even if Arabs were from different ideological camps, they nevertheless were able to cooperate on practical issues.[38]

Dostum's commander – the second person to confiscate the truck – was a harder nut to crack. Abu Zubaydah wrote about the event in his diary, which confirms it was a prolonged affair. The truck was held by Dostum's commander for seven months, from around September 1993 to April 1994.[39] Mustafa Hamid had no choice but to reach out to one of the most powerful and respected commanders in Afghanistan, Sheikh Jalaluddin Haqqani, to solve the crisis.

But in this case, even Haqqani was at a loss. "It is the most impossible thing in Afghanistan at the moment," he told Mustafa Hamid's messenger.[40] The problem was only solved due to the ever-shifting alliances of Afghan rebel leaders. After Dostum's commander confiscated the truck, Dostum joined in an alliance with Hekmatyar, and Hekmatyar in the end decided to help the Arabs get the truck back. The end of the story is that a substantial amount of weapons reached the Tajiks in the end – somewhere in the realms of ten tons, if we take Mustafa Hamid's account literally.[41]

---

[37] Details of the weapons transportation project are described in Hamid, *mashru' tajikistan*, and Abu Zubaydah, *The Abu Zubaydah Diaries, vol. 3*.

[38] Hamid, *mashru' tajikistan*, 28–29.

[39] Abu Zubaydah, *The Abu Zubaydah Diaries, vol. 4*, 9.

[40] Hamid, *mashru' tajikistan*, 31.

[41] According to Hamid, the Tajiks received two planeloads of weapons, which he estimated at four tons each, and one truckload. Hamid, *mashru' tajikistan*, 27.

The story of the Tajikistan project illustrates some common difficulties that foreign rebel groups encounter when operating in civil war settings. It supports the notion that failed states rarely constitute good "safe havens" for terrorists.[42] The unpredictable and violent environment of civil war makes them vulnerable and prone to be exploited – either by local bandits, or by various fighting factions who may have formerly posed as protectors. But even in war-torn Afghanistan, there were islands of relative peace and stability. Khost and Nangarhar were two such areas. Khost was controlled by Jalaluddin Haqqani's clan, while Nangarhar was under the control of the Nangarhar Shura led by the local warlord Haji Abdul Qadir.

Al-Qaida's Jihad Wal camp in Khost survived through the war because they came under protection of the Khost government. Their initial protector in the province had been Fayz Muhammad from Hekmatyar's party, but in 1993–94, the relationship between al-Qaida and Fayz Muhammad soured considerably. Fayz Muhammad was furious that al-Qaida had donated weapons to the Nahda Party, which was allied with his archenemy Ahmed Shah Massoud. He was constantly nagging the Arabs about buying their leftover ammunition and other equipment in order to use it in the civil war, but the Arabs refused. In the end, Fayz Muhammad's men physically assaulted Jihad Wal, and the Khost government had to intervene. The incident was so grave that the al-Qaida leadership in Sudan in the autumn of 1994 ordered Abu Ata' to evacuate Jihad Wal immediately.[43] The conflict was solved when the Khost government, which was dominated by Jalaluddin Haqqani's Zadran tribe, ensured al-Qaida continued protection in the province.

Abu Ata' stayed because Mustafa Hamid requested his help with training a new batch of Uzbek recruits who were due to arrive soon. Abu Ata' explained the situation in a letter to the al-Qaida leadership in Sudan dated September 4, 1994.[44] Al-Qaida's answer is not available, but the request was apparently approved. In the autumn of 1994, the al-Faruq camp was filled with Uzbek and Chechen recruits and the spirits of both trainers and trainees were high.[45] The Uzbeks and the Chechens were capable and highly motivated – unlike the first batch of Tajiks who

[42] *Al-Qaida's (mis)adventures in the Horn of Africa* (West Point, NY: Combating Terrorism Center, 2007): 14.
[43] AQ-SHPD-D-000-089, "A letter sent from the leader of a military group."
[44] Ibid.
[45] Hamid, *mashru' tajikistan*, 39.

had arrived in the spring of 1993, where some 80–90 percent deserted. The security issues of Jihad Wal were also solved for the time being. Meanwhile, the Pakistani authorities were tightening the noose of the Arabs in Peshawar.

UNWANTED GUESTS

"Your jihad is over!" said the Pakistani policeman with a satisfied grin on his face. He did not know who exactly it was that he had arrested, except that he was an Arab. And the Arabs had caused Pakistan nothing but trouble lately – if it were up to him they should all be arrested and deported back to where they came from.

"Damn it," thought Abu Zubaydah. "How did he know I was an Arab, even though I am wearing the Afghan white turban?" Normally he would bribe his way out of the situation, but there was an officer standing nearby, watching the scene. A bribe was out of the question. "I am with the United Nations," he said instead and showed his UN card. The policeman was disinterested. Probably he did not even know what a UN card was. "You can tell them inside the post," he said. Abu Zubaydah knew there would be no easy way out.[46]

Abu Zubaydah was arrested in March 1995 as part of a general crackdown on Arabs in the Peshawar area. It was not the first time that the police carried out such campaigns. Since 1992 the international community had been pressuring Pakistan to do something about the militant Arabs residing on their territory. Algeria and Egypt were experiencing campaigns of revolutionary violence in this period, connected to veterans from the Afghan-Soviet war. In Algeria, the Armed Islamic Group (GIA) and other Islamist guerrillas were involved in the Algerian civil war. In Egypt, al-Jama'a al-Islamiyya (JI) started a domestic terrorist campaign which by 1993 had killed some 120 people. Both countries accused Pakistan of hiding additional "terrorists" on their territory.[47] The United States joined the complaints – especially after the failed attack on the World Trade Center (WTC) on February 26, 1993. The main suspect in the case, Ramzi Yousef, escaped after the attack and was believed to be hiding in Pakistan. The United States was also concerned about Pakistan's support for Islamist guerrillas in Kashmir, and considered putting Pakistan on its notorious list of "State sponsors of terrorism." The

---

[46] The quotes are from Abu Zubaydah's own description of events in his diary. Abu Zubaydah, *The Abu Zubaydah Diaries, vol. 4,* 34–36.
[47] "Radical Arabs use Pakistan as base for Holy War," *New York Times,* April 8, 1993.

threat never materialized. Nevertheless, from early 1993 Pakistan was keen to demonstrate that it was not a terrorist state.

The authorities initially declared that all Arabs who did not have a legal reason to stay in Pakistan, must leave by January 31, 1993. The deadline was not immediately enforced. However, in April and May 1993 there was a wave of mass arrests of Arabs in Peshawar. It was in this context that Osama bin Laden and a number of associates relocated to Sudan. Others fled to Afghanistan where they were given shelter by Hekmatyar, Sayyaf or other mujahidin leaders.[48] Yet others were able to stay in Peshawar under cover of the many Arab NGOs that still operated in the city. Al-Qaida's Jihad Wal camp in Khost got at least one new resident in this period – the Egyptian Abu Hanifa, a former bomb maker from al-Jama'a al-Islamiyya. He would stay in Jihad Wal all through the civil war and the coming of the Taliban, hiding from Egyptian and Pakistani intelligence services. In the end, he became one of the nine Arabs that were killed in the US missile strikes on Khost on August 20, 1998.[49]

The Pakistani authorities did not have a consistent policy toward the Arabs. This was due, in part, to internal disagreements and, in part, to the relatively weak position of the Bhutto government. The political opposition used the Bhutto government's treatment of the Arabs as a pretext to tarnish the image of the regime. Arabs who were expelled to their home countries would surely face long prison terms, or even the death penalty. How could the Bhutto regime support such inhumane policies? Additionally, there was considerable pressure from Pakistani Islamist parties like Jamaat-e-Islami to leave the Arabs alone.[50]

The pestering of Arabs in Peshawar continued throughout 1994, albeit in a more subdued manner. In June 1994, a group of Arabs known as the "Khilafat Group" – which had previously refused to assist Mustafa Hamid's Tajikistan Project – were involved in a tribal feud in the remote Tirah Valley of Khyber Agency. The Arabs wanted to establish an Islamic caliphate on Pakistani soil and were sponsored by a local tribal leader. However, the other tribes in the area mobilized against them, resulting in a number of Arabs being killed. In August, four Egyptians were arrested in Peshawar, accused of belonging to the Khilafat group. In Pakistani newspapers the story took on a quite different flavor. It was alleged that the Arabs had set up the caliphate as cover for a range of "immoral"

[48] Ibid.
[49] Hamid, *mashru' tajikistan*, 61.
[50] "Arabs to be extradited, says Babar," *Dawn*, August 2, 1994; "The extradition question," *Dawn/LAT-WP News Service*, August 3, 1994.

activities including womanizing. The case led to a heated debate in Pakistan, with government representatives arguing the Arabs should be extradited while the Islamist opposition, fronted by Qazi Hussain Ahmad arguing for their innocence.[51] At the time of their arrest, Pakistan had just signed a formal extradition treaty with Egypt, and Interior Minister Nasrullah Babar promised that the Egyptians would be extradited in accordance with the treaty.

We do not know what happened to the Egyptians. What seems certain however, is that Pakistan continued their oppressive policies toward the Afghan-Arabs. In February 1995, the wanted WTC bomber Ramzi Yousef was apprehended in Islamabad. He was promptly extradited to the United States, despite protests from the Islamist opposition, which resented the idea of a Muslim being extradited to face trial in a non-Muslim country. After Ramzi's arrest, dozens of Arabs were arrested in Peshawar and elsewhere in a campaign to roll up Ramzi's network. In August, some sixty-five Egyptians were deported to Egypt in a chartered airplane sent by Egyptian authorities.[52] Pakistan's mass deportation of Arabs provides context for understanding why Taliban's refusal to expel Bin Laden in the late 1990s became an issue of such symbolic importance.

After Ramzi Yousef's arrest, it transpired that he was not only wanted for his role in the WTC bombings. He had also been involved in antiregime activities inside Pakistan, including a plot to assassinate Prime Minister Benazir Bhutto.[53] This is probably why Pakistan's reaction toward the Afghan-Arabs after Ramzi's arrest were so severe. But the problems did not end there. In November 1995, Egyptian militants carried out the first terrorist attack by Afghan-Arabs on Pakistani soil. A truck bomb exploded outside the Egyptian Embassy in Islamabad, killing sixteen and injuring dozens. The attack was part of an ongoing terrorist campaign against the Egyptian government, but it was also described as a revenge for Pakistan's deportation policies.[54] By now, it was clear that the Afghan-Arabs were not merely giving Pakistan a bad image abroad – they had become a threat to the Pakistani state itself.

---

[51] "Illegal Arabs involved in immoral acts: Haider," *The News*, August 3, 1994; "Arabs to be extradited, says Babar," *Dawn*, August 2, 1994.

[52] "WTC bombing suspect handed over to US," *Dawn*, February 10, 1995; "Arabs leaving country after crackdown in Ramzi case," *The News*, April 2, 1995.

[53] "Conspiracy to assassinate Benazir: Ramzi's men held in Lyari," *The News*, March 26, 1995.

[54] "Pakistan also was target, Egyptian group says," *Dawn*, November 22, 1995.

It was in this context that Abu Zubaydah was arrested at a checkpoint outside Peshawar in March or April 1995. They released him after three months. Perhaps they bought his cover story of being an asylum seeker registered with the UN. Or perhaps they were bribed by Abu Zubaydah's associates. We will never know for sure. Abu Zubaydah's story was plausible enough for the UN to believe him and to issue him official papers. The UN representative even visited him in jail and promised to plead his cause. "You look like a terrorist, but I know you well," he told Abu Zubaydah as he left. "Only if you knew!" thought Abu Zubaydah. He certainly had no love for the UN, or the "Infidel Nations" as he termed them, but in this case they proved to be useful to his cause.[55] By July 1995, Abu Zubaydah was back in business – a business that was becoming more difficult by the day.

Abu Zubaydah was one of few individuals that continued to facilitate training for Arabs in Afghanistan. By 1995, the Pakistani policies toward Arabs in Peshawar had forced these facilitation networks underground. Only a few training camps for Arabs were left in operation inside Afghanistan. Some of the camps were connected to Afghan mujahidin such as Hekmatyar or Sayyaf, who fought in the civil war. Other camps were run by Pakistani groups like Harakat ul-Ansar (HUA), who fought in Kashmir. Al-Qaida's old camp, al-Faruq, was used to train Tajiks, Uzbeks and Chechens. But very few camps offered basic training to Arabs who wanted to fight in Bosnia, Chechnya or elsewhere. Al-Qaida's al-Farouq camp had previously offered such training, but the courses were terminated in late 1992 or early 1993. After that, there was essentially one option left: Khalden.

Khalden was one of the longest operating training camps for Arab recruits in Afghanistan. It was located in Khost, most likely in the eastern part of the province on the border with Khurram Agency in Pakistan's Federally Administered Tribal Areas (FATA). It has often been described as an "al-Qaida camp" but there is little to substantiate this claim. Khalden was established by Abdullah Azzam's Services Office in the late 1980s or early 1990s, as a subsidiary to the famous Sada camp in Khurram Agency. In the fall of 1994 the Khalden camp was on the verge of shutting down, indicating the Services Office was withdrawing its support. The Services Office was experiencing pressure from Pakistani authorities in this period. Pakistani police in August 1994 raided the House of Martyrs, an Arab guesthouse in Peshawar, and arrested seven Arab

55 Abu Zubaydah, *The Abu Zubaydah Diaries, vol.* 4, 50, 60.

individuals, who were released only "after arduous efforts," according to Abu Zubaydah. In this period, Abu Zubaydah took over as Emir for the House of Martyrs, and established a close cooperative relationship with Ibn al-Shaykh al-Libi, the Emir of Khalden. From now on, "the work [the camp and the guesthouse] became integrated into one."[56]

It has been alleged that Khalden was financed by Bin Laden, but this is hard to substantiate. Abu Zubaydah had contact with lower-ranking al-Qaida members at Jihad Wal in the mid-1990s, but it is unlikely they had the means or authority to finance other training camps. During the Afghan civil war, it was individual entrepreneurs like Abu Zubaydah and Mustafa Hamid, and not al-Qaida, who kept the Arab training camps open.

When Afghan civil war started in 1992, al-Qaida stopped participating on the frontlines in Afghanistan. Al-Qaida, like most of the Afghan-Arab community in Peshawar, saw participation in the civil war as *fitna* (internal strife) rather than legitimate *jihad*. Initially, al-Qaida planned to continue using Afghanistan for training. But training in a civil war setting turned out to be challenging, for two reasons. First, Pakistan after 1992 changed their policies toward the Afghan-Arabs, hampering their freedom of movement within Pakistan. Second, al-Qaida's camps experienced pressure from Afghan mujahidin groups who wanted al-Qaida's weapons and ammunition for the civil war. Due to these challenges, in 1994 the al-Qaida leadership in Sudan considered closing the camps altogether. But the camps stayed open, largely due to the initiative of Abu Ata', the camp Emir, and with the protection of the local tribal government in Khost. This proved to be an advantage in 1996, when Bin Laden was forced to leave Sudan and once again re-locate al-Qaida's headquarters to Afghanistan.

[56] Abu Zubaydah, *The Abu Zubaydah Diaries, vol. 4*, 25, 30, 81.

3

Return of the Sheikh

In May 1996, Osama bin Laden returned to Afghanistan after being expelled from Sudan. He settled in the Eastern province of Nangarhar, where he was given refuge by old allies from the Afghan-Soviet war. But Bin Laden's position was vulnerable. The country was at civil war, and an obscure militia called the "Taliban" was on the march from the south. Bin Laden was eventually offered asylum in Afghanistan under the Taliban's protection. What characterized al-Qaida's early relationship to the Taliban?

FROM EXILE TO EXILE

In May 1996, an unscheduled flight descended upon Jalalabad airport. It had flown in from the Gulf, and carried Osama bin Laden and a group of his associates and family members. Jalalabad at the time was a relatively peaceful oasis in a country torn by civil war. The city was controlled by a coalition of ex-mujahidin commanders known as the Nangarhar Shura, who had declared neutrality in the war. Jalalabad was home to several foreign aid agencies and consulates, and was bustling with trade activity. Jalalabad was also the site of repeated attempts at peace negotiation between the Afghan factions warring over Kabul.[1]

When Osama bin Laden arrived in Jalalabad in May 1996, the peace efforts had just taken a leap forward. Rabbani and Hekmatyar, the two

---

[1] "Afghan factions alliance to have no effect on Nangrahar govt," *Business Recorder*, May 19, 1996; Mohammad Ali Imran, "Iran opens consulate in Jalalabad," *The Muslim*, June 10, 1996; "Jalalabad reaps economic reward of local peace," *The Muslim*, July 10, 1996.

main adversaries in the war, had decided to put their personal differences aside and join forces against a new threat from the south – an army of religious students led by an obscure mullah named Mohammed Omar.[2] Bin Laden had little knowledge of this new group, the "Taliban" as they were dubbed by the media, but neither were they of immediate concern to him. More importantly, he needed to establish good relations with the various factions that controlled Nangarhar.[3]

It is unclear precisely who had invited Bin Laden to Afghanistan. Most accounts agree that old allies of Bin Laden from the 1980s had invited him – political leaders and commanders who belonged to the four so-called fundamentalist mujahidin parties who had fought in the Afghan-Soviet war. The most detailed account of Bin Laden's return to Afghanistan was written in 2001 by Vahid Mojdeh, a former official in the Taliban's Ministry of Foreign Affairs.[4] According to Mojdeh, Bin Laden met with a group of Afghan commanders in Sudan in early 1996. During their meeting Bin Laden received their permission to settle in Nangarhar. The commanders were Engineer Mahmud (Hizb-e-Islami Khalis), Fazl al-Haqq (Hizb-e-Islami Hekmatyar) and Sazenoor (al-Ittihad al-Islami, led by Sayyaf). According to Mojdeh, Bin Laden flew to Jalalabad via the United Arab Emirates, in an airplane belonging to the Afghan-owned Ariana Airlines. Bin Laden's fourth eldest son Omar, who was onboard the plane, recalled in his memoirs that the plane was a Learjet chartered by the Sudanese government, and had flown directly to Jalalabad from Sudan with a refueling stop in Shiraz, Iran.[5] Whatever the truth, the accounts agree on one crucial point: It was not the Taliban who had invited Bin Laden to Afghanistan.

At Jalalabad airport, a small reception committee had gathered to greet the guests. There were probably no big names present at the airport to greet Bin Laden, although they may have given their consent to hosting Bin Laden prior to his arrival. Bin Laden's son Omar recalled that it took several weeks from Bin Laden's arrival in Nangarhar until he was able to meet the political leaders in the province. The Pakistani cleric Mullah Abdul Qawum Haqqani supports this account. He said that he met Bin Laden in Jalalabad in 1996 and helped him to arrange a meeting with the

---

[2] "New Afghan line-up," *The News*, May 15, 1996.

[3] Wright, *The looming tower*, 229.

[4] Vahid Mojdeh, *Afghanistan wa panj sal sultah taliban [Afghanistan under five years of Taliban sovereignty; Persian]*, 2nd ed. (Tehran: Nashreney, 1382 h.)

[5] Mojdeh, *Afghanistan wa panj sal*, 31–32; Sasson, N. bin Laden and O. bin Laden, *Growing up Bin Laden*, 139–143.

district governor of Jalalabad. Up until then, Bin Laden himself had been unable to arrange such a meeting.[6]

According to Bin Laden's former bodyguard, Abu Jandal, Bin Laden was greeted in Jalalabad by Engineer Mahmud. An article in *al-Hayat* from October 1996 substantiates this claim. It says that it was Engineer Mahmud who first hosted Bin Laden when he arrived in Afghanistan.[7] As we recall from Chapter 2, Engineer Mahmud was the Afghan commander in charge of Tora Bora when Bin Laden's men fought there in 1991–1992. According to Mojdeh, Engineer Mahmud was also one of the three men who had met Bin Laden in Sudan in early 1996 and invited him to Afghanistan. Omar bin Laden's account is slightly different; he recalled that they were met at the airport by a local commander named Mullah Noorullah, described as a powerful man in Jalalabad. Mullah Noorullah is probably identical to Haji Sazenoor (or Haji Saz Nur), a commander from Sayyaf's party.[8] Sazenoor, as we recall from Chapter 1, was one of the Afghan commanders who fought with Bin Laden's men during the Battle of Jalalabad in 1989. He was also a member of the three-man delegation described earlier by Mojdeh. In any case, the accounts agree that local commanders from Nangarhar, not high-level political leaders, met Bin Laden at Jalalabad airport.

In Nangarhar, Bin Laden had to start from scratch. According to Omar, they initially stayed at Sazenoor's house in Jalalabad while Bin Laden was setting up his own residence. Bin Laden was granted access to two properties in Nangarhar – a residence in or near Jalalabad city referred to as "Najm al-Jihad" and a hideout in Tora Bora.

Najm al-Jihad was a housing complex established by Yunus Khalis on the outskirts of Jalalabad city.[9] A Pakistani journalist, who visited Jalalabad in July 1996, recalled the "Bin Laden camp" at the site. At the time it was only a tent camp on a large field of grass, surrounded by a few strands of barbed wire and some Egyptian guards. The camp was meant for wives and children of the Arabs who had returned with Bin Laden to Afghanistan. "It's very dangerous here, the country is

---

[6] Sasson, N. bin Laden and O. bin Laden, *Growing up Bin Laden*, 154–156; Tor Arne Andreassen, "Hos Talibans læremester [Visiting the Taliban's mentor]," *Aftenposten*, October 19, 2001.

[7] Bergen, *The Osama*, 159; Ahmad Muwaffaq Zaydan, "*al-haraka a'tat al-aman li-ma la yaqill an 400 arabi wa rahabat bi-wujudihim. bin ladin wa 'al-afghan al-arab' fi manatiq saytarat taliban*," *al-Hayat*, October 5, 1996.

[8] Kevin Bell, *Usama bin Laden's 'Father Sheikh': Yunus Khalis and the return of al-Qai'da's leadership to Afghanistan* (West Point, NY: Combatting Terrorism Center, 2013): 57.

[9] For background on Najm al-Jihad, see Ibid., 55–61.

dangerous," said one Egyptian guard to the journalist. "I prefer the mountains. I feel safer there."[10]

Bin Laden also preferred the mountains. A few months after arriving in Jalalabad, he moved to a primitive mud-and-stone facility in Tora Bora, located "a twisting seven-hour drive" from the plains of Jalalabad.[11] The choice was no coincidence. Tora Bora had been the main site for al-Qaida's guerrilla operations in Afghanistan from late 1991 to April 1992. Back then, al-Qaida's men had worked directly with Engineer Mahmoud. Now, Engineer Mahmoud had seemingly returned the favor, by allowing Bin Laden to use the mountain as a hideout. The London-based Arab journalist Abdul Bari Atwan visited Bin Laden in Tora Bora in November 1996. "He loved that nature there. He loved the mountain. They were trying to have their own community, grow their foods," Atwan recalled.[12]

Although Bin Laden may have romanticized his stay at Tora Bora to visiting journalists, his move there was probably prompted by real security concerns. There are indications that powerful leaders in Jalalabad were against Bin Laden's presence in the province. In late July or early August 1996 the Nangarhar Shura, which was led by Governor Haji Abdul Qadir, denied Bin Laden's request for safe haven in the province. According to a cable from the US State Department, the Shura had decided that "... Bin Laden would not be allowed to work or live in their territory."[13] The information is partly substantiated by other sources. According to a former Taliban official, Haji Abdul Qadir was opposed to Bin Laden's presence in Nangarhar and wanted to expel him from the province prior to the Taliban's takeover.[14] After the Shura's decision, it was rumored that Bin Laden had disappeared to Kabul or that he was hiding in Sarobi, Hekmatyar's stronghold.[15] In reality, he probably went to Tora Bora and stayed there under the protection of his old ally, Engineer Mahmud.[16]

---

[10] "Little comfort for families of Mujahideen," *Pakistan Times*, July 12, 1996.

[11] Phil Hirschkorn and Peter Bergen, "Rare photos reveal Osama bin Laden's Afghan hideout," *CNN*, March 11, 2015.

[12] Ibid.

[13] Department of State (Washington) Cable, "Afghanistan: Whereabouts of extremist supporter Osama bin Laden," September 4, 1996.

[14] Author's interview with Afghan source (anonymized).

[15] "Department of State (Washington) Cable, "Afghanistan: Whereabouts of extremist supporter Osama bin Laden."

[16] According to Omar bin Laden, the Bin Laden family continued to live in Tora Bora until Bin Laden met with Mullah Omar in the spring of 1997. Leaked US intelligence confirms that Bin Laden continued residing in Nangarhar after 1996 and was under the protection of Engineer Mahmoud's deputy, Awal Gul, who was later captured and sent to Guantanamo. Sasson, N. bin Laden, and O. bin Laden, *Growing up Bin Laden*, 201;

The Taliban occupied the city of Jalalabad on September 11, 1996. Hajj Abdul Qadir fled to Pakistan, and the rest of the Nangarhar Shura decided to peacefully hand over the province to the Taliban. Coincidentally, both Engineer Mahmud and Haji Sazenoor were killed around this time by local criminals, which meant that Bin Laden lost his immediate protectors in the province.[17] It was now up to the Taliban to decide what to do with Bin Laden.

ENTER THE TALIBAN

On September 23, 1996, the Taliban movement took control over the Afghan capital Kabul and became *de facto* rulers of Afghanistan. The Taliban's supreme ruler, Mullah Mohammad Omar, appointed a number of acting ministers to run the administration in Kabul, while the seat of power remained in Mullah Omar's home province Kandahar. The new regime faced enormous challenges, the most urgent being the military threat from northern Afghan commanders and warlords who had refused to give up their territory to the Taliban. The war against these commanders would continue throughout the Taliban's reign, but was most intense in 1997 and 1998, when the Taliban struggled to capture the northern Afghan city of Mazar-e-Sharif.

It is unclear whether Bin Laden had an opinion of the Taliban at the time. The student movement was certainly known to the Arab world – its military advances in southern and eastern Afghanistan in 1995–1996 were being covered in the Arab press. Moreover, the Taliban were well-known among Afghan-Arabs in Peshawar. In 1995, *al-Jihad* magazine carried an interview with the leader of the Pakistani group Harakat al-Ansar, who praised the Taliban movement's advances.[18] In 1996, the Deobandi Scholar Abdul Qayum Haqqani – a known Taliban supporter – visited Bin Laden in Jalalabad. Although there are no indications that Bin Laden had direct ties to Taliban before 1996, Bin Laden had at least ties to individuals who were ideologically supportive of the Taliban.

AF-000782, "Recommendation for Continued Detention Under DoD Control (CD) for Guantanamo Detainee, ISN US9AF-000782DP [Awal Gul]," Department of Defense (Joint Task Force Guantanamo), February 15, 2008.

[17] Bell, *Usama bin Laden's 'Father Sheikh'*, 57; "'al-afghan-al-arab' ikhtaffu am tahawwalu ila 'taliban arab'? taliban wa kabul: ma'raka taqsim afghanistan," *al-Hayat*, September 30, 1996; Sasson, N. bin Laden, and O. bin Laden, *Growing up Bin Laden*, 173–74.

[18] Muhammad Salim, "al-yawm tahrir al-muslimin wa ghadan iqamat al-khilafa al-islamiyya," *al-Jihad*, no. 119 (March 1995): 20.

This suggests that Bin Laden may have been favorably inclined to accept the Taliban's ideology. But there are scarce indications that Bin Laden sought to establish relations to the Taliban before circumstances forced him to do so.

On their way toward Jalalabad, the Taliban had already encountered Arabs. The first encounter probably happened in Khost in 1995, where Arabs had been running training camps throughout the civil war. We know little of the details of these encounters, but it was most likely an undramatic affair. Al-Qaida's Jihad Wal camp in southern Khost was under the protection of the Khost government, which was controlled by Jalaluddin Haqqani's clan. When the Taliban came to Khost in 1995 Haqqani decided to ally himself with the Taliban instead of putting up resistance. This probably meant that the Khost government continued to run business as usual in the province – including hosting the Jihad Wal camp. The only foreign training camp affected by the Taliban's takeover appears to have been the camp of Hizb ul-Mujahidin – a Pakistani camp affiliated with Hekmatyar and Jamaat-e-Islami – which was shut down by Taliban and handed to another Pakistani group (Harakat ul-Ansar) in November 1996.[19]

Eyewitness accounts from this period confirm that the Taliban's takeover of Khost was a rather undramatic event for the Arabs. The first account is provided by Omar Nasiri, a French-Algerian jihadist who was a trainee in Khalden at the time. He says that after the Taliban's takeover of Khost a group of turbaned men came to visit the camp. They were not high-ranking Taliban members, but local representatives who came to the camp to ask for weapons. After having tea with the camp's leadership they left in peace, apparently convinced that the Khalden camp was no military threat to them.[20] The other account is given by Mustafa Hamid who stayed in the Jihad Wal area at the time. He does not mention any Taliban coming to the camp, but he says he sent a delegation to Gardez to offer the Taliban support in the form of training. "They did not even know how to shoot or clean their weapons" he recalled, rather condescendingly.[21] But again, their encounter was peaceful and it was with local Taliban and not with high-ranking leaders.

In other cases, the Taliban encountered Arabs who fought them violently. They were Arabs who had fought with Hekmatyar during the

[19] "Concern at reactivation of Afghan militant camps," *The News*, November 22, 1996.
[20] Omar Nasiri, *Inside the jihad: My life with Al Qaeda* (New York: Basic Books, 2007): 193–94.
[21] Hamid, *mashru' tajikistan*, 15.

Afghan civil war, and who defended his stronghold at Chahar Asyab south of Kabul.[22] In mid-1998, Abu Mus'ab al-Suri described the battles between Taliban and Hekmatyar's Arabs in 1994–1996 as having an overall negative effect on the relations between the Arabs and the Taliban. He claimed that the Taliban only saw "symbolic good" in the Arabs and in reality, "... the first Arab behavior they observed was their fighting with Hekmatyar. Even if it was a small group, they were still Arabs."[23] But these fighters were not associated with Bin Laden. Mustafa Hamid argued that the relationship between Arabs and the Taliban "took a decisive turn" when Bin Laden entered into an alliance with Mullah Omar after 1996.[24] This is supported by an *al-Hayat* account which suggests that the reason why the Taliban allowed Bin Laden and his followers to stay in Afghanistan was that he had not fought against the movement in the past.[25]

Most accounts agree that after the Taliban's takeover of Jalalabad in September 1996, there was a meeting between Taliban representatives and Bin Laden to determine the latter's future in Afghanistan. Many of the accounts emphasize the Taliban's humble attitude toward the Saudi guest and their immediate readiness to serve him.[26] Abu Mus'ab al-Suri recalled that when the Taliban arrived in Nangarhar, they sent a delegation to meet with Bin Laden in Jalalabad. They ensured him that he would be treated as an honorary guest of the country and even told him courteously, "we will not be your servants. We will serve the dust on which you walk."[27] Omar bin Laden's account is similar. He wrote that a Taliban delegation visited Bin Laden in Tora Bora shortly after Mullah Nourallah's death and ensured Bin Laden he would be under the protection of the Taliban. Internal al-Qaida sources from the time confirm the impression that the first meeting was cordial. In a letter written probably in mid-1997, Abu Hafs al-Masri recounted: "After [the Taliban] arrived in Jalalabad, we met with them and they gave us a warm welcome."[28]

[22] Ibid.
[23] Abu Mus'ab al-Suri and Abu Khalid al-Suri, "Noble brother Abu-Abdallah [Letter to Osama bin Laden dated July 17, 1998]," unpublished, courtesy Brynjar Lia, Andrew Higgins, and Alan Cullison.
[24] Hamid, *mashru' tajikistan*, 15.
[25] Zaydan, "*al-haraka a'tat al-aman.*"
[26] Abu Mus'ab al-Suri, *afghanistan wa al-taliban wa ma'rakat al-islam al-yawm* (Kabul: Markaz al-Ghuraba' lil-Dirasat al-Islamiyya, 1998): 26.
[27] Ibid., 26.
[28] AQ-SHPD-D-000-103, "Letter to Abu Khalid from Abu Hafs Al-Masri about cooperation of Taliban, Al Qaida and Pakistan," undated [ca. March–June 1997], Conflict Records Resource Center, Washington, DC.

Taliban officials have later insisted that "we did not invite Osama; we got him as a legacy."[29] As discussed, ex-mujahidin in eastern Afghanistan, not the Taliban, were responsible for Bin Laden's return to Afghanistan. However, once Taliban conquered Nangarhar, there is every reason to believe they gave him a courteous welcome. Taliban officials in Nangarhar, who spoke with the Pakistani journalist Rahimullah Yusufzai in October 1996, gave three reasons for hosting Bin Laden:

First, he was already in their territory when they took Jalalabad. Second, Bin Laden had assisted the Afghans a lot in their jihad against the Soviets. Third, the Taliban were not sure he was involved in terrorist activities, and had not yet seen convincing proof of his involvement.[30]

The Arab journalist Ahmad Zaydan wrote around the same time that Bin Laden sent an envoy to Mullah Omar in Kandahar, declaring his peaceful intentions:

The envoy, who visited the "Taliban" leadership's headquarters in Kandahar, told them that Osama bin Laden would support the movement ... The "Taliban" told the envoy that they welcome Osama bin Laden and the "Afghan-Arabs" that accompany him to stay in areas under their control, especially since they had not participated in the fight against the movement.[31]

Although the gist of the preceding accounts seem well documented, there is probably also information missing. Bin Laden was likely dependent on intermediaries to introduce him to the Taliban. Existing literature claims that Pakistan's Inter-Services Intelligence (ISI) played a role in introducing Bin Laden to Taliban officials.[32] These claims are somewhat problematic, because they are not well substantiated and probably based on the common perception at the time that Taliban was controlled by the ISI. Other sources suggest that Jalaluddin Haqqani introduced Bin Laden to the Taliban, which may be more plausible since there were historical ties between the two, and since Haqqani had already aligned himself with the Taliban by the time Bin Laden arrived in Afghanistan. However, they are contradicted by other sources, including the well-informed

---

[29] "America must give up its irrational attitude. An interview with Minister of Information of the Islamic Emirate of Afghanistan, Maulavi Qudratullah," *Taleban Home Page, New York Office*, July 19, 2000. For more examples of the Taliban's reasons for not handing over Bin Laden, see State Department Report, "U.S. Engagement with the Taliban on Osama bin Laden," July 16, 2001.

[30] Department of State (Peshawar) Cable, "Afghanistan: Taliban stall in permitting Western journalists access to Osama bin Laden," November 11, 1996.

[31] Zaydan, "*al-haraka a'tat al-aman.*"

[32] Rashid, *Taliban*, 138–39;

Arab journalist Ahmad Zaydan, who wrote in 1996 that it was Engineer Mahmoud who acted as an intermediary between Bin Laden and the Taliban prior to Engineer Mahmoud's death.[33]

By March 1997 Bin Laden had secured Mullah Omar's personal permission to stay in Afghanistan. On March 6, 1997, media reported that Bin Laden had met with Mullah Omar in Kandahar, and had offered the Taliban leader assistance in two areas he knew well from before: Construction and fighting. Bin Laden had agreed to carry out a few reconstruction projects, such as improving the road between Jalalabad and Kandahar, and to build a water channel to the agricultural fields in Kandahar. Moreover, he offered to put his fighters to the service of the Taliban, to assist them in their fight against mujahidin factions in Northern Afghanistan.[34] The account is substantiated by Abu Mus'ab al-Suri who recalled that in the beginning of the relationship between Bin Laden and the Taliban, Bin Laden made many promises to Mullah Omar such as urbanization projects, road building, economic projects and the provision of fighters to defend Kabul, "but the wind blew them away," as he wrote.[35] It is unclear if Bin Laden ever carried out the promised reconstruction projects. But whatever he may have promised, it was probably taken as credible. Bin Laden was known as a wealthy Saudi and a generous financier of the Afghan mujahidin movement. He had reportedly been involved in road construction projects in Eastern Afghanistan, having recently helped improve the road between Jalalabad and Torkham at the Afghan-Pakistani border.[36]

Indeed, many sources have emphasized that money was a central component of the initial alliance between Bin Laden and the Taliban. Former Taliban officials have claimed that Bin Laden had a deliberate strategy of buying his way into the Taliban's hearts. According to former Taliban Foreign Ministry official Vahid Mojdeh,

Osama and his loyalists were of course well aware of how to influence the Taliban, relying on their previous experiences with Mujahideen leaders. The purchase of expensive automobiles for Mullah Omar and his loyalists was the first step in that direction. Financial support in the war against the Taliban's opposition, in particular buying off the opposing commanders, proved to be an effective

[33] Zaydan, "*al-haraka a'tat al-aman.*"
[34] Ahmad Muwaffaq Zaydan, "*fi zill bawadir tahawwul fi al-siyasa al-pakistaniyya al-da'ima lil-haraka. bin ladin yuttafiq ma'a za'im 'taliban' ala tanfidh mashari' fi al-janub,*" *al-Hayat*, March 6, 1997.
[35] Lia, *Architect of global jihad*, 287.
[36] Zaydan, "*fi zill bawadir tahawwul fi al-siyasa al-pakistaniyya al-da'ima lil-haraka.*"

strategy ... Using his own financial assets, Osama bin Laden successfully positioned himself among the Taliban.[37]

But the size of Bin Laden's financial assets in 1996 is disputed. In the words of Steve Coll, Bin Laden was "close to financial bankruptcy" when he arrived in Afghanistan in 1996, because the Sudanese government had confiscated many of his personal assets.[38] All that remained was a modest amount of personal savings, in addition to donations from charities and wealthy individuals in the Gulf.[39] Omar bin Laden testified to the fact that his father was no longer a rich man in 1996. Their family "had been poor since 1994," he claimed, when Bin Laden's personal assets were frozen. But the situation did not become critical until 1998, when the Saudi regime banned charities from donating money to Bin Laden's cause. Omar recalled that for a period in 1998, Bin Laden barely had enough money to feed his family and fighters in Kandahar.

We were truly desperate for the first time, in such a low state that there was no money for food for our family, or for the enormous band of people who had gathered around my father.[40]

In the end, Bin Laden's financial contributions to the Taliban were probably more symbolic than strategically important. Although Bin Laden might have had access to a network of wealthy donors abroad, it is unlikely that his financial and monetary contributions to the Taliban regime ever exceeded those of the Taliban's major state sponsors; Pakistan, Saudi Arabia and the United Arab Emirates. Ahmed Rashid argues that Saudi and Pakistani intelligence gave a far more substantial contribution to the Taliban's car park and finances:

The Saudi intelligence chief Prince Turki al Faisal visited Kandahar in mid-June [1998], after which the Saudis provided the Taliban with 400 pick-up trucks and financial aid. Pakistan's ISI had prepared a budget of some 2 billion rupees (US$ 5 million) for logistical support that was needed by the Taliban.[41]

Due to the close ties between Bin Laden and the Saudi intelligence during the 1980s, it is possible that some of Bin Laden's "gifts" to Mullah Omar may have been conflated with those of the Saudi intelligence. Another possibility is that the Land Cruisers attributed to Bin Laden were in fact

[37] Mojdeh, *Afghanistan wa panj sal,* 163–64.
[38] Coll, *Ghost wars,* 332; The story of how the Sudanese government confiscated Bin Laden's assets is told in detail in Wright, *The looming tower,* 222.
[39] Coll, *Ghost wars,* 332.
[40] Sasson, N. bin Laden, and O. bin Laden, *Growing up Bin Laden,* 223.
[41] Rashid, *Taliban,* 72.

gifts left by rich Gulf Arabs who regularly came to Southern Afghanistan for falcon hunting and other recreation.[42]

There are many possible reasons that the Taliban decided to host Bin Laden. The initial decision is often ascribed to a mixture of Afghan cultural codes, Taliban's and Bin Laden's common identity as Muslims, Bin Laden's status as a former benefactor of the Afghan mujahidin movement, and his promises to provide the Taliban with financial and military assistance.[43] "Pashtun culture," which obligates a host to honor and protect his guests, has been described as a reason in itself, and may certainly have colored the initial meeting between the Taliban representatives and Bin Laden. Intermediaries, such as eastern Afghan commanders or Deobandi scholars who supported Bin Laden, may also have played a role in forging their ties.

Overall, the historical context must be taken into account. In August-September 1996, the Taliban was in the middle of a military campaign to take control over Kabul, which they achieved on September 27, 1996. After that, they were preoccupied with their goal of conquering Northern Afghanistan. Bin Laden's men were not involved in the civil war, and therefore posed no immediate threat to the Taliban's conquest for power within Afghanistan. There were simply no compelling reasons for the Taliban to expel him – at least not at the time. But this was soon about to change.

THE MEDIA WAR BEGINS

In August 1996, the London-based Arab newspaper *al-Quds al-Arabi* published Bin Laden's "Declaration of Jihad against the Americans Occupying the Land of the Two Holy Sanctuaries."[44] The "Declaration of Jihad" was issued before Bin Laden came under the Taliban's protection. This suggests that Bin Laden intended to use Afghanistan as a base for his war against the United States, even before he was offered asylum by the Taliban or knew about the opportunities the Taliban sanctuary would later offer al-Qaida.

Bin Laden's 1996 declaration was not merely reflecting a shift in al-Qaida's strategy – from support to Muslim revolutionaries worldwide,

---

[42] Author's interview with former Taliban official (anonymized).

[43] For example, see Department of State (Islamabad) Cable, "Afghanistan: The enigmatic Mullah Omar and Taliban decision-making," March 28, 1997.

[44] Osama bin Laden, "*i'lan al-jihad ala al-amrikyyin al-muhtallin li-bilad al-haramayn,*" *al-Quds al-Arabi*, August 23, 1996.

to direct confrontation with the "far enemy," the United States. The declaration can also be viewed as an escalation of a preexisting conflict between Bin Laden and the Saudi Arabian regime. Most of the declaration deals not with the crimes of the United States, but with the "infidelity" of the Saudi Arabian regime who invited US troops into the country after the Gulf War in 1991. For ideological and strategic reasons that will be dealt with later, Bin Laden did not declare *jihad* on the Saudi regime itself but rather, on the foreign "occupants" – the removal of which he saw as vital step toward reforming the political system in the country.

In addition to issuing the "Declaration of Jihad," Bin Laden conducted several international media interviews from Nangarhar: With Robert Fisk from *The Independent* in July 1996, with Abdul Bari Atwan from *al-Quds al-Arabi* in November 1996, and with Peter Arnett from CNN in March 1997.[45] The interviews were centered on the same topics as the "Declaration of Jihad" – the infidelity of the Saudi regime and America's perceived crimes toward the Muslim world in general and their "occupation" of Saudi Arabia in particular. Bin Laden praised the Khobar tower bombings in Riyadh on June 25, 1996, albeit not taking direct responsibility for them, and he threatened that there would be more attacks.[46]

These interviews were conducted in Nangarhar. It is possible that Bin Laden asked Sheikh Yunus Khalis for permission to meet the journalists in this period. Ayman al-Zawahiri recalled in 2002 that Bin Laden at some point asked Yunus Khalis for permission to give press interviews, whereupon the latter answered, "Why do you ask my permission? Do what you think is right."[47] Abu Jandal, Bin Laden's bodyguard, confirmed that leaders in Jalalabad "had no problem with" Bin Laden's declaration of *jihad* against America in 1996.[48] Other sources confirm that Bin Laden sought approval from a number of Afghan and Pakistani clerics for his 1996 declaration. In this context it may be true that Bin Laden

---

[45] Thomas Hegghammer, *Dokumantasjon om al-Qaida: Intervjuer, kommunikéer og andre primærkilder, 1990–2002* [Documentation on al-Qaida: Interviews, communiqués and other primary sources, 1990–2002] (Kjeller: Norwegian Defence Research Establishment (FFI), 2002): 18–24, 30–38.

[46] Later research has demonstrated that Bin Laden was, in fact, not involved in the planning or financing of the Khobar tower bombings. Thomas Hegghammer, "Deconstructing the myth about al-Qa'ida and Khobar," *CTC Sentinel* 1, no. 3 (February 2008): 20–22.

[47] Ayman al-Zawahiri, *al-tabri'a: risala fi tabri'at ummat al-qalam wa al-sayf min munqissat tuhmat al-khawa wa al-da'f* (Place and publisher unknown, 2008): 51.

[48] Khalid al-Hammadi, "Al-Qa'ida from within, as narrated by Abu-Jandal (Nasir al-Bahri)," part 3, *al-Quds al-Arabi*, March 28, 2005. Translated to English by Foreign Broadcast Information Service (FBIS).

discussed the fatwa with Yunus Khalis, whom he met with in Jalalabad in mid-1996, according to Omar Bin Laden.[49]

The "Declaration of Jihad" and the international media interviews served as yet another provocation to Bin Laden's main adversaries, the United States and Saudi Arabia. Both countries had put pressure on Sudan to expel Bin Laden in May 1996 and were continuing to trace Bin Laden's movements and activities in Afghanistan. The United States was concerned about Bin Laden's international terrorist activities and especially his sponsorship of "terrorist training camps" in Afghanistan where Ramzi Yousef, who carried out the World Trade Center bombing in 1993, had allegedly received training. For Saudi Arabia, Bin Laden was a troublesome political dissident who needed to be silenced.

Shortly after the Taliban's conquest of Kabul in September 1996, the United States started putting pressure on the Taliban to close all "terrorist training camps" on their territory and to expel Bin Laden. "The presence of Osama bin Laden in Afghanistan is not a positive development for Afghanistan," US diplomats were instructed to tell Taliban.[50] The Taliban's initial reaction was one of denial. Osama bin Laden is "not in areas controlled by the Taliban," said Mullah Jalil on September 18, 1996.[51] But after the Taliban came to power in Nangarhar, Bin Laden continued to live in properties associated with the Hizb-e-Islami Khalis in Najm al-Jihad outside Jalalabad, and in Tora Bora where he met Abdul Bari Atwan in November 1996.[52] By January 1997, the Taliban had publically admitted that Bin Laden was in areas under their control. According to the head of Taliban's Kabul administration, Mullah Rabbani, Bin Laden had been told "not to carry out terrorist activities" from the soil of Afghanistan.[53]

In reality, the Taliban did not control Bin Laden at this point or, at least, they did not prevent him from talking to foreign journalists. In March 1997, Bin Laden gave his first televised interview to Peter Arnett from the CNN. According to Peter Bergen, who produced the interview and

[49] Sasson, N. Bin Laden, and O. Bin Laden, *Growing up Bin Laden*, 154.
[50] Department of State (Washington) Cable, "Demarche to the Taliban on terrorism," September 18, 1996.
[51] Department of State (Islamabad) Cable, "Afghanistan: Taliban asserts "Arabs" have fled training camps; bin Laden's whereabouts unknown," September 19, 1996.
[52] Department of State (Islamabad) Cable, "Afghanistan: Bin Laden reportedly in Jalalabad," October 14, 1996; al-Hammadi, "Al-Qa'ida from within," part 4; and Hirschkorn and Bergen, "Rare photos reveal Osama bin Laden's Afghan hideout."
[53] Department of State (Peshawar) Cable, "Afghanistan: Taliban agree to visits of militant training camps, admit Bin Ladin is their guest," January 9, 1997.

accompanied Peter Arnett to Afghanistan, they arranged the interview directly with Bin Laden's Arab contacts in London and were not questioned by Taliban authorities on their way to interviewing Bin Laden.[54] The interview was held somewhere outside Jalalabad, possibly in Tora Bora where Bin Laden was said to be residing at the time.[55]

Saudi Arabia also started pressuring the Taliban to hand over Bin Laden. In the beginning of March, 1997, there were rumors that Saudi Arabia had asked the Taliban for Bin Laden's deportation. The pressure seems to have increased after Bin Laden's interview with the CNN.[56] Shortly after the interview, Bin Laden was summoned to meet with Mullah Omar in Kandahar. There are various second- and third-hand accounts of this meeting that say roughly the same thing: Mullah Omar expressed concern about Bin Laden's "aggressive" media statements and told him to not use Afghan territory for anti-Saudi activities. At the same time, Mullah Omar agreed in principle that the stationing of US troops in Saudi Arabia was wrong.[57] This suggests there was no principal ideological disagreement between the two. The disagreement mainly concerned the method and timing of Bin Laden's campaign.

The Saudi authorities also contacted Sheikh Yunus Khalis and asked him to encourage Bin Laden to return to Saudi Arabia. Khalis actually wrote Bin Laden a letter after this. "I urge you to go living near the two holy sanctuaries [Mecca and Medina]" he said in the letter, which is probably written around the end of March, 1997.[58] Responding to the pressure, the Taliban solved the problem in a way that would repeat itself later. When subject to international scrutiny, the Taliban would move the Arabs out of view or to areas where it was harder for foreigners to conduct surveillance and infiltration.

By the beginning of April 1997, Bin Laden had moved with his family and around a hundred followers to Kandahar, the heartland of the Taliban.[59] The official explanation was that he was moved for security

[54] For a first-hand account of the interview, see Bergen, *Holy War Inc.*, 1–23.

[55] Bergen, *Holy War Inc.*, 1–23; Behroz Khan, "Saudi Arabia seeking deportation of Bin Laden from Afghanistan," *The News*, March 3, 1997.

[56] Khan, "Saudi Arabia seeking"; Department of State (Washington) Cable, "Afghanistan: Saudi polcouns says they still want bin Laden," May 5, 1997.

[57] Department of State (Islamabad) Cable, "Afghanistan: Taliban official confirms that Mullah Omar asked bin Laden to refrain from "anti-Saudi" activities," March 27, 1997.

[58] AQ-PMPR-D-001-554, "Two letters to Osama bin Laden, one from Mowlawi Mohammed Yunis of the Islamic Party of Afghanistan and one from H. Ibn al-Sheikh," April 1, 1997, Conflict Records Resource Center, Washington, DC.

[59] AQ-MSLF-D-001-509, "A letter by Abd al-Aziz to Abu Hafs inquiring about the condition of Osama bin Laden following the publication of several news reports about the

reasons, but there was speculation he was moved so that the Taliban could better control his media activities.[60] The argument suggesting that Bin Laden was moved for security reasons is plausible. Nangarhar was a volatile region, and Bin Laden's local protectors had been killed the autumn before. According to some observers, the Taliban were in a hurry to move Bin Laden because of several armed groups that had arrived in Eastern Afghanistan.[61] However, others emphasize that the real reason for Bin Laden's move was that Taliban wanted to control his media statements. Mullah Mutawakkil later wrote that Bin Laden had been moved so that the Taliban could better control his activities – allegedly because Saudi Arabia had pressured them to do so.[62] Bin Laden in fact did not give any more international press interviews until a year later, in May 1998.[63] By moving Bin Laden to Kandahar in the spring 1997, and by promising to control his activities, the Taliban seemed to have solved the Bin Laden issue for the time being without compromising on their Islamic principles. Al-Qaida's leaders, for their part, were both pleased and encouraged.

"THE DUTIES TOWARD THE MOVEMENT"

The Taliban's conquest of Afghanistan, and their subsequent invitation of Bin Laden to Kandahar, was an unexpected turn of events for al-Qaida. This is evident from internal al-Qaida correspondence from that period. In a letter written probably in mid-1997, Abu Hafs states, "conditions in Afghanistan have developed in an unexpected way."[64] He goes on to describe the history of the Taliban movement and their strengths and weaknesses. Although he points out some weaknesses, such as the Taliban's lack of "sufficient administrative, organizational

---

Taliban's intention to hand him over to the Saudi Government," April 23, 1997, Conflict Records Resource Center, Washington, DC; Department of State (Washington) Cable, "Afghanistan: Saudi polcouns says they still want bin Laden," May 5, 1997; Ahmad Muwaffaq Zaydan, *"'taliban' ajilat fi naqlihi wa hadharatu min hajamat. bin ladin fi qandahar ba'idan an al-sahafa wa hirsan ala amnihi,"* al-Hayat, April 8, 1997.

[60] Zaydan, *"'taliban' ajilat fi naqlihi."*
[61] Ibid.; al-Hammadi, "Al-Qa'ida from within," part 9.
[62] Mutawakil, *Afghanistan aw taliban*, 46–47.
[63] This interview was conducted with ABC News journalist John Miller. Notably, the interview was conducted in Khost without the Taliban's permission. See Miller's own account of the interview, in John Miller, Michael Stone and Chris Mitchell, *The cell: inside the 9/11 plot and why the FBI and CIA failed to stop it* (New York: Hyperion, 2002): 176–192.
[64] AQ-SHTP-D-000-103, "Letter to Abu Khalid from Abu Hafs Al-Masri."

and political experience," there is little doubt that al-Qaida's overall impression of the Taliban at this point, is positive:

Thank God, our relationship with [the Taliban] is excellent. The Saudi consul and the Pakistanis came at the behest of the Americans, and they asked the Taliban to hand us over. The Taliban took a really excellent stand, even after the meetings with the press.[65]

The Taliban's welcoming attitude toward the Arabs in 1996–1997 was no doubt an important factor in Abu Hafs' praise of the Taliban. But the recurrent theme in his praise was the Taliban's adherence to Islamic law – from their implementation of *hudud* punishments to their banning of music and television. He also noted that Mullah Omar received the *bay'a* (oath of allegiance) of "more than 1,500 Afghan scholars" to become *amir al mu'minin* (Emir of the Faithful) and that the Taliban leadership was comprised of individuals "from different parties, not just one" – apparently, to reassure the reader that the Taliban is not just another faction in the civil war. It is evident from the letter that the author sees Taliban as a nascent Islamic state – manifested in their efforts to implement *Sharia* law on their territory. Importantly, he refutes conspiracy theories claiming that the Taliban is a creation of the Pakistani intelligence, suggesting instead that Pakistan and Taliban currently have a tactical alliance but that Pakistan, in the long run, will seek to replace the Taliban with a government that completely follows Pakistan's objectives.

He also claims that in meetings with Taliban leaders, "we felt their sincerity and resoluteness to establish the religion and to continue the jihad to Bukhara and Samarqand [i.e., into Central Asia]."[66] It shows that al-Qaida felt the Taliban were willing to sponsor – perhaps even participate in – Islamist revolutionary struggles outside their national borders. The point is important not because it reflects actual Taliban strategy – this we do not know for sure – but it illustrates the ideological connection between al-Qaida, and parts of the Taliban leadership. This ideological connection was crucial for their initial alliance.

At the end of the letter Abu Hafs outlines "The duties towards the movement." It is perhaps the most clearly formulated al-Qaida vision for Afghanistan from this time period:

[65] Ibid.
[66] Abu Hafs claims he met with the following Taliban leaders: Mullah Omar, Muhammad Hassan (Governor of Kandahar), Sheikh Ehsanullah (member of Taliban's inner shura) and Sheikh Hafeezullah (Minister of Planning and president of *jama'at al-amr bil-ma'ruf wal-nahi an al-munkar* [The organization for enjoining what is good and forbidding what is evil]). AQ-SHTP-D-000-103, "Letter to Abu Khalid from Abu Hafs Al-Masri."

The [Taliban] movement has demonstrated its sincerity in what it says and in the slogans it has raised. The movement is a capable Islamic entity and it is possible that it can be a turning point for the betterment of the Islamic world.

The movement needs a vision and it needs support. It needs someone who will give it a military strategy. And it needs to build a military force which is suitable for the situation in Afghanistan. Perhaps this is an opportunity for the Islamic world and the departure after that can be from the fortified base of Afghanistan, which nobody will dare to enter militarily again.[67]

Although the passage is open to some interpretation, it seems safe to assume that al-Qaida wanted to strengthen the nascent Islamic state in Afghanistan, hoping it could be used as a launch pad for spreading Islamic revolutions elsewhere.

Shortly after Bin Laden returned to Afghanistan in 1996, he declared war on the United States. Bin Laden's anti-American sentiment had been building up over time, but Bin Laden's expulsion from Sudan appears to have been the last straw. Bin Laden's declaration of *jihad* came at a time when al-Qaida enjoyed the protection of local tribal leaders on Afghanistan's periphery and thus, it had little to do with the Taliban's rise to power in Kabul.

In spring 1997, Bin Laden entered into an alliance with the Taliban and moved his family to Kandahar. By mid-1997 al-Qaida was convinced that the Taliban's state project was a project worth supporting. This was in line with al-Qaida's general philosophy of extending support to revolutionary Islamists, and a continuation of what they had done in Sudan and Somalia in 1992–1996. Initially, Bin Laden's offers of military and material assistance to the Taliban may have played into their decision to host him. Over time the Taliban's insistence on protecting Bin Laden became more and more costly to the regime, as Bin Laden's anti-American agenda provoked international pressure and, in the end, UN sanctions. The next chapter looks at how the Taliban regime dealt with their troublesome guest, and how Bin Laden in the end turned the situation to his and al-Qaida's advantage.

---

[67] AQ-SHTP-D-000-103, "Letter to Abu Khalid from Abu Hafs Al-Masri."

4

The Troublesome Guest

In 1996, Bin Laden declared war on the United States, and in 1997, al-Qaida started planning its first international terrorist attacks – the twin bombings of the US Embassies in Nairobi and Dar-es-Salaam. As a result of Bin Laden's provocations, Afghanistan was hit by US cruise missiles in 1998 and subject to UN sanctions from 1999. Bin Laden continued to pursue a strategy of international terrorism from the soil of Afghanistan, even if it harmed the Taliban's national interests. At the same time, Bin Laden provided political and material support to the Taliban, culminating with his public pledge of allegiance to Mullah Omar in the spring of 2001. The pledge symbolized the political subordination of Bin Laden to Mullah Omar – yet, his international terrorist campaign was in direct violation of Mullah Omar's orders. How do we explain the political relationship between Osama bin Laden and the Taliban?

DECLARATION OF *JIHAD*

In May 1996, an eleven-page Arabic booklet was being circulated in Peshawar. It called for Muslims to join a new, Islamic army to fight "the evil West and its Muslim protégés." Doors for training of the faithful Muslims to become part of the Islamic Army are open," it declared.[1]

It sounded like an al-Qaida propaganda booklet but it was not. Bin Laden had not yet returned to Afghanistan, and his declaration of *jihad* on the United States was still months away. The booklet was issued by a

---

[1] Ismail Khan, "Arab group threatens war against 'evil West, Muslim proteges'," *The News*, May 14, 1996.

group of Arabs who called themselves the "Khilafat" group. They were the same gang that had tried to declare a caliphate on Pakistani soil in 1993, and who had been ousted by the local tribes. In 1996, remnants of the group including the leader, the Jordanian Mohammed Eid al-Rifa'i, were believed to be hiding in Kunar in eastern Afghanistan.

Comprised of a few dozen Arabs, the group's booklet was hardly taken seriously. But when al-Rifa'i declared himself *amir al-mu'minin* (Leader of the Faithful) in June 1996, the Ulama in Kunar staggered. They promptly sentenced the "Arab warlord" to death, lest he repent his actions.[2] There could only be one *amir al-mu'minin* in Afghanistan and it was Mullah Omar, leader of the Taliban.

The death sentence was never carried out. Al-Rifa'i eventually escaped to Great Britain where he died of natural causes in 2006.[3] Meanwhile, Bin Laden took a very different approach in dealing with the Taliban. Bin Laden never declared himself leader of the Muslims and al-Qaida did not seek to control territory or declare a state in Afghanistan. Bin Laden did the exact opposite – he recognized Mullah Omar as the legitimate ruler of Afghanistan and swore a public oath of allegiance (*bay'a*) to him in 2001. There were both ideological and strategic reasons for doing this, which will be discussed later in this chapter. First, it is necessary to look at Bin Laden's relationship to the Taliban after Bin Laden moved to Kandahar in 1997.

As discussed previously, Bin Laden moved to Kandahar in April 1997 at the request of Mullah Omar. The Taliban's purpose of moving Bin Laden was probably to both protect him from foreign intelligence agents, and to control his media statements. It appears that the Taliban succeeded in silencing Bin Laden for a while. Bin Laden's last, major interview with foreign journalists was given to Peter Arnett and Peter Bergen from the CNN in Nangarhar in March 1997.[4] After that, there were no more interviews with Bin Laden until May 1998, when he gave several unsolicited interviews to foreign journalists from al-Qaida's training camp complex in Khost.

---

[2] Mohammad Ali Imran, "Afghan Ulema declare death for Arab warlord," *The Muslim*, June 21, 1996.
[3] Nibras Kazimi, "The Caliphate attempted," *Current Trends in Islamist Ideology* vol. 7 (2008), 16–17.
[4] Bin Laden also gave an interview to Robert Fisk around the same time. Two articles about the interview were published in *The Independent*. Robert Fisk, "Muslim leader warns of a new assault on US forces," *The Independent*, March 22, 1997; and Robert Fisk, "The man who wants to wage holy war against the Americans," *The Independent*, March 22, 1997.

Meanwhile, on February 23, 1998, the London-based newspaper *Al-Quds al-Arabi* had printed a declaration signed "The Global Islamic front for Jihad against the Jews and Crusaders." The declaration later became known as Bin Laden's universal declaration of *jihad* against the United States. It was signed by Bin Laden and four other Islamist leaders: two Egyptians, Ayman al-Zawahiri and Rifaʻi Taha, and two Pakistanis, Sheikh Mir Hamza and Maulana Fazlur Rehman. A much-quoted section of the statement reads:

> The ruling to kill the Americans and their allies – civilians and military – is an individual duty for every Muslim who can do it in any country in which it is possible to do it, in order to liberate the al-Aqsa mosque and the holy mosque from their grip, and in order for their armies to move out of all the lands of Islam, defeated and unable to threaten any Muslim.[5]

It is unclear if the February 1998 declaration had any direct effect on the relationship between Bin Laden and the Taliban. Publically, the Taliban sought to diminish the "fatwa's" importance and denied outright that Bin Laden had anything to do with it.[6] The United States put moderate pressure on the Taliban at this time, asking them in April 1998 to "control" Bin Laden. In return, the Taliban declared that the soil of Afghanistan should not be used as a base for terrorists.[7]

But an internal conflict between Mullah Omar and Bin Laden soon became apparent. It was caused not so much by the content of Bin Laden's fatwa but by the fact that Bin Laden decided to meet foreign journalists on the soil of Afghanistan without informing Mullah Omar beforehand. In May 1998, Bin Laden, Ayman al-Zawahiri, and Abu Hafs al-Masri held a press conference in one of the training camps in Khost province. The press conference was attended by the two Pakistani journalists Rahimullah Yusufzai and Jamal Ismaʻil.[8] In the same period, Bin Laden carried out a new press interview with a Western journalist – John Miller from ABC news. The interview was given from somewhere in Eastern Afghanistan – probably one of the Khost training camps – again without the Taliban's permission.[9]

5 Osama bin Laden, quoted in Hegghammer, *Dokumentasjon om al-Qaida*, 143.
6 State Department Report, "U.S. Engagement with the Taliban on Osama bin Laden," July 16, 2001.
7 Ahmad Zaydan, "*muhadathatahu shamilat al-irhab wa al-mukhaddarat wa huquq al-marʼa … wa mudifu bin ladin qallalu min ahamiyyit tahdidatihi. richardson fi afghanistan aqnaʻa ʻtalibanʼ bi-hudna li-badʼ al-hiwar*," al-Hayat, April 18, 1998.
8 Rahimullah Yusufzai, "The best story of my career," *Newsline*, January 10, 2010.
9 Miller, Stone and Mitchell, *The cell*, 176–192.

Both Rahimullah Yusufzai and the Syrian jihadist Abu Mus'ab al-Suri, who lived in Kabul at the time, could testify that Bin Laden's press conference had infuriated Mullah Omar. Yusufzai claimed the Taliban leader called him after the press conference, saying "How can he hold a press conference without my permission? There is only one ruler. Is it me or Osama?"[10] According to Yusufzai, Mullah Omar's resentment had been building up over some time – he "particularly resented Mr. Bin Laden's flamboyant grandstanding – his blood-curdling declarations against America, phony fatwas for which he had no religious authority, and news conferences scripted to exaggerate his power."[11]

Abu Mus'ab al-Suri gives further details concerning the conflict between Bin Laden and Mullah Omar. Al-Suri was considered a close ally of the Taliban regime.[12] At the same time he was well integrated into the Arab community in Afghanistan. Although he was not member of al-Qaida, he most likely had access to sources close to the events.

In a private letter to Bin Laden, which is dated July 19, 1998, al-Suri discusses the al-Qaida leader's "latest troublemaking" with the Taliban – apparently referring to Bin Laden's May 1998 press conference and the controversy it created both within the Taliban leadership, and among Arab jihadists in Afghanistan. Al-Suri confirms that it was not the content of Bin Laden's 1998 "fatwa" that was the main source of conflict between him and Mullah Omar – rather, it was Bin Laden's unruly behavior within Afghanistan. According to al-Suri, the Taliban had permitted Bin Laden to fight "on the condition of silence," and that

[in] many meetings, some of which I attended, the Taliban told you "if you wish to fight America and your adversaries then do so without much talk and shouting from our land, as our condition is critical."[13]

This suggests that the disagreement between Mullah Omar and Bin Laden was mainly of a strategic nature. Mullah Omar was not opposed to Bin Laden's plan of fighting Americans, however, he disagreed to the timing and methods of Bin Laden's campaign. Mullah Omar wanted the Taliban to consolidate their power within Afghanistan before getting involved

---

[10] Alan Cullison and Andrew Higgins, "Once-stormy terror alliance was solidified by cruise missiles," *Wall Street Journal*, August 2, 2002.

[11] Ibid.

[12] Lia, *Architect of global jihad*, 240–41.

[13] Abu Mus'ab al-Suri and Abu Khalid al-Suri, "Noble brother Abu-Abdallah [Letter to Osama bin Laden dated July 17, 1998]," unpublished, courtesy Brynjar Lia, Andrew Higgins and Alan Cullison.

in conflicts elsewhere. If Bin Laden wanted to fight from Afghanistan he therefore had to "fight in silence," or go somewhere else.

But the conflict between Bin Laden and Mullah Omar also had a personal dimension to it. Al-Suri's letter reveals that there were deeper issues at stake than a disagreement over war-fighting strategy. Bin Laden was challenging Mullah Omar's authority within Afghanistan. According to al-Suri, Bin Laden justified his disobedience to Mullah Omar by claiming that his actions were in line with Islamic law. A section of al-Suri's letter reads,

The strangest thing so far was Abu-Abdullah [Bin Laden]'s saying that he won't listen to the leader of the faithful when he asked him to stop giving interviews. He said let's see what Islamic law dictates ... Since when is the guest entitled to resort to Islamic law concerning excessive demands on the host?[14]

The context is important. In order to cover his back, Bin Laden had managed to enlist the support of a number of Afghan, Pakistani, and Saudi *ulama* who had endorsed his 1996 and 1998 declarations of war against the United States. Bin Laden's alliance with the Deobandi scholar Mufti Nizamuddin Shamzai was of particular importance.[15] Mufti Shamzai was the leader of the Deobandi madrasa at Binori Town in Karachi, and was highly respected among the Taliban's most important allies in Pakistan; the political party Jamiat-e-Ulema Islam (JUI), the charity organization al-Rashid Trust, and Deobandi militant outfits who directly supported the Taliban's fight against the Northern Alliance. It put Mullah Omar in a delicate situation. He could not oppose the rulings of the most powerful Deobandi clerics in the region without losing religious legitimacy. This would weaken his position and possibly create splits within the Taliban.[16]

Bin Laden seemed to be fully aware of Mullah Omar's dilemma, and used it to his advantage. According to al-Suri, Bin Laden had been blaming the Taliban for "letting down the sacred matters [or land]." From the context, we understand that he is referring to the Taliban's attempts at silencing Bin Laden's propaganda campaign and thereby obstructing his efforts to liberate "the sacred land," that is, Saudi Arabia. Al-Suri is

[14] Ibid.

[15] See, for example, Ahmad Muwaffaq Zaydan, "'*taliban*' *ahatat al-liqa*' *bi-ajwa*' *min al-takattum. ibn ladin istaqbal wafdan min ulama*' *al-yaman*," *al-Hayat*, November 30, 1998; Gunaratna, *Inside Al Qaeda*, 62–63.

[16] This argument was also used by Taliban's Foreign Minister, Mullah Mutawakkil in conversations with US representatives. See, for example, Department of State (Islamabad) Cable, "Osama bin Laden: Taliban spokesman seeks new proposal for resolving bin Laden problem," November 28, 1998.

defending the Taliban's position by stating that "... they [the Taliban] are not the ones who let down the sacred matters ... but its [Saudi Arabia's] people and ulama."[17]

Here, we see the contours of a more fundamental, theological disagreement between Bin Laden and Mullah Omar: When is *jihad* warranted and for whom? As far as is known, Mullah Omar never contested Bin Laden's claim that Saudi Arabia was "occupied" by the Americans. However, he expressed the classical view that *jihad* was an individual duty for the Saudi Arabians only, and that the struggle was to take place within the country's borders.[18] Bin Laden, on the other hand, saw *jihad* as an individual duty for all Muslims, and that the struggle against the Americans had no geographical limits. According to Bin Laden's view, the Taliban regime had no right to obstruct Bin Laden's propaganda activities in Afghanistan; if they did, they would be shirking their religious duties.

Bin Laden was challenging the religious credentials of Mullah Omar by setting him up against the religious authorities and scholars who supported Bin Laden's fatwa against the Americans. Al-Suri warned that Bin Laden's challenges to Mullah Omar's authority could have far-reaching consequences. Not only did it have the potential of creating internal splits within the Taliban – it could damage the Taliban's relations with the Muslim world. Al-Suri was worried that Bin Laden's provocations would force the Taliban to enforce sanctions on the Arabs in Afghanistan. This would damage the Taliban's reputation in the Muslim world and cause them to lose support, because

The world won't understand that the Taliban have given the Arabs what they deserve due to their poor policies and relations. They will think that the Taliban have given in to enemy demands to the disfavor of the Arabs and the sacred.[19]

In his letter, al-Suri does not hide the fact that his criticism of Bin Laden has a personal dimension to it. He is worried that all Arabs in Afghanistan – including himself – would suffer from Bin Laden's provocative behavior. He claims that the Khalden training camp and the Pakistani camps had already been shut down because of Bin Laden's "whims."[20] Al-Suri summarizes the mood in Kabul in July 1998:

[17] Abu M. al-Suri and Abu K. al-Suri, "Noble brother Abu-Abdallah."
[18] Department of State (Washington) Cable, "Afghanistan: Taliban's Mullah Omar's 8/22 Contact with State Department," August 23, 1998.
[19] Abu M. al-Suri and Abu K. al-Suri, "Noble brother Abu-Abdallah."
[20] It is unclear if the camps really closed at this point. If they did, it was probably a temporary measure. For example, Ahmed Ressam claimed that he had attended the Khalden camp for 5–6 months from end of April 1998. Abu M. al-Suri and Abu K. al-Suri, "Noble brother

The results of this crisis can be felt even here in Kabul and other places. Talk about closing down the camps has spread. Discontent with the Arabs has become clear. Whispers between the Taliban with some of our non-Arab brother [sic] have become customary.[21]

Al-Suri does not hide his bitterness toward Bin Laden, whom he believes may "strike a deal" with the Saudi regime, or go back to Sudan. Al-Suri and many of the other Arab mujahidin had nowhere else to go – if they returned to their home countries, they would most certainly face legal prosecution.[22] By pursuing his narrow goals, Bin Laden was jeopardizing the sanctuary of all the Arabs in Afghanistan. Al-Suri told Bin Laden, "We are in a ship that you are burning on false or mistaken grounds ... What right have you got to destroy our and others' homes!" According to al-Suri, the Arabs were left with few alternatives. Either they have to "stay silent and suffer the consequences" of Bin Laden's behavior, or, they may be forced to go to the Taliban and Mullah Omar and "... tell them that Abu-Abdullah [Bin Laden] only represents himself and his group of guards but not the Arabs." It was not an ideal solution, as it would reveal internal dissent among the Arabs. It "involves the obvious harm of hanging our dirty laundry for others to see," as he put it.[23]

The gist of al-Suri's message is that if Bin Laden continued his undermining activity toward the Taliban regime, it would have destructive consequences for the Taliban and the Arab community in Afghanistan. Since the Taliban is stuck between a rock and a hard place, only Bin Laden himself can prevent this negative trend from developing. Al-Suri's advice to Bin Laden is clear:

You should apologize for any inconvenience or pressure you have caused, agree to apply mutual shura and commit to the wishes of the leader of the believers [Mullah Omar] on matters that concern his circumstances here.[24]

Al-Suri's letter puts the conflict between Bin Laden and Mullah Omar into a larger context. The main problem for Mullah Omar appears to have been Bin Laden's behavior within Afghanistan: his refusal to obey Mullah Omar's orders to keep a low profile, and challenging Mullah

Abu-Abdallah." "A terrorist's testimony [Ahmed Ressam's testimony before the Federal District Court of the Southern District of New York, July 2001]," *PBS Frontline,* undated.

[21] Abu M. al-Suri and Abu K. al-Suri, "Noble brother Abu-Abdallah," July 17, 1998.
[22] Ibid.
[23] Ibid.
[24] Ibid.

Omar's authority by enlisting the support of powerful *ulama* – all for the sake of furthering his own interests before the interests of the Taliban state.

Scoffing at Bin Laden's arrogance and love of media attention, al-Suri notes, "I think our brother has caught the disease of screens, flashes, fans, applause ..."![25] When reading al-Suri's letter one must keep in mind that it was written by one of the more strong-minded and outspoken leaders in the Arab community. Al-Suri had more than one personal grudge toward Bin Laden that may have colored his observations.[26] Nevertheless he claimed that his resentment toward Bin Laden was shared by many Arab leaders, including Abu Hafs al-Masri and other members of Bin Laden's immediate circle.

In the end, Bin Laden followed al-Suri's advice to respect Mullah Omar's orders because his next interviews in December 1998 were with the Taliban's permission, and with the presence of officials from the Taliban's Ministry of Foreign Affairs. But before that, he managed to provoke Mullah Omar once again.

THE US MISSILE STRIKES

On August 7, 1998, al-Qaida carried out its first major terrorist attack against American interests – the near-simultaneous bombings of the US embassies in Kenya and Tanzania that killed some 220 people. The embassy bombings provoked military reprisals in the form of a number of US missile strikes on purported al-Qaida-bases on Afghan soil, carried out on August 20. "We recognize these strikes will not eliminate the problem," said US Defense Secretary William Cohen shortly after the attacks. "But our message is clear. There will be no sanctuary for terrorists and no limit to our resolve to defend American citizens and our interests ... against these cowardly attacks."[27] The American Secretary of State, Madeleine Albright, did not hesitate with placing the blame for the attacks on Bin Laden and the Taliban. She demanded that the Taliban surrender Bin Laden so that they could interrogate him in the case. "If they want us to recognize them, they are obliged to not give sanctuary to individuals who are regarded terrorists."[28]

[25] Ibid.
[26] Lia, *Architect of global jihad*, 58–59; Author's interview with former Taliban official (anonymized).
[27] "U.S. missiles pound targets in Afghanistan, Sudan," *CNN*, August 20, 1998.
[28] Ibid.

In public, Mullah Omar strongly condemned the US missile strikes on Khost and repeated his previous statements that the Taliban would not surrender Bin Laden to any third party.[29] The Taliban leader was reportedly furious at what he saw as a violation of Afghanistan's sovereignty and indicated that there would be no more talks with the United States. On August 26, he was quoted as saying, "What is there left to talk about now ... everything ended after the rocket attacks."[30]

At this point, Mullah Omar started openly criticizing US foreign policies toward the Middle East. According to a US government cable, Mullah Omar called the US State Department in Washington on August 22, 1998 and spoke with Michael E. Malinowski, the US director for Pakistan, Afghanistan, and Bangladesh Affairs. Reportedly in a "careful and controlled manner," he advised the US government that the missile strikes on Afghanistan had been counterproductive to the United States, since they would increase hostility in the Islamic world against the United States. He suggested that President Bill Clinton must resign and the United States should withdraw its forces from Saudi Arabia, since the Islamic world sees the US forces there as a threat to Islam's holiest sites. He said that he has seen no evidence that Bin Laden is guilty of the East African embassy bombings, and that "getting rid of one individual would not end the problems posed to the U.S. by the Islamic world."[31]

There is little doubt that the missile strikes made Mullah Omar more distrustful of the United States. Basing on this, the literature has tended to draw the conclusion that the missile strikes brought the Taliban leader and Bin Laden closer together. However, when discussing the Taliban regime's reactions to the US missile strikes, it is crucial to differentiate between their reactions to the outside world and their internal reactions toward Osama bin Laden. Based on available empirical evidence, there were no significant changes in the Taliban's internal policies toward Bin Laden.

---

[29] Wikalat al-Anba', an Afghan news agency based in Pakistan, quoted Mullah Omar as saying, "It is absolutely impossible for us to hand over Osama to America." Hassan Sandarusi and Muhammad Salah, *"tazahurat fi duwal arabiyya wa islamiyya. rusia wa al-sin wa al-yapan tantaqidu al-ijra' al-amiriki. britanya wa faransa tu'ayyidan...,"* al-Hayat, August 22, 1998.

[30] *"washington ta'udd qarar ittiham diddahu li-idfa' siffa qanuniyya ala mulahaqatihi. 'taliban' tarfud ardan amirikiyyan li-l 'hiwar' bi-sha'n usama bin ladin,"* al-Hayat, August 26, 1998.

[31] Department of State (Washington) Cable, "Afghanistan: Taliban's Mullah Omar's 8/22 Contact."

The Arabs in al-Qaida were not sure how Mullah Omar would react to the news of the East African embassy bombings. Only a few hours before the missile strikes, Bin Laden was gathered with a group of al-Qaida members and other Arabs in Kabul. Mustafa Hamid, who was present at the meeting, recalled that they were talking about the East African bombings and how they would affect the situation in Afghanistan. They wondered why the American reaction was delayed, and saw it as a sign of weakness. But it was not the American reaction that worried them most; it was that of the Taliban, they said. The Taliban had neither approved nor allowed the East African bombings to happen. Hamid was worried that there would be tension between Bin Laden, who had hurt the Taliban's interests, and the Taliban.[32]

Abu Mus'ab al-Suri, who had seen the tension building up over months, said after the missile strikes that he expected a harsh response from Mullah Omar and that the Taliban would close down Bin Laden's camps.[33] But the reaction was not as strong as al-Suri expected. The Taliban did not accuse Bin Laden of being behind the embassy strikes. An internal al-Qaida document found in 2011 suggests that at the time of the 1998 Embassy bombings, "the Taliban opposition [to Bin Laden] wasn't apparent or even clear."[34] Taliban's lack of interest in the US Embassy bombings is reflected in the Taliban's internal reactions toward Bin Laden. These reactions were not spurred by the East African bombings, but by Bin Laden's media activities afterward.

Bin Laden gave at least two media statements after the embassy strikes. On August 18, Bin Laden's organization, the Global Islamic Front, issued a communiqué in which they praised the act and warned of new attacks against America.[35] Two days later, Bin Laden probably felt compelled to ease the pressure on the Taliban leadership. On August 20, Ayman al-Zawahiri delivered a statement by phone to the Pakistani journalist Rahimullah Yusufzai, which was claimed to be from Bin Laden. Bin Laden's statement explicitly denied "… any involvement in the Nairobi and Dar es Salaam bombings,"[36] although it called on Muslims to continue fighting Jews and Americans.

[32] Hamid, *mashru' tajikistan*, 58.
[33] Lia, *Architect of global jihad*, 292.
[34] "06 Ramadan," November 11, 2002. From "Bin Laden's Bookshelf, Declassified Material - May 20, 2015," *Office of the Director of the National Intelligence*, Washington, DC.
[35] Muhammad Salah, "'al-jabha al-islamiyya al-alamiyya': tahdhirat jadida lil-amirikyyin. albright tutalib 'taliban' bi-taslim usama bin ladin," al-Hayat, August 19, 1998.
[36] Quoted in Bergen, *The Osama*, 224.

On August 22–23, the Taliban's Inner Shura (i.e., the top leadership) held a meeting during which several members, including the governor of Kandahar, Mullah Hassan, put pressure on Mullah Omar to take measures against Bin Laden.[37] We do not know the details of their discussions, but other sources give a good indication of Mullah Omar's stance on the issue and his immediate reactions toward Bin Laden.

The sources confirm that Mullah Omar was not so much troubled by the terrorist attacks in East Africa, as by the fact that Bin Laden was issuing statements without his permission. The Pakistani newspaper, *The News,* quoted Mullah Omar as saying after the strikes, "It is impossible to have two distinct and parallel Emirates in Afghanistan … We have a central authority that is led by the Taliban, and it should be obeyed."[38] The article was written by Rahimullah Yusufzai who allegedly spoke with Mullah Omar by phone on August 23. The same article said that Mullah Omar had sent a delegation to Bin Laden, asking him to "show restraint and leave it to the Islamic Emirate of Afghanistan to take the required measures to defend itself and give an appropriate answer to the US attack on its soil."[39]

Initially, Mullah Omar reacted to Bin Laden the same way as he had done in the past – by sending him a letter asking him to stop issuing threatening statements. On August 25, *Wikalat al-anba',* a Pakistan-based news agency used by the Taliban, quoted Mullah Omar as saying from his headquarters in Kandahar,

I sent a letter to Bin Laden yesterday, in which I clearly asked him to not issue military and political statements against anyone from our soil … Osama's hostile remarks against the Americans, given from our soil, angered me and I stressed to him that he shall not do that … [Bin Laden] broke his pledge to not use our soil to issue such statements, after I previously also had forbidden him to do that.[40]

The account of Mullah Omar's letter is substantiated by al-Qaida's internal documents. In September 2000, an al-Qaida member was jotting down the main points of a speech Bin Laden was giving to a group of members. The topic of the speech was the history of the jihadist movement. "The mujahidin struck at a time when many of the leaders had

[37] Department of State (Islamabad) Cable, "Pakistan/Afghanistan reaction to U.S. air strikes," August 24, 1998.
[38] "*ba'dama ablaghahu za'im al-haraka 'istiya'ihi' min tasrihatihi. bin ladin wa'ada 'taliban' bi-waqf al-tahdid min afghanistan,*" *al-Hayat,* August 25, 1998.
[39] Ibid.
[40] Ibid.

surrendered from armed struggle," the notebook reads.[41] In the context, the statement probably refers to the deradicalization processes taking place in Egypt from 1997 onward, during which a large number of Egyptian militants, in particular members of al-Jama'a al-Islamiyya (JI) refrained from violent activity.[42] The "strike" most likely refers to the East African Embassy bombings on August 7, 1998, which were the only major al-Qaida operations carried out at the time. According to the same notebook, the next points of Bin Laden's speech dealt with "the letters received by the sheikh asking him to stop his speeches and incitement," and "the sheikh's mistake in sending the *bayan*," which probably refers to the statement of the Global Islamic Front in the aftermath of the Embassy bombings, or Bin Laden's statement on August 20, given by al-Zawahiri by phone.[43]

It seems clear that it was one of these statements that had angered Mullah Omar, not the East African Embassy bombings themselves. This is further substantiated by Mullah Mutawakkil, who noted in a meeting with US representatives in Islamabad in November 1998:

... while the U.S. believed that bin Laden was the head of a terrorist network, the Taliban could only charge him with two particulars. The first was an unauthorized news conference in Khost *and the statement he had made following the airstrikes*. These violated the Taliban-imposed prohibition on his speaking out [author's emphasis].[44]

It supports the hypothesis that Mullah Omar – like many others in Afghanistan and Pakistan at the time – did not know, or did not want to know anything about Bin Laden's role in international terrorism. At the same time, the Taliban reacted promptly every time Bin Laden was seen to violate Mullah Omar's direct orders not to talk to the press.

The US missile strikes led to increased international pressure on the Taliban, especially from its major ally in the Middle East, Saudi Arabia. On September 19, 1998, a Saudi delegation led by the intelligence chief,

---

[41] AFGP-2002–801138, "Various admin documents and questions," Combating Terrorism Center, West Point, NY: 59.

[42] For a more detailed study of this process, see Omar Ashour, *The de-radicalization of jihadists: Transforming armed islamist movements* (London: Routledge, 2009): 90–109.

[43] A US embassy cable suggests that it was Bin Laden's statement on August 21, given by al-Zawahiri by phone, that angered Mullah Omar; not the statement of the Global Islamic Front. Department of State (Islamabad) Cable, "Pakistan/Afghanistan reaction to U.S. air strikes."

[44] Department of State (Islamabad) Cable, "Osama bin Laden: Taliban spokesman seeks new proposal for resolving Bin Laden problem," November 28, 1998.

Prince Turki al-Faisal, flew in to Kandahar to meet with Mullah Omar.[45] Al-Faisal had been on a secret visit to Afghanistan that previous June and asked the Taliban to expel Bin Laden to Saudi Arabia. According to al-Faisal, at the June 1998 meeting Mullah Omar had "agreed in principle" to hand Bin Laden over to Saudi Arabia, and they had "agreed to jointly convene a committee to discuss the details of the Bin Laden handover."[46]

In September 1998, al-Faisal returned to Kandahar and demanded that Osama be handed over to him. But this time, Mullah Omar refused to comply. To the surprise of the foreign delegation, he said that he had never promised to hand over Bin Laden to Saudi Arabia, and that "there could have been a mistake by the interpreters" during the previous meeting.[47] According to Iftikhar Murshed, Pakistan's special envoy to Afghanistan who himself was present at the meeting, the event developed into a bickering between Mullah Omar and Prince Faisal. Prince Faisal reportedly became furious and suggested that Mullah Omar should learn Arabic in order to avoid such misunderstandings in the future. In return, Mullah Omar blamed Prince Faisal for allying himself with the Americans. "God has given you everything but yet you cannot defend yourselves against puny Iraq and therefore you invited the Americans into your country to protect you and to fight your battles."[48] Needless to say, the Saudi prince returned to Saudi Arabia insulted and empty-handed. A few days after the meeting, Saudi Arabia announced that they would break diplomatic ties with the Taliban regime.[49]

Mullah Omar had by now used "Bin Laden-like" rhetoric several times to defend his political decisions – giving rise to speculations that Mullah Omar was influenced by Bin Laden's ideology. However, there are few sources that can substantiate this claim. Mullah Omar's rhetoric about Saudi Arabia was not particular for Bin Laden – rather it reflected

---

[45] See, for example, Department of State (Islamabad) Cable, "Afghanistan: Tensions reportedly mount within Taliban as ties with Saudi Arabia deteriorate over bin Laden," September 28, 1998; Murshed, *Afghanistan: The Taliban years*, 300–301.

[46] Erich Von Follath and Stefan Aust, "Und dann schrie Mullah Omar [And then screamed Mullah Omar]," *Der Spiegel* 11 (2004): 119.

[47] Murshed, *Afghanistan: The Taliban years*, 301.

[48] The gist of Murshed's account is confirmed by Turki al-Faisal in an interview with *Der Spiegel* in 2004. Murshed, *Afghanistan: The Taliban years*, 301; Von Follath and Aust, "Und dann schrie Mullah Omar," 119.

[49] Turki al-Dakhil, "*tarhib irani bi-qarar al-sa'udiyya talab rahil al-qa'im bi al-a'mal al-afghani*," *al-Hayat*, September 24, 1998; "*al-sa'udiyya taqta' ilaqatiha al-diblumasiyya ma' taliban li-istimrariha fi istikhdam aradiha li-iwa' al-irhabiyyin*," *al-Sharq al-Awsat*, September 26, 2001.

the widespread sentiments of the Saudi *Sahwa* that originated in 1991 when the Saudi regime allowed the US to establish military bases on its soil. There are other sources indicating that Bin Laden was hardly in a position to influence Mullah Omar ideologically.[50]

A few days after the debacle between Mullah Omar and Prince Faisal, on September 21–23, 1998, the Taliban conveyed a Grand Shura in Kabul. The Grand Shura was different from the Inner Shura that had met in Kandahar the month before. During the Grand Shura, a council of around 1,500 *ulama* from across Afghanistan was convened in Kabul to discuss a number of topics and give policy advice to Mullah Omar. Officially, they were to discuss five topics. Four of them were related to the Taliban regime's ongoing conflict with Iran, and the fifth was concerned with the legitimacy of the Taliban government. However, there were rumors that the *ulama* council would discuss other topics as well, including the "Bin Laden issue." A US embassy cable quoted a "well-informed contact" saying that Mullah Omar had authorized the council "to take a final decision on the presence of Osama bin Laden on Afghan territory."[51] The same information appeared in *al-Hayat* on September 23. The newspaper's sources held it as likely that the council would allow Bin Laden to stay in Afghanistan, on the condition that he respect the laws of the Islamic Emirate and avoid giving political statements or carrying out operations from Afghan territory.[52]

The *ulama* conference was convened only two days after Mullah Omar's debacle with Prince Turki al-Faisal, which had stirred controversy within the Taliban. This may have contributed to bringing the Bin Laden issue to the discussion table during the conference. Taliban's prime minister in Kabul, Mullah Rabbani, was reportedly frustrated with Mullah Omar for causing a diplomatic crisis between the Taliban regime and Saudi Arabia.[53] It is likely that the event had led to a renewed debate concerning Bin Laden's status in Afghanistan.[54]

---

[50] For a more thorough discussion of Bin Laden's purported ideological influence on Mullah Omar, see Stenersen, *Brothers in Jihad*.

[51] Department of State (Washington) Cable, "Afghanistan: Taliban convene Ulema, Iran and bin Ladin on the agenda," September 25, 1998.

[52] Ahmad Muwaffaq Zaydan, "*al-ulama' al-afghan yabhathun fi mas'alat ibn ladin*," *al-Hayat*, September 23, 1998.

[53] Department of State (Islamabad) Cable, "Afghanistan: Tensions reportedly mount within Taliban."

[54] It was Mullah Rabbani who had decided to convene the *ulama* conference in Kabul. As Mullah Rabbani was known as an opponent of Bin Laden, the purpose of bringing up

Sources from inside the Arab community in Afghanistan have confirmed that Mullah Omar convened an *ulama* council to discuss the fate of Bin Laden.[55] Captured documents give further indications that the Bin Laden issue was brought up by the Taliban for public discussion after the US missile strikes. A booklet printed by the Taliban's Ministry of Education in late 1998 or early 1999 contained a number of essays written by Afghan, Pakistani, and Arab intellectuals discussing the status of Osama bin Laden in Afghanistan. They argued from religious, legal, and political points of view that Bin Laden had the right to receive protection by the Taliban in Afghanistan. The line-up of authors includes theologians, such as the Pakistani Mufti Abdul Rahim, the deputy leader of al-Rashid Trust, but also, various Afghan professors in economy, law, and political science.[56] The document indicates that the Taliban's decision to protect Bin Laden after the US missile strikes found acceptance far outside Mullah Omar's inner shura. In other words, it was not a decision by a small, "fundamentalist" faction within the Taliban. This perspective has rarely been presented in existing literature on Afghanistan. Part of the reason for this is probably that few Afghans after 9/11 would be willing to admit they supported the Taliban's decision to host Bin Laden in the 1990s.

We do not know if Mullah Omar actually authorized the Shura in 1998 to "make a final decision on Bin Laden's status." But we know that the day after the Shura's last session, on September 24, Mullah Omar sent a fax to the US government saying that the Taliban regime will not and cannot change its policies as they are based on Islam. The tone of the letter is uncompromising:

Our policy is clear Islamic policy. We cannot change it. It is not up to us to change it. We have no power or authority to change it. Almighty God has obligated us to follow this policy. If you have objections to our policy or our deeds, or if you call it un-Islamic, that is not right. All Muslims of the world agree this is Islamic, but if you still believe that it is not Islamic, then we can try to convince you.[57]

Although it seems to leave room for some dialogue ("then we can try to convince you"), the tone of the letter differs noticeably from Mullah

---

the Bin Laden issue might have been to settle disagreements between him and Mullah Omar. Department of State (Washington), Cable, "Afghanistan: Taliban convene Ulema."

[55] Harun, *al-harb ala al-islam*, 440.

[56] The names of the Afghan professors have been withheld in accordance with CRRC's policy on protection of Personally Identifiable Information (PII). AQ-SHPD-D-000-809, "Loose pages of a book about Usama Bin Laden," 1419 h [April 1998–April 1999]. Conflict Records Resource Center, Washington, DC.

[57] Department of State (Washington) Cable, "Message to Mullah Omar," October 1, 1998.

Omar's phone conversation with the US State Department a month earlier. In the phone conversation on August 22, he had defended his decision to protect Bin Laden, saying that he had seen no evidence of Bin Laden's guilt. In the September 24 letter, he did not explicitly defend Bin Laden, but only referred to the fact that Muslim people think that Bin Laden is not guilty: "Muslims believe that the Osama bin Laden issue is just an excuse made by the U.S. and this is harming the U.S."[58] In the last statement, the question of evidence and guilt was not mentioned at all. Instead, Mullah Omar emphasized that the Taliban's policies are unchangeable since they are based solely on Islamic law and the will of Muslims. It appears as if the question of Bin Laden's guilt had been rendered irrelevant. One possible interpretation of these events is that the *ulama* council in Kabul did indeed rule that Bin Laden cannot be expelled to the United States – and that Mullah Omar is conveying this view to the US administration in his September 24 letter. This would at least explain the uncompromising tone of the letter.

Meanwhile, there was an internal battle within the Taliban concerning how to cope with Bin Laden. The question was probably not so much about whether to expel him to the United States – as this would be a highly radical step to take at the time – although several Taliban officials expressed that they wished Bin Laden out of their country. As discussed earlier, the Taliban was in a difficult position because a number of religious scholars in the region had already sanctioned Bin Laden's political agenda. As a compromise, several Taliban officials started pushing Mullah Omar to take measures against Bin Laden in order to restrict his activities while residing on Taliban-controlled territory. Mawlawi Wakil Ahmad Mutawakil, who called for increased restrictions on Bin Laden's activities, hoped that this would eventually cause Bin Laden to leave of his own free will, and thus save the Taliban from the awkward position it found itself in. In a meeting with US officials on November 28, 1998, Mutawakil said,

There appear to be two ways to deal with the problem. One would be to expel him [Bin Laden] by force, which would cause internal problems for the Taliban. The other would be to restrict his activities in such a way that he would decide to leave of his own volition, as was being done. This was what the Taliban hoped would result from their current policy.[59]

---

[58] Ibid.
[59] Department of State (Islamabad) Cable. "Osama bin Laden: Taliban spokesman seeks new proposal," November 28, 1998.

During the autumn of 1998, Bin Laden made efforts at appeasing the Taliban leadership. At the end of August 1998, Mullah Omar received a written promise from Bin Laden that he will not carry out attacks against any other country.[60] Also, Bin Laden started praising the Taliban leader publicly and privately. In November 1998 he wrote letters to several Deobandi scholars in Pakistan asking them to support the Taliban regime and incite the Pakistani people to fight for the Taliban – although he also promoted his anti-American agenda in these letters.[61] At the end of 1998, Mullah Omar was still reluctant to impose harsher restrictions on Bin Laden's media activities. But after a series of fatal interviews in December that year, even Mullah Omar agreed that there could be no more interviews with Bin Laden.

BIN LADEN'S LAST INTERVIEW

On December 24–25, 1998, Bin Laden gave a series of interviews to international media from a remote area of Helmand or Kandahar.[62] It appeared to be a new direct violation of the orders given by Mullah Omar, but eyewitness accounts give strong indications that the Taliban were informed of Bin Laden's new media appearance, and had approved it beforehand.

The Pakistani journalist Jamal Isma'il traveled to Kandahar to interview Bin Laden on behalf of *al-Jazeera*. He arrived in the city late one evening in December 1998 and spent the night in the Taliban's guesthouse. The next day, a Taliban regime official in Kandahar was informed of his arrival. The official appeared to be well aware of Isma'il's errand and put him in touch with Bin Laden's men. Shortly afterward, Isma'il was met by a group of Arabs led by Abu Hafs al-Masri and eventually taken to a provisional tent camp a three-hour drive from Kandahar city, where his now infamous interview with Bin Laden took place.[63] From his story, it is evident that at least a local Taliban official in Kandahar knew

---

[60] *"ba'dama ablaghahu za'im al-haraka 'istiya'ihi' min tasrihatihi,"* al-Hayat, August 25, 1998.

[61] On bin Laden's letter to Mufti Jamil Khan: See *"ibn ladin yahudd al-pakistaniyyin ala da'm harakat 'taliban',"* al-Hayat, November 19, 1998. On Bin Laden's letter to Mufti Shamzai: See Zaydan, *"'taliban' ahatat al-liqa' bi-ajwa' min al-takattum."*

[62] Jamal Isma'il stated the interview took place in southern Helmand. Fadil Harun recalled that the interviews were held in "a faraway place close to Arghandabi [a district northwest of Kandahar city]." Fadil Harun was not present at the actual interview. Isma'il, *bin ladin wa al-jazira*, 102; Harun, *al-harb ala al-islam*, 381.

[63] Isma'il, *bin ladin wa al-jazira*, 137–138.

that a foreign journalist had come to interview Bin Laden. Rahimullah Yusufzai is more explicit; he claimed that two officials from the Taliban's Foreign Ministry were present during his interview with the al-Qaida leader:

Two Taliban Foreign Ministry officials who had accompanied us from Kandahar, and a dozen Bin Laden men, including his teenaged son Mohammad, listened in rapt attention as [Bin Laden] spoke.[64]

The Taliban had probably granted Bin Laden permission to conduct the interviews on the condition that he denied having any direct role in the East African embassy bombings. During the interviews Bin Laden did, in fact, speak highly about the Taliban and specifically denied that he had given the order to carry out the bomb attacks in Kenya and Tanzania.[65] But he also made statements that were highly provocative to the United States, such as the now infamous statement that it was "a religious duty" for Muslims to acquire nuclear and chemical weapons.[66]

Bin Laden's remarks led to increased American pressure on the Taliban. On December 30, 1998, American officials met with Sayed ur-Rehman Haqqani, the Taliban's ambassador in Pakistan, and expressed anger over Bin Laden's recent media escapades. The American official was furious with Bin Laden's statements and said that they could no longer trust the Taliban. Haqqani's reaction supports the interpretation that the interviews had indeed been given at the Taliban's permission, but that Bin Laden had unexpectedly provoked the United States.[67] According to a US embassy cable describing the meeting, Haqqani explained,

Bin Laden was supposed to use the interview to deny involvement and any support for terrorist activities. However, he did not do this; he did not do what he promised. The Taliban are not supportive of what he [Bin Laden] said. We did not want this; it was a mistake. His comments complaining about [the US-British bombing of] Iraq went too far: The Taliban cannot support [Bin Laden's]

---

64 Yusufzai, "The best story of my career."
65 Isma'il, *bin ladin wa al-jazira*, 121–122.
66 For a further analysis of Bin Laden's statements concerning Weapons of Mass Destruction, see Anne Stenersen, *Al-Qaeda's quest for Weapons of Mass Destruction, 1996–2008: The history behind the hype* (Saarbrücken: VMD, 2008); Hegghammer, *Dokumantasjon om al-Qaida*, 54.
67 Mawlawi Mutawakil and Mullah Omar allegedly responded to the U.S. accusations by saying that Bin Laden had issued the threats due to "pressure from journalists." State Department Report, "U.S. Engagement with the Taliban on Osama bin Laden," July 16, 2001.

comments against Americans. It is not our policy. He will not be allowed to give any more interviews. This is honestly what happened.[68]

It is interesting to note how Bin Laden describes his relationship to the Taliban during the interviews. On one hand he confirms that he adheres to the orders of Mullah Omar:

> We do not work independently here. On the contrary, we are in a country that has an *amir al-mu'minin*. We are obligated by Sharia to obey him as long as this does not contradict God. We have committed ourselves to this country, and we call on people to support it . . . [69]

However, some obstinacy seems to shine through. Although he denies involvement in international terrorist attacks, he is reluctant to let Mullah Omar "silence" him – that is, stop him from his incitement activities:

> Due to the situation in Afghanistan, there is a view among the Taliban that we should not move from Afghan soil against any other state. As everyone knows this was decided by *amir al-mu'minin*. But we will continue with the incitement, God willing, and there is no stop to our limited effort during this period.[70]

It is worth recalling Bin Laden's attitude to Mullah Omar's orders in the summer of 1998, when he said that he would not stop giving interviews even if Mullah Omar had asked him to do so. According to al-Suri he had said, "let's see what Islamic law dictates."[71] We also recall that Deobandi clerics in Pakistan had supported Bin Laden's call for *jihad* against the Americans, and that Sheikh Yunus Khalis, a political leader of high religious stature in Eastern Afghanistan, probably had permitted Bin Laden to give interviews at an earlier stage. In December 1998, it appears that Bin Laden still saw it as a legal right to continue inciting his followers – but he eventually had to bow to Taliban pressure.

In the meeting between US officials and the Taliban ambassador, Sayed ur-Rehman Haqqani on December 30, the United States put increased pressure on the Taliban. The Taliban would be held responsible for any terrorist attack carried out by Bin Laden, the US officials said, and Haqqani promised to convey the message to the Taliban leadership in Kandahar.

---

[68] Department of State (Islamabad) Cable, "Osama bin Laden: Charge underscores U.S. concerns on interviews; Taliban envoy says bin Laden hoodwinked them and it will not happen again," December 30, 1998.
[69] Isma'il, *bin ladin wa al-jazira*, 137–138.
[70] Ibid.
[71] Abu M. al-Suri and Abu K. al-Suri, "Noble brother Abu-Abdallah."

In early 1999, it appears that Mullah Omar agreed to physically restrict the movements and communications of Bin Laden. The most vivid account of this event was given by the Taliban's representative to the UN, Abdul Hakeem Mujahid. In an interview with the New York Times published in March 1999, he said that on February 10, 1999, there had been clashes between a group of Taliban guards and Bin Laden's bodyguards. The Taliban guards had attempted to take over responsibility for Bin Laden's security, but Bin Laden's men had refused. Three days later, Taliban guards allegedly took control over Bin Laden and confiscated his satellite equipment and phone. Their task was to isolate him and ensure that he would not communicate with foreigners. During the event, Bin Laden was "expelled" from Kandahar to a remote place in the mountains.[72]

This contradicted the official explanation of Mullah Omar's office in Kandahar, which said that Bin Laden had disappeared "to an unknown place," without informing them of his new destination.[73] The US administration doubted the truth of the statement. They saw it as another attempt by the Taliban to avoid complicity in hosting Bin Laden, and to protect him against new attacks. Conveniently, the "disappearance" of Bin Laden happened shortly after the Taliban received threats from the US embassy in Islamabad that they must expel Bin Laden or face the consequences.

The Taliban's official statements regarding Bin Laden must be seen in light of the local context. The Taliban at the time were facing pressures from two sides – from the United States, who wanted them to expel Bin Laden, and from the Taliban's home audience – primarily conservative Muslim networks in Afghanistan and Pakistan. On February 20, 1999, media reported that mullahs in Afghanistan had warned Mullah Omar against bowing to US demands.[74] If the Taliban expelled Bin Laden, they would be seen as giving in to US pressure, and risk losing legitimacy among local and regional supporters. The Taliban's spokesmen in Kandahar were concerned about facing a popular backlash should it

---

[72] Tim Weiner, "Terror suspect said to anger Afghan hosts," *New York Times*, March 4, 1999; Muhammad Salah, "*taliban tanfi anba' an itlaq rusas ma'a harasihi. afghanistan: ibn ladin yu'awid al-zuhur qariban,*" *al-Hayat*, May 3, 1999; and author's interview with former Taliban official (anonymized).

[73] Isma'il, *bin ladin wa al-jazira*, 234.

[74] "*al-safir al-afghani fi al-qahira: ibn ladin mawjud fi mantiqat taliban,*" *al-Hayat*, February 20, 1999.

become known that they had fallen out with Bin Laden or tried to restrict his anti-American activities. They were left with few options other than to say that Bin Laden had "disappeared."

However, other sources confirm there was conflict between Bin Laden and Mullah Omar in early 1999. In February 1999, the director of the Binori mosque in Karachi, Mufti Nizamuddin Shamzai, called for an immediate intervention of the *ulama* in order to end the dispute between Mullah Omar and Bin Laden.[75] The fact that high-ranking clerics like Mufti Shamzai were involved, confirms that the Bin Laden issue was not only a bilateral matter between the United States and the Taliban leadership – it was a real dispute between Bin Laden and Mullah Omar.

After the events in early 1999, Bin Laden and Mullah Omar must have reached some sort of compromise. From then on, there were no more interviews with Bin Laden. This is significant, considering Bin Laden's strong belief in the power of the media. Between January 1999 and December 2001, Bin Laden spoke with a foreign journalist on only one occasion: In a short interview with the Kuwaiti newspaper *al-Ra'i al-Amm*, published November 13, 2000, he denied involvement in the attack on the US destroyer *USS Cole* on October 10 that year, which killed seventeen sailors. Moreover, he denied having any links to a group of suspected terrorists that had recently been arrested in Kuwait.[76] Contrary to previous statements he made no calls for *jihad* against the Americans. Whether consciously or not, he seems to have followed the advice of fellow Arabs in Afghanistan who had called on him to stop violating the orders of Mullah Omar.[77]

---

[75] Ahmad Muwaffaq Zaydan, "*ala amal tahqiq shurut al-i'tiraf al-dawli ba'd ibti'adiha an ibn ladin. taliban tuharrim al-mukhaddarat wa tatlaf mahasilaha,*" *al-Hayat*, February 20, 1999.

[76] Hegghammer, *Dokumantasjon om al-Qaida*, 88.

[77] The most outspoken of these advisors were Abu Mus'ab al-Suri and Mustafa Hamid, but they claimed that people in Bin Laden's inner circle held the same opinions. Several members of Bin Laden's Shura council were reportedly against Bin Laden's behaviour – in particular Sayf al-Adl, Mustafa Abu al-Yazid, and others, according to Hamid. Al-Suri claimed that many of Bin Laden's closest advisors, including Ayman al-Zawahiri, had the same attitude. Sayf al-Adl himself complained after 2001 that Bin Laden had not followed advice but made his own decisions – in particular with regards to the September 11 attacks. Mustafa Hamid, *The history of the Arab Afghans from the time of their arrival in Afghanistan until their departure with the Taliban*, serialized in *al-Sharq al-Awsat*, December 8–14, 2004, Part 7; Abu M. al-Suri and Abu K. al-Suri, "Noble brother Abu-Abdallah"; and "Al Adl letter," June 13, 2002, Combatting Terrorism Center, West Point, NY.

UN SANCTIONS

The last major event to challenge the relationship between Taliban and Bin Laden prior to 9/11 was the announcement on October 15, 1999 of UN Resolution 1267, which called for sanctions against the Taliban regime unless they expel Osama bin Laden from their territory. The Taliban were given one month to respond. To the outside world, the Taliban took an uncompromising stance – the regime's spokesmen refused to expel Bin Laden on religious and cultural grounds, as they had done in the past.

However, internally the issue was not taken lightly. In late October or early November, a group of *ulama* in the Taliban's Fatwa Department (*dar al-ifta'*) sent a note to Mullah Omar, stating that they had "agreed to surrender Osama bin Laden to the Chinese or Iranian Embassy."[78] The text of this note is not available in full. However, the *ulama* must have been aware of the potential harm that UN-imposed sanctions would cause the Islamic Emirate. Hence, they may have concluded that the Taliban leadership's insistence on protecting Bin Laden was no longer justifiable from a religious point of view, because it would most certainly cause harm to the Muslims in Afghanistan.

Higher-ranking *ulama*, including the Taliban's Grand Mufti, Sheikh Abd al-Ali Deobandi, and the head of the Islamic Emirate's Special Court, Sheikh Ahmadi, did not agree to the Fatwa Department's recommendations. They decided to involve the Union of Afghan Ulama (*ittihad ulama afghanistan*, hereafter referred to as "the Ulama Union"), an independent committee of Afghan scholars who were based in Quetta, Pakistan at the time. On November 8, 1999, Taliban's Sheikh Ahmadi met with the Ulama Union and asked them to "investigate the problems that are currently facing Afghanistan" and the next day the Taliban's Grand Mufti, Sheikh Abd al-Ali, attended a meeting with the Ulama Union. He invited them to Kandahar to discuss the issue with the Taliban's Fatwa Department (*dar al-ifta'*), to make a joint resolution that could be presented to Mullah Mohammad Omar.

On November 11, 1999, the Ulama Union of Afghanistan issued a statement addressed to Mullah Omar:

We think that if Osama was surrendered, America would also demand that we remove the veil of the women, do away with the *hudud, qisas* and other punishments and put an end to the divine laws ... this situation will be a pretext for

---

[78] Ittihad Ulama Afghanistan, "*al-fatwa bi-sha'n ikhraj usama bin ladin,*" 3 Sha'ban 1420 [November 11, 1999], quoted in *al-mizan li-harakat taliban* by Yusuf al-Uyayri (place unknown: Markaz al-Dirasat wa al-Buhuth al-Islamiyya, 2001): 76–77.

them [the Americans] to create an infidel government. The Afghan people and the world's Muslims and religious students will turn away from them [the Afghan Government], and not support them at all. There will be a rift between them. They will look upon the religious student and scholar of this movement as agents of America ... Therefore, I say with certainty that this act – surrendering Osama bin Laden – is not permitted, legally or politically. This act must not be carried out because it would be like declaring war on God.[79]

Mullah Omar's answer to the letter was issued on the same day. He assured the Union of his view that "if he [Bin Laden] is surrendered, the banner of infidelity will be raised and if he is not surrendered, the banner of Islam will be raised."[80] Like previous and later statements, Mullah Omar reiterated his belief that the issue is not about Bin Laden but rather, a battle between Islam and unbelief.

It is unknown to what extent the Ulama Union had any sway over the Taliban's political decisions. As noted earlier, the Union was not a formal part of the Taliban regime but an independent body located in Quetta, Pakistan. However, the Ulama Union's involvement in the case indicates that there was an internal conflict within the Taliban regime that required consultation from a "neutral" third party. The Taliban's Grand Mufti may have decided to involve the Ulama Union because he knew they would support his and Mullah Omar's own views. But it is also possible that the Taliban preferred to contact that Ulama Union, rather than convening a national-level Shura, in order to draw less media attention to the dispute. In any case, this illustrates that the Taliban regime was divided on how to respond to the sanctions regime imposed by the UN on October 15, 1999. As before, the Taliban chose the least controversial way out of the dilemma.

The events described so far in this chapter suggest that the Taliban's repeated decisions to protect Bin Laden in Afghanistan were influenced by a complex set of reasons. The aim of this book is not to explain the Taliban regime's political decision-making processes. However, their policies toward Bin Laden in the 1990s and early 2000 are so vital to the history of al-Qaida, that they can hardly go uncommented. There are two common explanations for why the Taliban hosted Bin Laden in Afghanistan in spite of the harm it caused the regime: The first is that the Taliban were dependent on Bin Laden's military and material contributions to the

[79] Ibid.
[80] Mullah Mohammad Omar, "radd amir al-mu'minin ala risala," 3 Sha'ban 1420 [November 11, 1999], quoted in al-Uyayri, al-mizan li-harakat taliban (Place unknown, Markaz al-Dirasat wa al-Buhuth al-Islamiyya, 2001): 77–78.

Taliban's war against Massoud. The second is that Bin Laden was protected in Afghanistan by a group of "fundamentalists" within the Taliban, including Mullah Omar, who ruled the country through a peculiar mix of Pashtun honor codes and literal interpretations of Islamic law.

The first argument is easiest to repudiate. The Taliban welcomed Bin Laden's offers of military and material assistance in 1997 and later, but these contributions were not vital to the Taliban's survival. As I will argue in Chapter 7, Bin Laden's fighters did a commendable job on the Taliban's front lines but their contributions were still dwarfed by those of Afghan commanders such as Haqqani, and even by other foreign fighter groups such as Uzbeks and Pakistanis. Over time, al-Qaida's military operations became more qualitatively important – the prime example being the assassination of Ahmed Shah Massoud on 9 September, 2001. However, al-Qaida only started carrying out strategically important operations for the Taliban in mid-2001. But the major Taliban decisions to expel or not expel Bin Laden came in September 1998 (involving the Grand Shura in Kabul), and in October/November 1999 (involving Taliban's Fatwa department and the neutral Afghan Ulama Union in Quetta).

The second argument to explain why the Taliban hosted Bin Laden – that the decision was taken by a small group of "fundamentalists" who ruled the country according to their own whims – is weakened by the narrative presented in this chapter. As argued, the "Bin Laden issue" was a source of great controversy within the Taliban, and the Taliban's leaders did not take the issue lightly. In 1998 and 1999 Mullah Omar repeatedly sought the opinions of scholars outside Taliban's inner circle to get advise on how to deal with Bin Laden. The regime was in fact facing an impossible dilemma: Expelling Bin Laden would be highly controversial and possibly lead to splits within the movement, and loss of religious legitimacy. Mullah Omar himself said it candidly in 1998: "If I expel or surrender Bin Laden, it will be my end."[81] But if the Taliban did not surrender Bin Laden, the Taliban would face international pressure and sanctions and in the worst case, military attack. The Taliban in the end chose the lesser of the two evils: They publically continued to offer Bin Laden sanctuary, while implementing various measures to minimize the damage he caused. This would buy the Taliban time while searching for a more permanent solution to their dilemma.

---

[81] Ahmad Muwaffaq Zaydan and Turki al-Dakhil, *"mas'ud yuballigh 'al-hayat' asr aska-riyyin pakistaniyyin fi shimal kabul. tawaqqu' darba amirikiyya jadida li-'taliban' bi-sabab ibn ladin,"* al-Hayat, October 21, 1998.

The Taliban were not a monolithic organization, and were therefore divided on what this permanent solution should be, and how urgently it should be pursued. Overall, officials within the Taliban were mainly pursuing two options: Either, Bin Laden had to be judged in a Sharia court acceptable to both the United States and the Taliban. This line was pursued by Taliban's Minister of Foreign Affairs, Mullah Mutawakil, in various meetings with US diplomats.[82] Alternatively, Bin Laden had to be convinced to leave Afghanistan of his own free will, but it was imperative to the Taliban that his exit be framed as voluntary.[83] According to one account, Mullah Omar at one point asked Bin Laden outright to leave Afghanistan.[84] Other accounts suggest that Taliban officials hoped that their restrictions on Bin Laden's communications, enforced from 1999, would eventually persuade Bin Laden to leave Afghanistan on his own.[85]

Bin Laden did not leave Afghanistan. Instead, he exploited the Taliban's internal weaknesses and turned the whole situation to his and al-Qaida's advantage. Instead of propagating al-Qaida's cause through the international media, Bin Laden built an active recruitment network in the Gulf and started using the Taliban's status as "Islamic state" to draw recruits to Afghanistan. Bin Laden's public pledge of allegiance to Mullah Omar in the spring 2001 must be viewed in this context.

PLEDGE OF ALLEGIANCE

In the spring of 2001, Osama bin Laden publically confirmed that he had pledged an oath of allegiance (*bay'a*) to Mullah Omar.[86] The first public statement of the pledge was given in a videotaped speech that was broadcast on a Deobandi conference in Pakistan and subsequently referenced on *al-Jazeera*.[87] In June 2001, Bin Laden again spoke about his pledge to

---

[82] Department of State (Islamabad) Cable, "Osama bin Laden: Taliban spokesman seeks new proposal," November 28, 1998.

[83] See, for example, Ahmad Muwaffaq Zaydan, "*shukuk fi muwafaqat amirika … wa al-iraq wa al-shishan wajhatan muhtamilatan. ibn ladin yuwafiq ala mughadarat afghanistan shart an tatakattam taliban ala makanihi*," al-Hayat, October 30, 1999.

[84] Sasson, N. bin Laden, and O. bin Laden, *Growing up Bin Laden*, 247.

[85] Department of State (Islamabad) Cable, "Osama bin Laden: Taliban spokesman seeks new proposal"; and Mustafa Hamid, "*bin ladin wa harakat taliban: sina'at al-harb wa al-hazima*," Mafa al-Siyasi – Adab al-Matarid [Mustafa Hamid's blog], May 3, 2010.

[86] Part of this subchapter is based on a blog post the author wrote with Phillip Holtmann, "The Three Functions of UBL's "Greater Pledge" to Mullah Omar (2001–2006–2014)," *Jihadology*, January 8, 2015.

[87] Ahmed Zaydan, "*bin ladin yubayi'u za'im taliban*," Al-Jazeera, April 10, 2001.

Mullah Omar, confirming it was a "greater pledge" (*bay'a uzma*) and not just a temporary one, to a group of followers in Afghanistan.[88]

The story of Bin Laden's pledge to Mullah Omar has not been fully told before. The dominant narrative so far has been that of Mustafa Hamid. Hamid claimed that he was the first Arab militant in Afghanistan to pledge allegiance to Mullah Omar in 1998. He then tried to persuade Bin Laden to do the same. Bin Laden was hesitant, but in the end, he agreed to letting Mustafa Hamid give Mullah Omar the pledge on Bin Laden's behalf. This "pledge by proxy" was later interpreted as symptomatic of the weak relationship between the Taliban and Bin Laden, where the pledge was nothing but a "façade of allegiance."[89] Given Mustafa Hamid's somewhat ambivalent relationship to Bin Laden, this interpretation makes sense.

However, the Bin Laden tape from June 2001, which did not surface until 2014, strengthens the impression that the pledge was in fact genuine.[90] Answering a question from the audience, Bin Laden states that his pledge to Mullah Omar is indeed a greater pledge (*bay'a uzma*). Explaining why he gave the pledge, he quotes a prophetic tradition saying that "the one who dies without a pledge in his throat [i.e., has not uttered a pledge], dies an ignorant death." He then defends the right of Mullah Omar to assume the title *amir al-mu'minin* (Leader of the Faithful) even if he is not from the tribe of Qureysh, the Prophet Muhammad's tribe.

Bin Laden's words are meant to answer a common theological objection to Mullah Omar's status as Leader of the Faithful. Prospective al-Qaida recruits, especially from Bin Laden's homeland Saudi Arabia, were reluctant to accept Mullah Omar's status because they believed that only members of the Quraysh tribe can be elected as Leader of the Faithful. This was no trivial point for al-Qaida, which, from 2000, had been working actively to bring recruits from the Peninsula to its training camps in Afghanistan. Gulf Arabs often believed in a literal interpretation of Islamic texts and legitimizing the Taliban from a theological point of view was therefore essential to recruitment. As there was no clear-cut foreign occupation of Muslim land in the region, as had been the case in 1980s Afghanistan, al-Qaida instead framed going to Afghanistan

[88] Bin Laden, "*bushrayat lil-shaykh usama.*"
[89] Vahid Brown, "The facade of allegiance: Bin Laden's dubious pledge to Mullah Omar," *CTC Sentinel* 3(1) (2010), 1.
[90] The videotape was published by al-Qaida's media company al-Sahab in 2014, seemingly to criticise a rival jihadi leader, Abu Bakr al-Baghdadi, for declaring himself caliph in June 2014.

as *hijra* (migration) – alluding to Prophet Muhammad's *hijra* from Mecca to Medina in 622 CE. In this context it was essential to prop up Taliban-led Afghanistan as a true Islamic state and Mullah Omar as its legitimate ruler.

This chapter has discussed the political relationship between Bin Laden and the Taliban. For the Taliban, the status of Bin Laden in Afghanistan was a highly contentious issue, and it was not taken lightly, neither by Mullah Omar nor by the rest of the Taliban leadership. The Taliban in the end decided to protect Bin Laden in Afghanistan in spite of the harm it caused the regime, simply because they viewed other options as even more harmful. Bin Laden, on his part, used the Taliban's internal weaknesses to his advantage. In early 1999 he managed to reach a compromise with Mullah Omar in which he would stop issuing statements and interviews, while continuing to pursue his own agenda in private.

Bin Laden's compromise with Mullah Omar meant that al-Qaida could not take direct responsibility for terrorist attacks, and Bin Laden could not give media interviews to promote his anti-American campaign. In the end, these restrictions were a small price to pay compared to the enormous benefits al-Qaida would get from their alliance with the Taliban. By recognizing the authority of Mullah Omar, al-Qaida was able to reap the benefits of living in an Islamic state, without having to carry the burdens of statehood.

From late 1998, al-Qaida's recruitment strategy was expanded – from issuing public calls for *jihad* to building up a recruitment network in the Gulf that would encourage devout Muslims to go to Afghanistan for *hijra* (migration) to experience life in a true Islamic state. Once in Afghanistan, the recruits were absorbed into al-Qaida's network of guest houses and training camps where many of them would be introduced to Bin Laden's political ideas. This particular arrangement facilitated al-Qaida's organizational expansion in 2000–2001, which is the subject of the next chapter.

5

Training under the Taliban

In 1996–2001, al-Qaida built an infrastructure in Afghanistan. It was comprised of residences for al-Qaida members and their families; of guest houses, and of course, militant training camps. The number of al-Qaida camps in Afghanistan tends to be exaggerated, because training camps have been conflated with non-military installations; because training camps were situated at various locations at various times; and because several of the training camps described as "al-Qaida camps" were in fact run by other militant groups. This chapter tells the history of al-Qaida's training camps in Afghanistan, whereas Chapter 6 talks about the training camps of other militant groups. What was the purpose and function of al-Qaida's training camps in Afghanistan under the Taliban?

THE AL-FARUQ CAMP IN KHOST

When Bin Laden returned to Afghanistan in May 1996, al-Qaida already had access to a cluster of training camps at Jihad Wal in Khost. The most famous of these camps was al-Faruq. The camp was named after Umar al-Faruq, the second Caliph of the Muslims, famous for a number of military victories including the conquest of Persia in 651 CE.[1] During the Taliban regime, al-Faruq changed location several times, but never changed its name.

As we recall from Chapter 2, al-Qaida's camps in Khost had been maintained by Abu Ata' al-Sharqi during the Afghan civil war. Al-Qaida's own training activity at the site had been minimal. Al-Qaida had allowed

[1] Harun, *al-harb ala al-islam*, 64.

other groups such as Tajiks, Uzbeks, and Chechens, to use the site. Al-Qaida had provided support in the form of a few trainers and logistics.

At some point, probably after Bin Laden's return to Afghanistan in 1996, al-Qaida resumed control of activities in al-Faruq. We know little of al-Qaida's training activities there in 1996–1998. Abu Jandal, who worked as a bodyguard for Bin Laden in the late 1990s, said he had been sent to attend a "concentrated course" in al-Faruq around February 1997, shortly after joining al-Qaida.[2] An individual named Abu al-Harith, who later became a training camp manager for al-Qaida, attended al-Faruq at the end of 1997 before going to fight on the Taliban's frontline north of Kabul.[3] It appears that admittance to al-Faruq was selective, and that training was offered on an ad hoc basis rather than as regular courses.

Bin Laden at the time wanted to re-establish al-Qaida in Afghanistan and strengthen the organization with new members. Some of the first Arabs who were recruited into al-Qaida in 1996 was a group (referred to in some sources as the "Northern Group") already present in Afghanistan. The group had tried, but failed to enter the Tajik civil war. They were subsequently invited to meet with Bin Laden in Nangarhar. One of the group's members was Abu Jandal, who later worked as a bodyguard for Bin Laden.[4] It appears that Bin Laden specifically targeted Saudis and Yemenis for recruitment – both among the "Northern Group" and among volunteers who came to Afghanistan through separate recruitment networks.

Al-Qaida did not have strong recruitment networks at this time, but got access to a limited number of recruits through the Khalden camp. Khalden had been founded by Abdullah Azzam's Services Office in the late 1980s. It continued to run throughout the Afghan civil war, thanks to the efforts of Ibn Sheikh al-Libi and Abu Zubaydah. In 1996, Ibn Sheikh was still Emir of the camp and Abu Zubaydah assisted him from Pakistan. Until it closed down in mid-2000, Khalden was the main gateway for new recruits entering Khalden. As such, it was also a gateway for joining al-Qaida.

[2] al-Hammadi, "Al-Qa'ida from within," part 4.
[3] MO-000244, "Recommendation for Continued Detention Under DoD Control (CD) for Guantanamo Detainee, ISN US9MO-000244DP [Abdulatif Nasser, aka Abu al-Harith]," Department of Defense (Joint Task Force Guantanamo), October 22, 2008; and AFGP-2002-800321, "Information from the Military Committee Al-Mujahideen Affairs Office," court filing, *Alsabri v. Obama*, United States District Court, District of Columbia, 2011.
[4] al-Hammadi, "Al-Qa'ida from within," part 4.

Khalden was in a different geographic location than al-Qaida's camp. Information about its exact location is surprisingly hard to come by, but it was most likely situated in Eastern Khost, close to the border with Pakistan, and usually accessed via Khurram agency in Pakistan, or Khost city. Al-Faruq was located in the Jawur valley in southern Khost, and accessed via Mir Ali in northern Waziristan. This would explain why Abu Ata', Mustafa Hamid, Fadil Harun, and other eyewitnesses who visited the al-Faruq camp in the 1990s never mentioned seeing or passing Khalden.[5]

The purpose of Khalden was to offer training to militant Islamists, regardless of group affiliation. Some of the trainees in Khalden were members of national-revolutionary groups such as the Armed Islamic Group (GIA). Others came as individuals, using the camp as a gateway to fight in Bosnia or Chechnya. Although trainees had various political motivations for seeking training, the camp leadership appears to have been apolitical. Political and doctrinal discussion among trainees was discouraged.[6]

Khalden has often been described as an "al-Qaida camp." Although this is not accurate, there was a degree of coordination with al-Qaida, especially after Bin Laden's return to Afghanistan in 1996. In March 1997, Ibn Sheikh sent Bin Laden a group of recruits with a letter stating they would remind Bin Laden of "the days of Jaji" – presumably referring to the first contingent of Bin Laden fighters in al-Ma'sada in 1987.[7] In May the same year, Abu Ata' sent a letter to Abu Hafs al-Masri, in which he discussed setting up a training program for a group of Gulf Arabs in al-Faruq. He planned to draw the recruits from Khalden, or alternatively, to coordinate with Abu Zubaydah in Peshawar so that the recruits are sent directly to al-Faruq instead of Khalden.[8] The correspondence indicates that al-Faruq at the time was a small training camp compared to Khalden, and that Ibn Sheikh and Abu Zubaydah had more effective recruitment networks in the Gulf than Bin Laden. Over the next three years, the power relationship between Khalden and Al-Qaida would change drastically.

---

[5] See, in particular, Omar Nasiri's and Abu Zubaydah's detailed accounts of how they travelled to Khalden. Nasiri, *Inside the jihad,* 130–133; Abu Zubaydah, *The Abu Zubaydah Diaries,* Vol. 1.

[6] Nasiri, *Inside the jihad,* 192; "A terrorist's testimony."

[7] AQ-PMPR-D-001-554.

[8] AQ-MCOP-D-000-922, "Personal letter regarding training and other issues from Abu Ataa al Sharqi to Abu Hafs," May 1, 1997, Conflict Records Resource Center, Washington, DC.

In August 1998, al-Qaida was running a basic course and a tactics course in al-Faruq with some 70 trainees in total.[9] This is the first clear indication that al-Qaida had expanded the training activity in al-Faruq. We do not know the identity of the trainees or the content of the courses, but they likely resembled those given in al-Faruq in the early 1990s, and in al-Faruq after it was moved to Kandahar in 2000. In the basic course, recruits were taught physical fitness, small arms, and how to use explosives. In the tactics course they were taught how to operate in small guerrilla units. The purpose of these courses was to prepare the recruits for frontline service. The purpose was also to identify promising candidates for joining al-Qaida.[10]

According to Mustafa Hamid, Bin Laden at the time wanted to make al-Faruq into a permanent training facility for al-Qaida, and he even contemplated moving his family there.[11] The US missile strikes on Khost on August 20, 1998 derailed the plan. Al-Faruq and al-Siddiq were partly destroyed in the strikes, whereas al-Qaida's administrative headquarters at Jihad Wal was almost completely destroyed. Six or seven Arabs were killed – one in Jihad Wal, another in al-Siddiq and four or five trainees in al-Faruq. Eighteen Pakistanis were killed in nearby Pakistani camps.[12]

The strikes boosted the anti-American sentiment in the region, especially among Taliban and their supporters in Pakistan who saw the strikes as an unwarranted assault on Islam and Muslims. The notion that Bill Clinton carried out the strikes to take attention away from the Monica Lewinsky affair became a long-standing joke in Islamist circles. The strikes themselves were ridiculed because they appeared to have missed their intended targets. The Al Shifa Pharmaceutical plant that was hit in Sudan did not contain any chemical weapons, and Bin Laden was not in Khost at the time of the strikes.

Arab insider sources tell a different story. Although no high-ranking al-Qaida members were killed in the strikes, they succeeded in destroying al-Qaida's camp infrastructure in Khost. Perhaps more importantly, they reinforced myths about the precision and reach of US military technology. Both Mustafa Hamid, and the Syrian jihadist Abu Mus'ab al-Suri, were in awe of the precision of the US missiles that had destroyed

[9] Hamid, *mashru' tajikistan*, 64.

[10] AQ-TRED-D-000-996, "Description of several courses in al-Qaeda training program for new recruits," undated [ca. 1998–2001], Conflict Records Resource Center, Washington, D.C.; al-Hammadi, "Al-Qa'ida from within," part 5.

[11] Hamid, *mashru' tajikistan*, 63.

[12] Hamid, *mashru' tajikistan*, 70–71; al-Hammadi, "Al-Qa'ida from within," part 9.

al-Qaida's camps. Hamid, for instance, noted in his memoirs that in al-Siddiq camp, the United States had "put one missile in every of the five rooms that had been prepared for Bin Laden and his family."[13] The point here is not the factual accuracy of Hamid's account but the feelings it conveys: The US missile strikes were a stark reminder that al-Qaida was facing a formidable and technologically superior foe. As a consequence, al-Qaida became more cautious about the security of their camps and of communications security in general.

AL-QAIDA EXPANDS

After the US missile strikes in August 1998, al-Qaida was at a cross-roads: Bin Laden had declared war on the United States, al-Qaida had carried out its first international terrorist attacks against American interests, and the United States had responded by destroying al-Qaida's camps. Despite the destruction of al-Qaida's training camps in Khost, al-Qaida still viewed the East African operation a success: The attacks and their aftermath had granted al-Qaida maximum publicity, without destroying the relationship between al-Qaida and their hosts, the Taliban. Al-Qaida was ready to start a period of expansion. Fadil Harun recalled that al-Qaida's Shura council called a meeting sometime after the US missile strikes,

... in order to organize the inner organization, and to gather the ranks of the youth again, and to take proper security measures in order to wage the new war; and to activate the training camps, and to put in place new security measures for the new arrivals. Osama had closed the door for joining al-Qaida, and then opened it again after the East Africa operations because many of the umma's youth came to Afghanistan after those operations.[14]

On November 28, 1998, Abu al-Faraj al-Libi was summoned to a top secret meeting in Kandahar with al-Qaida's "Joint Chiefs of Staff" (*hay'at al al-arkan*). It was the first time that al-Qaida used the term "Joint Chiefs of Staff," indicating that some kind of re-organization had indeed taken place. Abu al-Faraj was, at the time, chief of al-Qaida's training branch. He was asked to present at the meeting an organizational chart for the camps, a budget, and a description of present training activities. Abd al-Hadi al-Iraqi was also summoned to the meeting. He was to present a

---

[13] Abu Mus'ab al-Suri made similar remarks in his writings. Hamid, *mashru' tajikistan*, 70; Lia, *Architect of Global Jihad*, 6.

[14] Harun, *al-harb ala al-islam*, 380.

similar report about al-Qaida's contributions to the Taliban's frontline north of Kabul.[15] We do not know the content of the Chiefs of Staff meeting, which was scheduled for December 7, 1998. However, it is clear that al-Qaida was not going to be paralyzed by the missile strikes on Khost.

In 1999, the al-Faruq camp was temporarily located at the Mes Aynak copper mine in Logar.[16] In November 1999 it was moved to a location right north of Kabul known as Murad Beg. At Murad Beg, al-Qaida held an advanced training course known as the "cadre course." It lasted "for several months" and the purpose, according to Fadil Harun, was to educate future al-Qaida leaders. The course differed from the basic course and the tactics course in that it was open to sworn al-Qaida members only, and the course employed some of the most experienced trainers al-Qaida had to offer.[17]

The existence of a cadre course in November 1999 indicates that al-Qaida was in a period of expansion. The last time al-Qaida organized a cadre course – as far as we know – was in late 1992, shortly before al-Qaida launched its training mission to Somalia. Several of the cadre who graduated from that course, became part of the East African training mission. Similarly, in November 1999, al-Qaida was about to embark upon a big training project – this time, in southern Afghanistan.

In spring 2000, al-Qaida moved the al-Faruq camp to its final location – the Gharmabak Ghar mountains some 60 kilometers northwest of Kandahar City.[18] At the same time, al-Qaida intensified the recruitment efforts targeting the Arabian Peninsula. According to leaked US intelligence information, al-Qaida already had recruiters in Saudi Arabia and Yemen who had been active from at least 1999. The recruiters singled out candidates at mosques and public events, and facilitated their travel to Kandahar. These networks probably contributed to recruiting candidates for al-Qaida's cadre course in Murad Beg in November 1999.[19]

---

[15] AQ-MSLF-D-001-422, "Top secret letter from Ahmed bin 'Abd al-Aziz to Abu Alfaraj, the subjects: The meeting of Chief of Staffs for the Security and Military Committees," December 7, 1998; and AQ-PMPR-D-001-421, "Letter from Ahmad bin 'Abd al-'Aziz to 'Abd al-Hadi in regards to a meeting of the general staff of the Security and Military Committee," December 7, 1998, Conflict Records Resource Center, Washington, DC.

[16] *The 9/11 Commission report* (New York: W. W. Norton), 157.

[17] Harun, *al-harb ala al-islam*, 397–400.

[18] According to one source, regular training courses were held at al-Faruq, Kandahar from April 6, 2000. AQ-TRED-D-001-406, "Various topics pertaining to al-Qaida operations and possibly al Farouq from personnel, weapons, equipment, training etc," undated, Conflict Records Resource Center, Washington, DC.

[19] According to leaked US intelligence sources, one of these networks were operating in Ta'iz and Aden, and led by Sheikh Abu Ali al-Yafi, aka Marwan Jawan. Jawan recruited

At some stage, al-Qaida must also have increased its sources of funding. Bin Laden's fourth son Omar had recalled that Bin Laden was literally broke in 1998, and that the family barely had money to buy food.[20] Although there are few primary sources about al-Qaida's funding in this period, Bin Laden throughout the 1990s probably continued to use and expand on fundraising networks, especially in the Gulf region, that were established during the Afghan-Soviet war.[21] Moreover, leaked US intelligence information suggests that several of the recruits who traveled to Afghanistan in the late 1990s and early 2000s – whether to train in al-Qaida's camps, or to experience life in the Taliban's Islamic state – brought personal donations with them.[22]

From mid-2000, the recruitment campaign was intensified when the charismatic Saudi Sheikh Yusuf al-Uyayri started vouching for al-Qaida. The aim of the recruitment campaign was to encourage Gulf Arabs to go to Afghanistan to receive training in al-Qaida's camps, and to experience life in a true Islamic state. Al-Qaida was further assisted by radical Saudi scholars such as Hamid bin Uqla al-Shu'aybi, who from late 2000 issued fatwas in support of the Taliban regime.[23]

During 2000 and 2001, several hundred recruits would attend training in al-Faruq. A majority of them were from the Arabian Peninsula. For example, of 126 new recruits arriving in Kandahar during August and September 2000, 74 percent were from either Saudi Arabia or Yemen. But recruits came to join al-Faruq from a number of different countries. In the sample mentioned earlier, no less than eighteen different countries were represented.[24]

a Yemeni named Khaled Ahmad, who went to Afghanistan in 1999 and trained under Fadil Harun in al-Faruq outside Kabul, suggesting he was part of al-Qaida's cadre course. YM-000242, "Recommendation for Continued Detention Under DoD Control (CD) for Guantanamo Detainee, ISN US9YM-000242DP [Khaled Ahmad], Department of Defense (Joint Task Force Guantanamo), April 7, 2008.

[20] Sasson, N. Bin Laden, and O. Bin Laden, *Growing up Bin Laden*.
[21] *The 9/11 Commission report*, 169–172.
[22] See, for example, KU-00028, "Recommendation for Continued Detention Under DoD Control (CD) for Guantanamo Detainee, ISN: US9KU-000228DP [Abdullah Kamel Abdullah]," Department of Defense (Joint Task Force Guantanamo), December 27, 2005.
[23] Hegghammer, *Jihad in Saudi Arabia*, 121–122.
[24] The count is based on the following three documents: "*tawziy' al-akhwa al-qadimin bi-tarikh 9/5/1421* [Distribution of the brothers arriving August 9, 2000]; *kashf bi-asma' al-akhwa al-qadimin bud'an min tarikh: 18/06/21*" [List of names of brothers arriving from September 16, 2000]; and *kashf bi-asma' al-akhwa al-qadimin min tarikh: 29/06/21 to 04/07/21*" [List of names of brothers arriving from September 27, to October 1, 2000]. All documents are part of AFGP-2002–800321, "Information from the Military Committee Al-Mujahideen Affairs Office," Court filing, *Alsabri v. Obama*, United States District Court, District of Columbia, 2011.

Al-Qaida decided to accommodate for all types of recruits, including those recruited outside al-Qaida's own recruitment networks in the Gulf. An internal al-Qaida document, which is probably from 1999 or later, describes how al-Qaida should deal with "those young men who were recruited in Afghanistan or who came to us outside of the official channels":

There is no doubt in my mind that some of them, if not all, are sincere. It is also possible to find agents among them. Generally, those seniors who are already in the field must be separated from the newcomers, even though both of them are subject to the same training program.[25]

The document goes on to describe a training scheme for the recruits. After completing the basic course, the recruits have to "spend at least two months on the frontline" in order to test their sincerity and motivation. "The Emir of the camp must send a special report on the young men who wish to work with us," said the document. After completing service at the frontline, "the commander of the front must send another report on the young men."[26] The rest of the document is missing, but it seems clear that al-Qaida by 2000 had not only expanded its organization; it had also expanded its role inside Afghanistan. From being a close-knit organization around Bin Laden, al-Qaida was now acting as a "Services Office" for incoming volunteers. This created both opportunities and challenges for al-Qaida.

As illustrated in the introduction of this book, al-Qaida in 2001 was a bureaucratic organization. The Office of Mujahidin Affairs, which was located next to the Haji Habash mosque in Kandahar city, took care of the initial screening of recruits. The office registered new arrivals, collected personal items for safe-keeping, and provided lodging in nearby guesthouses. The office announced the start of new training courses in the Kandahar area – usually in al-Faruq, but occasionally in more specialized camps such as the Abu Ubaydah camp at Kandahar airport, or a facility in Kandahar city known as "the Clinic." Recruits who wanted to attend training had to register their names at the office and await approval before being shipped to the camp on a designated date.[27]

---

[25] AQ-TRED-D-000-996, "Description of several courses in al-Qaeda training program for new recruits."

[26] Ibid.

[27] See, for example, "*jadwal mawaʻid bud' al-dawrat* [date schedule for the start of courses], January 15–20, 2001; "*iʻlan hamm* [important announcement]," February 27, 2001; "*dawrat al-ittisalat raqam* 2 [Communications course no. 2]," February 18, 2001, in AFGP-2002-800321, "Information from the Military Committee Al-Mujahideen Affairs Office."

A collection of registration forms, found in Afghanistan after the US-led invasion in 2001, gives a snapshot of the activity in al-Qaida's training camps. From August 2000 to August 2001, more than 400 trainees registered for courses in Kabul and Kandahar (Table 5.1). Some trainees are presumably registered in more than one course. On the other hand, the list of courses is most certainly incomplete – suggesting that 400 is a moderate estimate of the number of trainees attending al-Qaida's camps in that period.

Al-Qaida had, by mid-2000, designed a comprehensive training scheme with three main components: (1) Basic and advanced military training to enable recruits to fight conventional to guerrilla type conflicts, such as on the Taliban's frontline north of Kabul, (2) Specialized courses to enable recruits to take part in revolutionary activity or international terrorism abroad, and (3) Cadre-development program to strengthen al-Qaida's own organization. The training scheme reflected how al-Qaida by now had developed into a strong organization. It was carrying out essential tasks such as cadre development, and nonessential tasks such as supporting other militant groups with training. The next sections discuss al-Qaida's training courses in detail.

BASIC AND SPECIALIZED COURSES

Basic training in al-Qaida's camps consisted of the basic course and the tactics course, in addition to courses on certain weapons. According to Abu Jandal, the basic and tactics course was divided into three periods as follows:

- Screening period (*ayyam al-tamhis*): fifteen days, physical exercise.
- Basic training period (*al-fatra al-ta'sisiyya*): forty-five days, basic training on weapons, explosives, and map reading.
- Tactics course (*dawrat al-taktik li-harb al-asabat*): forty-five days, advanced training on guerrilla tactics.[28]

We recall that al-Qaida's original basic course had four weeks of training on the "fundamentals" such as small arms, military explosives, and map reading. The "fundamentals" course was followed by two weeks of tactics training and two weeks of artillery training (Table 1.1). Al-Qaida's training courses in 2000–2001 were longer. The "fundamentals" period was extended from twenty-eight days to forty-five days, or sixty days including

---

[28] al-Hammadi, "Al-Qa'ida from within," part 5.

TABLE 5.1 *Example of courses held in al-Qaida-run camps, 2000–2001*

Course	Camp	No.	Start	End
IED manufacture course	Abu Khabab	?	Feb 27, 2000	
Artillery Course		o	July 7, 2000	
Information Security Course	Kabul	25	Aug 24, 2000	Sept 25, 2000
Basic Course		16		Sept 8, 2000
Basic Course		12		Sept 15, 2000
Basic course		8		Sept 17, 2000
Documents course		10	Jan 15, 2001	
Tactics course 1		33	Jan 20, 2001	
Artillery+Anti-Aircraft course		25	Jan 20, 2001	
Armor course		8	Jan 20, 2001	
Security course		16	Jan 20, 2001	
Security course		16	Jan 20, 2001	
Execution course		20	Jan 20, 2001	
Execution course		20	Jan 20, 2001	
Communications course		10	Jan 20, 2001	
Communications course 2	Clinic	8	Feb 18, 2001	
Documents course 2	Airport	11	Feb 19, 2001	
Security course 3	Airport	12	Feb 19, 2001	
Sniper course 1	Airport	9	Mar 20, 2001	
Tactics course 2	Al-Faruq	35	Mar 24, 2001	
Artillery course 2	Al-Faruq	28	Mar 24, 2001	
Execution course		2	May 16, 2001	
Explosives course (special)		15	June 4, 2001	
Information course		12	June 4, 2001	
Execution course		?	June 4, 2001	
Security course		20	June 5, 2001	
Anti-Aircraft course		7		Aug 24, 2001
Artillery course		7	Aug 25, 2001	
Trainers Preparation course		20	Undated	
TOTAL		**405**		

Note: The table is mainly compiled from AFGP-2002–800321, "Information from the Military Committee Al-Mujahideen Affairs Office," and AQ-MISC-D-001-034, "Recommendation letters to Abu Khabab to attend training at the toxin session and requests for aluminium powder and other materials for the toxin training, training requests for other brothers, and letters of other matters," February 27, 2000, Conflict Records Resource Center, Washington, DC.

the screening period. The tactics training and artillery training were separate courses. After completing one or both courses, recruits who wanted to join al-Qaida were expected to serve on the Taliban's frontlines.[29]

Al-Qaida's basic military education was meant to enable recruits to participate in conventional to guerrilla type conflicts. This is evident because skills taught in these courses included small arms, map reading, first aid, and basic infantry tactics. Al-Qaida recognized that participation in classical *jihad* (guerrilla war to liberate occupied Muslim territory) was the primary goal and motivation of many recruits coming to Afghanistan. In the late 1990s, the war in Chechnya was a source of motivation for many recruits, thanks in part to the horrific images of Muslim suffering that spread rapidly throughout Europe and the Middle East, coupled with homemade videos of heroic Arab fighters struggling to rectifying the wrongs. Among the iconic commanders of that era was Khattab – the Saudi fighter who had a short stint in al-Qaida's al-Faruq camp in the early 1990s, before making a name of his own in Tajikistan, and later in Chechnya. Some of the recruits who came to Afghanistan in the late 1990s and early 2000s planned to move on to Chechnya after receiving training.[30]

However, in 2000 it was almost impossible for foreign fighters to join the conflict in Chechnya. The Chechen rebels and their Arab supporters, including Khattab, experienced major setbacks in the winter of 1999–2000, when Vladimir Putin – then Russian Prime Minister – ordered Russian troops to enter Chechnya and seize the capital, Grozny. Meanwhile, al-Qaida provided an alternative – the Taliban's frontlines north of Kabul. As will be detailed in the Chapter 7, al-Qaida manned several positions on the Taliban's frontline north of Kabul. Al-Qaida used the frontline systematically to train and test new members. One of the challenges in this regard was to convince new recruits coming to Afghanistan that fighting Massoud was a legitimate *jihad*. To remove any doubt, in November 2000 the influential Saudi Sheikh Hamud bin Uqla al-Shu'aybi issued a fatwa saying it was legitimate (*mashru'*) to fight with the Taliban against its opponents [i.e., Massoud and his allies] "who are supported by the forces of disbelief like America, Great Britain and Russia."[31]

---

[29] See, for example, AQ-TRED-D-000-996, "Description of several courses in al-Qaeda training program for new recruits."

[30] On recruits wanting to go to Chechnya: See, for example, AFGP-2002-000091, "Notes from Abd al-Hadi," Combating Terrorism Center, West Point, NY.

[31] Hamud bin Uqla al-Shu'aybi, "*su'al an shara'iyyit hukumat al-taliban*," 02/09/1421 h. [November 28, 2000].

The part of al-Qaida's training program that taught basic military skills was the largest and probably most resource demanding of al-Qaida's training activities. Al-Qaida required that its own members go through the courses and serve on the Taliban's frontlines as commanders – if not, it was not possible to advance internally in al-Qaida.[32] This suggests that al-Qaida viewed itself as an elite military unit, in addition to being a clandestine organization. At its core, al-Qaida needed cadre who were skilled in conventional and guerrilla warfare because al-Qaida's long-term strategy required a group of revolutionary cadre.

Another type of training given in al-Qaida's camps were the specialized courses. The purpose of these courses are best described in an internal document found in Afghanistan, where unfortunately some pages are missing. The document indicates that al-Qaida trained its own members to do "internal work" (*al-ʿamal bil-dakhil*) and that it planned to offer the same type of training to other groups.[33] Based on the context, it is understood that *internal work* must refer to clandestine militant activity inside Muslim countries, supporting either revolutionary violence or attacks on American targets. Al-Qaida frequently used the term *external operations* (*amaliyyat kharijiyya*) to refer to militant activity outside the Muslim world.

The document proposes that "internal work" requires special crews (*atqum*) specialized in the following four fields: Information gathering (*maʿlumat*), execution (*tanfidh*), explosives (*mutafajjirat*), and document forgery (*watha'iq*).[34] The required specialties correspond with names of training courses offered by al-Qaida in 2000–2001. At least one of these courses (the document forgery course) were not held in al-Faruq, but on the training site referred to as The Airport.[35] This was likely the Abu Ubaydah Camp at Kandahar Airport, which was used by al-Qaida to teach specialized courses and skills. The Kandahar Airport facility was the most infamous of al-Qaida's training facilities in Afghanistan because it was associated with the planning and preparation of al-Qaida's international terrorist attacks.

From January to June 2001, al-Qaida offered several courses in "execution" (*al-tanfidh*). In al-Qaida parlance, these courses most likely

[32] AFGP-2002-000112, "Al-Qa'ida staff count public appointments," Combating Terrorism Center, West Point, NY.

[33] AQ-TRED-D-000-996, "Description of several courses in al-Qaeda training program for new recruits."

[34] Ibid.

[35] "*dawrat al-watha'iq raqam* 2 [Documents course no. 2]," in AFGP-2002–800321, "Information from the Military Committee Al-Mujahideen Affairs Office."

trained operatives to execute violent attacks in urban settings as opposed to guerrilla attacks in rural areas. In *The Encyclopedia of Jihad*, written in the early 1990s, *qism al-tanfidh* refers to a team of operatives specifically tasked with carrying out assassinations and kidnappings.[36] Other jihadist training manuals associated with the word *al-tanfidh* describe topics such as pistol shooting, how to plan a secret meeting and how to plan an assassination.[37]

Al-Qaida also planned to offer special courses to other jihadi and insurgent groups. They included courses in document forgery; a specialized course in explosives (including topics such as blasting, sabotage, and booby-traps); a course in how to make homemade explosives; and finally, a three-month trainers preparation course.[38] We do not know if al-Qaida offered these courses to anyone prior to 9/11. The existence of the course outline is nevertheless an indication of al-Qaida's broad ambitions in Afghanistan. Trainer preparation courses would typically be given to insurgents who need to build military capability from the bottom, such as the Somali militants trained by al-Qaida in the early 1990s, or the Tajik rebels trained by Mustafa Hamid's group in al-Faruq around the same time. Courses in document forgery allow groups to operate across international borders. Courses in explosives can be used in a wide range of conflict types but specialized courses in homemade explosives (HME) are typically given to groups who operate underground in peaceful countries.

Al-Qaida assisted other groups with training in other ways as well. In September 1999, Hassan Mahsum, the leader of the East Turkestan Islamic Movement (ETIM) participated in a thirty-day advanced security course in Kabul. According to an internal document, Hassan Mahsum audited the course in the capacity of being "Emir of the Turkestani brothers."[39]

Due to lack of documentation from other high-level al-Qaida courses, we do not know if this was a widespread phenomenon. However, it seems clear that al-Qaida shared operational knowledge with selected representatives of other groups. Again, these activities must be interpreted

---

[36] *mawsu'at al-jihad, al-juzz al-awwal: al-amn wal-istikhbarat*, 2nd electron. ed. (Afghanistan: Maktab al-Khidamat, 1424 h. [2003]): 413–414.

[37] Based on text search in an archive of jihadi training manuals stored at the Norwegian Defence Research Establishment (FFI), Kjeller, Norway.

[38] AQ-TRED-D-000-996, "Description of several courses in al-Qaeda training program for new recruits."

[39] "*khitab istilam* [receiving letter]," August 24, 2000; and "*khitab irsal* [Dispatching letter]," September 25, 2000, in AQ-TRED-D-000-996, "Description of several courses in al-Qaeda training program for new recruits."

in light of how al-Qaida viewed itself and its role in Afghanistan – not primarily as a clandestine terrorist organization but as an instigator and enabler that would support other militant groups according to ability. Al-Qaida's mission in Afghanistan may be seen as a continuation of al-Qaida's first training mission to Somalia in 1993, except that al-Qaida no longer had to travel to support islamist groups elsewhere. In Afghanistan, the islamist groups came to al-Qaida.

THE CADRE COURSE

The final component of al-Qaida's training scheme in Afghanistan was al-Qaida's own cadre-development program. This program is relatively well documented through the eyewitness accounts of Fadil Harun, and internal documents found in Afghanistan. The most comprehensive source is a twelve-page, handwritten booklet called "Fundamental Qualifying Courses to Prepare the Cadre of al-Qaida".[40]

The booklet describes a comprehensive education program resting on the following five pillars: Islamic, military, security, management, and political courses. The advanced security course held in Kabul in September 1999, in which ETIM leader Hassan Mahsum participated, was part of the "security courses" pillar. Within each pillar the student would progress from basic first-level courses to more advanced second- and third-level courses.

Although the focus of the cadre course was clearly on military and security courses, the candidates were supposed to complete a wide range of courses including handwriting improvement and Qur'an recitation. As an example, the content of the Islamic courses pillar was outlined as shown in Table 5.2. Unsurprisingly, the first- and second-level courses emphasize core texts and concepts of Salafi-Jihadism such as *al-wala' wal-bara* (loyalty and disavowal) and Qur'anic chapters legitimizing armed *jihad*, such as *surat al-anfal* and *surat al-bara'a*. Other parts of the syllabus seem to teach standard religious knowledge such as prayer and recitation rules and the forty hadith of al-Nawawi, taught to give students an introduction to the fundamentals of Islamic Law.

The "military studies" is the most comprehensive and probably most resource-demanding part of al-Qaida's training program. On the first

---

[40] Original title: *al-dawrat al-ta'hiliyya li-i'dad kawadir al-qa'ida al-asasiyya*. In AFGP-2002-000112, "Al-Qa'ida staff count public appointments."

TABLE 5.2 *Content of the "Islamic courses" pillar of al-Qaida's cadre education program*

3rd level	Al-sira al-nabawiyya, Kitab al-fawa'id by Ibn al-Qayyim, Explanation of surat al-baqara from the mukhtasir of Ibn Kathir, Explanation of surat al imran, Explanation of surat al-an'am.
2nd level	Jurisprudence and rules of jihad, Rules of prayer, Explanation of surat al-bara'a, The second twenty Hadith of al-Nawawi, with memorizing.
1st level	Simple beliefs, including al-wala wal-bara, Explanation of surat al-anfal, Evolvement of the stages of jihad, The first twenty Hadith from the forty Hadith of al-Nawawi, with memorizing, Rules of recitation and intonation.

level, recruits complete the basic course, tactics course, and "some specialized weapons courses" (such as artillery, sniping, etc.) On the second level, recruits develop their leadership skills through the platoon and battalion commander courses, and "other specialized courses." On the third level, we find the cadre course, in addition to "advanced specialized courses." Between courses, recruits are expected to serve at the frontline to get battlefield experience and to prove themselves as commanders.

The most detailed description of al-Qaida's cadre course – that is, the third and last stage of military education – can be found in the memoirs of Fadil Harun. He claimed he attended an early version of the course in al-Faruq in 1992, and worked as an instructor in a similar course held north of Kabul in 1999. The course in 1999 was held at al-Faruq's temporary location at Murad Beg. The goal was to "educate a new group that would belong to al-Qaida and that would be specialized in leading training camps and fronts." Most of the twenty-four trainees that had been selected for the course were Saudis and Yemenites, underlining the fact that al-Qaida was targeting Saudis and Yemenis for recruitment – not only to carry out international terrorist attacks but to serve as mid- and high-ranking leaders in the organization.[41] The program included a four-week basic course in small arms, followed by courses in explosives, topography, and tactics. The practical lessons were supplemented by

[41] Harun, *al-harb ala al-islam*, 397, 403.

religious and political lectures. The lecture series, according to Harun's memoirs, looked something like this:

- Osama bin Laden – "Issues of the Muslim Ummah"
- Abu Muhammad al-Masri – "Palestine and World Politics"
- Fadil Harun – "The East Africa Operation"
- Abu Osama al-Libi – "The Algerian Civil War" (arguing against the GIA's killing of Muslims during the war).[42]

It is notable that Fadil Harun was selected to lecture on the East African Operation. As further described in Chapter 8, Harun was the only member of the terrorist cell that managed to flee East Africa after the attacks, and join al-Qaida in Afghanistan. His survival ensured, presumably, that the tactical lessons from this operation were transferred to new generations of al-Qaida cadre.

Al-Qaida's cadre course at Murad Beg was not open for members of other militant groups. However, other groups were welcome to attend the political lectures given at the camp. The Kurds, Tajiks, and Uzbeks were invited to attend, as were the groups of Abu al-Layth al-Libi, leader of a Libyan Islamic Fighting Group (LIFG) faction, and Hassan Mahsum, the founder of ETIM.[43] The purpose, presumably, to spread Bin Laden's political ideas to other groups in Afghanistan.

We do not know what happened to the twenty-four recruits at Murad Beg – except for one Yemeni nicknamed Abu Usama al-Adani, who ended up in the US detention facility at Guantánamo Bay. According to leaked US intelligence information, al-Adani served at the Bagram frontline at various periods after completing the course, and in December 2001 he was commanding a group of Arabs at Tora Bora.[44] If it is true, it means that the Yemeni was following a rather typical career path of al-Qaida – starting with the basic course and advancing to become a midlevel operational commander.

The booklet describing al-Qaida's cadre education program describes this career path in detail. Overall, the booklet states that "the training camp plays a big role initially to appraise and categorize the brothers."[45] The best candidates are selected for more advanced training. Then, trainees are supposed to spend a period of time "in an operational program,

---

[42] Harun, *al-harb ala al-islam*, 402–403.
[43] Ibid.
[44] YM-000242, "Recommendation for Continued Detention Under DoD Control (CD) for Guantanamo Detainee, ISN US9YM-000242DP [Khaled Ahmad]."
[45] AFGP-2002-000112, "Al-Qa'ida staff count public appointments."

like the front for example, ... to discover and get to know other sides of his personality, and to confirm what was recorded about him during training." Afterward, the trainee is instructed to take more advanced courses, which will complete the formal training. Then, he will be assigned to "the areas of service" (*amkan al-khidma*) like the frontline or guarding "or any other type of work in order to reach his real potential." Then, after a certain period he will be selected to join the cadre course.[46]

According to this program, the recruits would move back and forth between the training camps and the frontline, which, until spring 2001, meant the frontline north of Kabul, and after spring 2001 also included positions in Takhar province in northern Afghanistan. The frontline service had several functions. During the trainee's first visit to the frontline he was expected to complete a set of courses in artillery and other heavy weapons. It was also a test for the trainee to see how he would endure the harsh battlefield conditions. When the trainee completed the cadre course, he would be sent to "work" in al-Qaida – which would mean either at the frontline, in administration, or as instructor in a training camp. Trainees who were sent to the frontline at this stage would typically work as commander or subcommander of small groups of fighters.[47]

Al-Qaida's cadre-development program was based on continuous evaluation, starting from the moment the recruits entered basic training. An internal al-Qaida document gives insight into some of al-Qaida's evaluation processes. In September 2000, twenty-four recruits graduated from al-Qaida's advanced security course in Kabul. In a report sent to Abu Hafs al-Masri [aka Ahmad Abd al-Aziz], the instructor in the course lists the candidates and their grades, ranging from *ya'tamid alayihi – jayyid jiddan* (dependable – very good) to *kusul* (lazy).[48]

Table 5.3 provides a definition of the grades. They suggest that trainees were evaluated according to their leadership qualities as well as the level of their skills. In other words, al-Qaida's cadre program emphasized the development of military leaders, similar to education within regular armies.

The four top grades were awarded to trainees with good to excellent skills and who were either "capable of leading a team," or "in need of time and experience with the men before being able to lead a team." Only four of the twenty-five graduates fell in those categories. Ten graduates

---

[46] Ibid.

[47] AFGP-2002-000112, "Al-Qa'ida staff count public appointments."

[48] "*khitab irsal* [Dispatching letter]," September 25, 2000, in AQ-TRED-D-000-996, "Description of several courses in al-Qaeda training program for new recruits."

TABLE 5.3 *Definition of grades used in al-Qaida's advanced security course, September 2000*

Grade	Grade name	Definition
1	Dependable – very good	Capable of leading a team and very high level of skills.
2	Hard-working – excellent	In need of time and experience with the men before being able to lead a team, but excellent skills.
3	Dependable – good	Capable of leading a team and high level of skills.
4	Hard-working – good	In need of time and experience with the men before being able to lead a team, but good level of skills.
5	Hard-working – acceptable	Team member. Active, energetic and industrious. Needs more time to gain experience.
–	Bored and hard-working – good	Exerts effort, needs time to understand many matters. It is recommended that he be tried at other things.
–	Makes effort – good	Cooperates with his brothers, exerts great effort in administrative work at a good level, and is trying out other types of work.
–	Makes effort – acceptable	Cooperates with his brothers, exerts effort in administrative work at an acceptable level, and is trying out other types of work.
–	Acceptable	Cooperates with his brothers and is trying out other types of work.
–	–	Must increase the number of Muslims.
–	[blank]	Lazy, has very low motivation for work, needs time to put his heart and mind to work.

fell in the category of "team members." The rest fell into the lower grades, suggesting they would be better off working in administration or pros- elytizing (da'wa).[49]

One of the top students in the class of September 2000 – and described as "capable of leading a team" – was Adnan El Shukrijumah aka Ja'far al-Tayyar. He was a Saudi who grew up in Florida and who started fre- quenting training camps in Afghanistan in 1999. Sometime after 2001, he became involved with al-Qaida's External Operations Cell and in 2010, he was placed on the FBI's list of most wanted terrorists with a USD $5 million reward on his head.[50]

These internal documents show that al-Qaida's system of education was comprehensive, rigid, and ambitious. Al-Qaida did not simply edu- cate operatives capable of planning and carrying out international terror- ist attacks. The main goal was to educate military leaders for al-Qaida's organization that could take on a range of tasks – from leading units on a battlefield to building clandestine underground networks in the "interior" (i.e., the Middle East), to providing military assistance to local insurgencies.

This provides at least a partial answer to a puzzle that plagued the Western intelligence community for years after 9/11. How could al-Qaida survive so long, in spite of the arrest and killing of so many of their mid- and high-level operatives in Pakistan after 2001? The founda- tion was laid already in the early 1990s when al-Qaida started its first "cadre course" in the Khost province of Afghanistan. We do not know how many cadre courses al-Qaida held after 1996 – only one is docu- mented in the primary sources but most likely there were more. In any case, the existence of a cadre course, and its re-activation in Afghanistan in late 1999, suggests that building a resilient organization was a core part of al-Qaida's strategy in this period.

Al-Qaida's training activities in Afghanistan in 1996–2001 had stra- tegic as well as idealistic purposes. This duality can be traced back to al-Qaida's charter from 1988, which divided al-Qaida's work into essen- tial and nonessential tasks. One of the core, but nonessential tasks of al-Qaida was to provide support and guidance to other militant groups. This explains why al-Qaida offered training and assistance to other mili- tant groups who came to Afghanistan. It may also explain why al-Qaida

[49] Ibid.
[50] Federal Bureau of Investigation, "Adnan G. El Shukrijumah," accessed March 7, 2016, www2.fbi.gov/wanted/terrorists/terelshukrijumah.htm.

offered Hassan Mahsum, a Chinese Uighur separatist leader, to audit one of al-Qaida's advanced courses on security.

However, al-Qaida's training activities in Afghanistan also had a strategic purpose. The purpose was to educate cadre for al-Qaida's organization who would be qualified to take on a range of tasks in the future. Al-Qaida's cadre course covered a wide variety of subjects including political, Islamic, and administrative topics. During the course, the recruits were expected, *inter alia*, to memorize the forty Hadith of al-Nawawi; to practice their handwriting; and to serve for extended periods at the Taliban's frontline. The purpose was to create a pool of skilled, reliable and battle-hardened personnel.

The existence of the cadre course illustrates how al-Qaida by now had developed into a semiprofessional military organization. It had a system for receiving new recruits. It had formal entry procedures. It had a rigid training program in which only the most dedicated and talented recruits were offered to enter al-Qaida. The recruits were graded according to their leadership abilities as well as the level of their skills. There were set job descriptions and standing operating procedures for camps and guest houses. This does not mean that al-Qaida was a regular army. But their activities described here suggest they had ambitions that went far beyond international terrorism.

Al-Qaida's professionalism made it stand out from other militant groups in Afghanistan. This helps explain how al-Qaida managed to get a privileged position with the Taliban regime, even as the Taliban sought to regulate the activities of foreign fighters in Afghanistan, which is the topic of the next chapter.

6

Taliban's Policies toward the Arabs

Al-Qaida did not run their training camps in Afghanistan in a vacuum. Afghanistan in 1996–2001 became a safe haven for a number of militant Islamist groups from the Middle East, North Africa, Pakistan, and Central Asia. These groups had various degrees of connections to each other and to the Taliban regime. Due to increasing external pressures as well as internal security threats, the Taliban from 1999 sought to regulate the activities of foreign militants on their territory. How were al-Qaida's activities in Afghanistan shaped by the competitive environment of foreign militants and by the Taliban regime's policies toward the Arabs?

"A GOOD AND BROTHERLY FEELING"

Abu Mus'ab al-Suri left the meeting with Mullah Omar in Kandahar, feeling relieved. It was mid-1999 and Mullah Omar had just granted him permission to open an independent training camp in Kabul. It would be co-located with one of the Taliban's Army divisions at Qargha, and supported by the Taliban's Ministry of Defense.[1] Before going back to Kabul, al-Suri decided to stop by bin Laden's office to inform him of his project. Al-Suri was not very fond of bin Laden, and he certainly had no desire to join al-Qaida. But no harm in keeping them informed. Who knew, it might start a new page of brotherhood and cooperation ...[2]

[1] The wording is based on al-Suri's own recollections of the event, as he described it in a private letter. AFGP-2002-001111, "Letters to Abu Khabab," undated [ca. 1999], Combating Terrorism Center, West Point, NY.
[2] Ibid.

Al-Suri later recalled the event in a private letter to his friend Abu Khabab:

I stopped at Sheikh Abu Abdullah's [Bin Laden's] group and met Abu Hafs and Abu al-Khayr ... I suggested to turn a new page of brotherhood and cooperation ... However, Abu Hafs asked us to cancel the project altogether and said he will be talking with them [the Taliban]. I refused his suggestion, however, I offered to cooperate with him in any way he wants but he cannot cancel ours or anybody else's project. The meeting ended with a good and brotherly feeling.[3]

Al-Suri's account suggests that al-Qaida had an ambivalent attitude to Arabs who wanted to establish their own training camps in Afghanistan. Al-Qaida was not too fond of such initiatives – presumably because it would lead to internal competition among the Arabs – but in the end, it was up to the Taliban regime to decide who should run camps. If the Taliban approved, there was not much al-Qaida could do. This narrative, which is further elaborated later, contradicts the common assumption that bin Laden had a privileged position with Mullah Omar and was able to influence the latter's decisions. Al-Qaida had, to some extent, a privileged position with the Taliban but it was primarily due to their professionalism and willingness to serve the Taliban's state.

Al-Suri opened *al-Ghuraba'* ("The Strangers") camp in the fall of 1999. It was situated at Qargha, an old military garrison northwest of Kabul. Afterward al-Suri wrote a letter to the Emir of the garrison, Amir Khan Haqqani, to request weapons, supplies, Taliban ID cards and living quarters for three families and seven individuals.[4] Al-Suri's group cooperated on the frontline with Sayf ul-Rahman Mansour, a Taliban division commander at Qargha, and son of the famous mujahidin commander Nasrullah Mansour from Paktiya.[5] It is unknown how many trainees went through al-Suri's camp, but his military influence in Afghanistan remained minimal. According to Mustafa Hamid, in early 2001 al-Suri only had "between ten and twenty" fighters on the Kabul front.[6]

Al-Suri was a strategist and theoretician, more than a military commander. On September 18, 1999, a flyer from al-Suri's group invited Arabs in Afghanistan to a series of political lectures about the "new

---

[3] Ibid.
[4] AQ-MISC-D-001-264, "Abu Musab al-Suri's datebook from Afghanistan in 1999 with names and some addresses of al-Qaeda members, Taliban officials and others; mentions al-Qaeda guest house at Qargha," undated [circa January 2000–March 2000], Conflict Records Resource Center, Washington, DC, 80.
[5] Ibid., 81.
[6] Hamid and Farrall, *The Arabs at war in Afghanistan*, 275.

world order" and the "arenas of battle today" among other things, at the al-Ghuraba camp.[7] Al-Suri was to some extent known in al-Qaida circles for his historical and strategic writings. He was also known for being a vehement critic of Bin Laden, but this was probably for personal, more than ideological reasons.[8] Al-Suri often agreed with al-Qaida on ideological and strategic questions. Some of al-Suri's writings directly supported al-Qaida's agenda in Afghanistan, such as the booklet *Afghanistan, Taliban, and the Battle for Islam Today*, which argued that it was legitimate to fight under the Taliban's banner.[9]

At least two other independent Arab camps were established in Afghanistan in the fall of 1999 with permission from the Taliban: a camp in Kabul associated with the Libyan Islamic Fighting Group (LIFG), and a camp in Herat run by the Jordanian militant Abu Mus'ab al-Zarqawi.[10] The Libyan camp was established by a LIFG splinter faction led by Abd al-Hakim Bilhaj (aka Abu Abdullah al-Sadiq). Bilhaj had split from LIFG in 1998, after LIFG was crushed in Libya by the Ghaddafi regime. Bilhaj believed the revolutionary struggle in Libya was a lost cause, and instead sought to participate in conflicts elsewhere. From 1999, the LIFG splinter faction fought on the Taliban's frontlines north of Kabul.[11] The Libyan group remained small – according to Mustafa Hamid, the Libyans only had "eleven fighters" on the frontline in the spring of 2001.[12] But the group had prominent personalities including Abu al-Layth al-Libi, who became a key Arab commander in northern Waziristan after 2001.

Abu Mus'ab al-Zarqawi was a Jordanian militant who had fought in Afghanistan in the early 1990s. Then he returned to Jordan, got involved in subversive activity, and was eventually imprisoned by Jordanian authorities. When he was released from prison in 1999, he returned

---

[7] AQ-MCOP-D-000-041, "Letter from Abu Massab to Abu Khabab; An invitation to Sheikh Abu-Mussab al-Suri and Sheikh 'Isa al-Masri to attend a meeting, from the administration of the military camp of the strangers of Qargha Division," undated [before September 19, 1999], Conflict Records Resource Center, Washington, DC.

[8] Lia, *Architect of global jihad*, 278–292.

[9] It is also notable that Ayman al-Zawahiri in his memoirs from 2008 praised al-Suri's writings, in particular, al-Suri's *mulahadhat haula al-tajruba al-jihadiyya fi suria* from 1991 and *da'wat al-muqawama al-islamiyya al-alamiyya* from 2004. Al-Zawahiri, *al-tabri'a*, 55; al-Suri, *afghanistan wa al-taliban*.

[10] Mary Anne Weaver, "The short, violent life of Abu Musab al-Zarqawi," *The Atlantic*, June 8, 2006.

[11] Tawil, *Brothers in Arms*, 158; LY-000708, "Recommendation for Continued Detention Under DoD Control (CD) for Guantanamo Detainee, ISN US9LY-000708DP [Ismael Ali Bakush], Department of Defense (Joint Task Force Guantanamo), January 22, 2008.

[12] Hamid and Farrall, *The Arabs at war in Afghanistan*, 275.

to Afghanistan and opened a training camp in Herat to train militants primarily from Jordan and Syria.[13]

According to Sayf al-Adl, it was al-Qaida who helped al-Zarqawi establish the camp. Sayf al-Adl's account is supported by Mustafa Hamid, who claimed that Bin Laden helped al-Zarqawi in order to prevent al-Zarqawi from working with Bin Laden's rival, Abu Mus'ab al-Suri.[14] Whatever al-Qaida's motivation, it seems plausible that al-Qaida had some hand in establishing al-Zarqawi's camp. As far as is known, al-Zarqawi had no contacts in the Taliban government who could speak his cause. He therefore needed an intermediary from among the Arabs who knew the Taliban well.

Sayf al-Adl admitted that al-Zarqawi was a controversial figure among al-Qaida's leaders, due to his "uncompromising" views on issues such as takfir, modus operandi, and how to deal with the Saudi regime. However, as Sayf al-Adl summarized, "It was both unfair – in terms of jurisprudence – and incorrect – in terms of the movement – to abandon every brother or group with whom we might have minor disagreements."[15]

Sayf al-Adl claimed he held an initial meeting with al-Zarqawi where they discussed the terms of their agreement.

One of the topics we discussed was that we were not seeking full allegiance from Abu-Mus'ab or his companions. Rather, we wanted coordination and cooperation to achieve our joint objectives. We explained to him that we were ready to provide him with special training for every distinguished individual or group from his side. We pledged to coordinate with the fraternal brothers of the Taliban movement to avoid any obstacles in the future.[16]

Prior to establishing the Herat camp, al-Zarqawi and his two original companions from Jordan went through a forty-five-day training program in one of al-Qaida's camps. This was in line with the initial agreement between al-Zarqawi and Sayf al-Adl. Al-Adl probably also helped al-Zarqawi secure approval from the Taliban for opening the Herat camp. Sayf al-Adl does not recount this event, but following the pattern of other Arab camps, the Taliban must have approved the project on some level. Over time, al-Zarqawi's group established a good relationship with the Taliban governor of Herat, who gave material support to Zarqawi's camp.[17]

---

[13] Weaver, "The short, violent life of Abu Musab al-Zarqawi."

[14] Hamid and Farrall, *The Arabs at war in Afghanistan*, 257.

[15] Sayf al-Adl, *tajrubati ma'a abi mus'ab al-zarqawi*, undated, Minbar al-Tawhid wal-Jihad, accessed October 12, 2011. www.tawhed.ws/pr?i=6477.

[16] Ibid.

[17] "*kunt jaran li-abu mus'ab al-zarqawi*," Shabakat Ana al-Muslim, June 27, 2006, accessed March 8, 2016. www.muslm.org/vb/showthread.php?167769.

Abu Mus'ab al-Suri wrote that by the end of 1999 there were fourteen "camps, groups and formations" in Afghanistan officially recognized by the Taliban. Nine of them were Arab and three were non-Arab. Al-Qaida, al-Suri's group, al-Zarqawi's group, and LIFG were among the Arab groups. The others were the Moroccan Islamic Fighting Group, the Egyptian Islamic Jihad, the Egyptian al-Jama'a al-Islamiyya, the Algerians, the Tunisians, the Khalden camp, and the Abu Khabab camp.[18]

To say that all the mentioned groups were "officially recognized" by the Taliban regime is perhaps an exaggeration. Some of the groups mentioned earlier had by 2000 received permission from the regime to run camps. We know little about the other groups. The North African militants were based in the Nangarhar province, primarily in Jalalabad city and the Derunta camp complex northwest of Jalalabad. The Khalden camp was located in Khost and run by Ibn Sheikh al-Libi. Members of the two Egyptian groups were based in Kabul and Kandahar. As all these areas were under Taliban control, it can be assumed that the groups who ran training camps – such as those in Derunta and Khost – had some level of understanding with Taliban government representatives, at least on a local level.

According to the primary sources reviewed here, al-Qaida did not have a consistent attitude toward other Arab camps. Al-Suri claimed that al-Qaida tried to hamper his project, while Sayf al-Adl claimed that al-Qaida voluntarily offered help to al-Zarqawi to open a camp in Herat. Al-Suri's experiences may have been a result of the personal differences between him and bin Laden. In any case, all the accounts strengthen the impression that it was the Taliban, not al-Qaida, who decided who should run camps. The Taliban's policies toward the Arab training camps are further detailed in the next section.

TALIBAN'S THIRTEEN POINTS

In early 2000, the Taliban regime attempted to put a set of restrictions and regulations on Arab training camps. This appears to be the first well-documented attempt by Taliban to regulate the Arab presence in Afghanistan and to enforce rules on the Arab community as a whole. This shift in attitude may have been prompted by increased pressure from abroad, including the UN, United States, and Pakistan, to close alleged "terrorist training camps" on Afghan soil. On October 4, 1999 a Pakistani

[18] al-Suri, *da'wat al-muqawama*, 727.

delegation visited Kandahar and met with Mullah Omar. The purpose was to ask the Taliban to close down training camps for Pakistani militants, and to arrest and hand over suspected Pakistani terrorists.[19] Four days later on October 8, the United States placed al-Qaida on its list of foreign terrorist organizations. On October 15, the UN Security Council adopted Resolution 1267, demanding that the Taliban hand over Osama bin Laden or face international sanctions. After the Taliban's Ulama investigated the issue and concluded that they could not hand over bin Laden, UN sanctions were imposed from November 15, 1999.

We do not know exactly what prompted the Taliban to put regulations on the Arabs – whether Pakistani pressure, the UN sanctions, the US "terror listing," or a combination of the three. Abu Mus'ab al-Suri's diary notes provide useful hints. In early 2000, al-Suri met with a Taliban official (possibly Mullah Rabbani, as the name "Rabbani" was scribbled on the top of the page) to discuss the background for the restrictions put on Arabs. As the piece gives unique insight into the reasoning behind the Taliban's political decisions it is worth quoting at length:

> He [Taliban official] claims to have been asked by officials in some of the countries he visited about specific individuals who need to be extradited. This is a result of infiltration, because the officials are unaware of what is going on among you [the Arabs].
>
> He [Taliban official] claims that as a result of being infiltrated, many countries have been able to collect information about you [the Arabs] and we [the Taliban] became baffled by how they gathered all this information about you. Even Masud, Hikmatyar, and Sayyaf are accusing you of being terrorists after you fought along their side [in the Afghan-Soviet war] . . .
>
> Therefore, we [the Taliban] must manage our affairs secretly and refute all rumors and allegations that are being used to place more pressure on us. You [the Arabs] must reexamine your units and ranks and extensively check the background of every newcomer and collect all necessary information . . .[20]

According to al-Suri's notes, the Taliban's primary concern at the time was infiltration of the Arab community in Afghanistan by foreign agents, who subsequently accused the Taliban of hosting terrorists on their soil. Sometime before March 3, 2000, the Taliban issued a set of thirteen points meant to regulate the presence of the Arabs. The thirteen points state, among other things, that all foreigners who enter Afghanistan must register at a central office and carry official ID papers; they have to live

[19] Shakil Shaikh, "Taliban to hand over 150 terrorists to Pakistan," *The News*, October 6, 1999.

[20] AQ-MISC-D-001-264, "Abu Musab al-Suri's datebook from Afghanistan," 2–3, 12.

in designated areas; and they cannot talk to foreign media or organize press conferences. Any participation in "jihad" must be approved by the Taliban.[21] The content of the thirteen points seems to confirm that Taliban's primary concern was infiltration, and that they wanted to solve the problem by hiding away the Arab training camps from foreign eyes. It should be noted that the Taliban in principle were not against the idea of foreigners participating in militant struggle ("jihad") as long as it be approved by the Taliban government beforehand.

The thirteen points caused a stir in the Arab community, as reflected in the diary notes of Abu Mus'ab al-Suri. It appears that al-Suri, in coordination with other Arabs, worked out a response to the Taliban. The "collective concerns" of the Arabs, according to al-Suri were as follows: (1) training camps; (2) family issues, living expenses, and residences; (3) identification and ID cards, and (4) political and jihadi activities abroad. For al-Suri, registration and ID cards was out of the question. "I have no doubt that any information in possession of the Taliban will be obtained by Pakistan and others and thus, our enemies," he wrote. He also believed the Arabs "should be free to reside anywhere in the Emirate without any restrictions," and that "we need training camps, not the termination of training." Finally, about jihadi activities abroad, "we recommend that each group discusses the issue with the authorities of the Emirate individually." On the issue of the registration and ID cards, al-Suri was uncompromising: "We refuse the registration and the ID cards," he noted along with what appeared like a threat: "We inform the Taliban that we are getting ready to leave."[22]

After Taliban issued the thirteen points, there were one or several meetings between Arabs and Taliban officials, probably including Mullah Omar himself, to reach a compromise solution. According to al-Suri's diary notes he discussed the issue of the thirteen points with Abu Layth al-Libi, Abd al-Hadi and Muhammad Salah. Abd al-Hadi is probably Abd al-Hadi al-Iraqi, al-Qaida's overall frontline commander in Afghanistan. Muhammad Salah probably refers to Nasr Fahmi Nasr (aka Muhammad Salah), responsible for "finances and general relations" in Ayman al-Zawahiri's faction of Egyptian Islamic Jihad.[23] Abu Layth al-Libi was

---

[21] AQ-TBGD-D-000-003, "13 clauses concerning immigration policies for Taliban-era Afghanistan," undated [ca. January – March 2000], Conflict Records Resource Center, Washington, DC.

[22] AQ-MISC-D-001-264, "Abu Musab al-Suri's datebook from Afghanistan," 23, 28–30, 32–34.

[23] Camille Tawil, "*al-suba'i lil-hayat: iran salamat majmu'a min al-masriyyin wa 12 a'ila min "al-jama'" adat tawwa'an*," *al-Hayat*, December 13, 2003.

member of the LIFG faction that fought on the Taliban's frontline from 1999. This suggests that the Taliban's restrictions on Arabs concerned all Arab groups in Afghanistan including al-Qaida.[24]

The Taliban never managed to enforce the thirteen points in their original form. However, developments in 2000 suggest that the new regime was at least partly enforced. A few months after the points were issued, al-Qaida moved the al-Faruq camp to the Gharmabak Ghar mountains northwest of Kandahar City. It was a desolate area with ample space for training camps and shooting practice, but more importantly, it was an area far removed from people. Parallel to opening al-Faruq, al-Qaida established the Office of Mujahidin Affairs in Kandahar city where all new recruits had to register and leave their official ID papers for safe-keeping. These security measures were very much in line with the original proposal of the Taliban. The main difference being that it was the Arabs themselves, not the Afghans, that kept rosters of new recruits and who detected and interrogated suspected spies among their ranks.[25]

The notion that Taliban ordered al-Qaida to move the al-Faruq camp to Kandahar in order to get it out of the public view is plausible. Taliban had behaved in a similar manner in other cases. In 1997, Osama bin Laden was offered to move from the volatile Eastern province of Nangarhar to Taliban's heartland in Kandahar. A few months later, an al-Qaida guest-house in Kabul was moved by the Taliban to the outskirts of the city because they believed it was under surveillance by Saudi intelligence.[26]

It was probably around this time that an Arab Liaison Committee (*lajnat al-irtibat al-arabiyya*) was established to coordinate requests from the Arabs to the Taliban regime.[27] The committee had six members, as listed in Table 6.1.

---

[24] Al-Suri does not mention meeting Mullah Omar. However, another, anonymous account says that Muhammad Salah was in a delegation that met with Mullah Omar to discuss the relationship between the Taliban and the Arabs. Presumably, the delegation was going to discuss the thirteen points. AQ-MISC-D-001-264, "Abu Musab al-Suri's datebook from Afghanistan"; the meeting between Muhammed Salah's delegation and Mullah Omar is described in "*kunt jaran li-abu mus'ab al-zarqawi.*"

[25] Al-Qaida arrested and interrogated several suspected "spies" – as described, for example, in SY-000489, "Detainee Assessment Brief ICO Guantanamo Detainee, ISN US9SY-000489DP [Abd Al Rahim Abdul Raza Janko], Department of Defense (Joint Task Force Guantanamo), June 30, 2008.

[26] AQ-MCOP-D-001-149, "Al-Qaida letters," undated [circa 1997], Conflict Records Resource Center, Washington, DC.

[27] AFGP-2002-000100, "This document contains a flyer addressed to all Arab immigrants. The flyer lists the Islamic Emirate officials' names that would assist the Arab immigrants in entering the Emirate," undated, FMSO/Internet Archive.

TABLE 6.1   *The Arab Liaison Committee to the Taliban, ca. spring 2000*

Name	Title	Location	Group
Ibn Sheikh	Emir of Khalden camp	Khost	Independent
Ali Abu Zar'a	Unknown	Unknown	Unknown
Abd al-Hadi al-Ansari	Frontline commander	Kabul	Al-Qaida
Muhammad Salah	Manager of finances and general relations	Unknown	Egyptian Islamic Jihad
Abu Mus'ab al-Suri	Emir of al-Ghuraba camp	Qargha	Independent
Abu Mus'ab al-Zarqawi	Emir of Herat camp	Herat	Independent

The members of the liaison committee probably represented individuals in charge of training camps or frontline sections recognized
by the Taliban: Ibn Sheikh ran the Khalden camp in Khost, Abd
al-Hadi al-Iraqi [aka al-Ansari] was in charge of al-Qaida's fighters
on the Taliban's frontline, Muhammad Salah was the Egyptian Islamic
Jihad's representative to the Taliban; al-Suri and al-Zarqawi ran camps
in Qargha and Herat, respectively. The only member of the committee
that cannot be positively identified is Ali Abu Zar'a. Following the logic
outlined earlier, Abu Zar'a may be a representative of the LIFG faction
of Abd al-Hakim Belhaj (aka Abu Abdullah Al-Sadiq) which fought on
the Taliban's frontline at the time; or one of the North African groups
in Jalalabad.

The purpose of the liaison committee was likely to coordinate material support from the Taliban to the various Arab factions. According to
al-Suri's diary, typical requests from the Arabs included everything from
housing to vehicles, food, and personal expenses. It should be noted that
the Arab liaison committee included groups that did not support the
Taliban militarily. Al-Zarqawi in particular did not believe in sending
fighters to the Taliban's frontlines. Nevertheless, the Taliban recognized
al-Zarqawi's right to run a training camp for Arabs in Herat. This suggests that Taliban supported Arab training camps for ideological reasons,
not because they were dependent on Arab fighters or money.

The Taliban's thirteen points specify that the Arabs should only
contact the Taliban through an official point of contact. The establishment of the liaison committee contributed to reducing the number of
contact points between Taliban and the Arabs, giving Taliban more
centralized control over the communication. From the Taliban's side, the

thirteen points specified that all communication with the Arabs should go through Mullah Abdul Razzaq, the Taliban's Interior Minister in Kabul.[28]

There are some individuals missing from the liaison committee – for example, Abu Khabab, who ran an explosives and poisons training camp in Derunta outside Jalalabad. Internal al-Qaida correspondence suggests that Abu Khabab in the fall of 1999 or early 2000 moved his training camp to Qargha outside Kabul and joined al-Qaida.[29] This would explain why he did not have any independent relationship to the Taliban. Moreover, the Qargha training site was already represented on the committee by Abu Mus'ab al-Suri, who was a good friend of Abu Khabab. Abu Khabab's move was in line with the Taliban's policy at the time to move camps from the volatile areas in the periphery to areas under Taliban control. But the Taliban never managed to get all militant groups on the periphery to move to the center. For example, North African militants continued to use Jalalabad and adjacent areas for training in 2000 and 2001 – even after Taliban attempted to close the Derunta camps in mid-2000.[30]

THE CLOSURE OF KHALDEN

Another effect of the Taliban's new policies toward the Arabs was the closure of the Khalden camp in Khost. Khalden had been operating since the late 1980s, and was the longest-running training camp for Arabs in Afghanistan. According to Mustafa Hamid, Khalden was situated in a volatile border area that was subject to clashes between Pakistani forces and local tribes, forcing the Arabs in the end to evacuate the camp.[31] Abu Zubaydah said that he requested help from bin Laden in re-opening the camp, but bin Laden refused. Abu Zubaydah later thought that bin Laden may have convinced the Taliban to permanently close the camp, but it is unlikely that bin Laden had much sway over the Taliban in such

[28] AQ-TBGD-D-000-003, "13 clauses concerning immigration policies for Taliban-era Afghanistan."

[29] AFGP-2002-001111, "Letters to Abu Khabab"; AQ-MCOP-D-000-041,"Letter from Abu Massab to Abu Khabab"; and AQ-MISC-D-001-033, "Letter to Abu Khabab from Abu al-Bara'a," undated, Conflict Records Resource Center, Washington, DC.

[30] As indicated, for example, in MO-000075, "Update Recommendation to Transfer to the Control of Another Country for Continued Detention (TRCD) for Guantanamo Detainee, ISN: US9MO-000075D [Lahassimi Najib], Department of Defense (Joint Task Force Guantanamo), June 3, 2005.

[31] Hamid and Farrall, *The Arabs at war in Afghanistan*, 259–260.

matters.[32] More likely, the Taliban refused to protect the camp because it was situated too close to the Afghan-Pakistani border. This would be in line with the Taliban's policies at the time of moving training camps from the periphery to areas under tighter Taliban control. The purpose was not so much to control what was going on in the camps, but to ensure that the Arabs kept a low profile to not cause diplomatic embarrassment for the Taliban. The Khalden camp was hardly low profile; it had long been rumored to be a "terrorist" training camp and it was easy to conduct surveillance of the camp, due to its location on the Afghan-Pakistani border.[33]

Taliban may have supported the Khalden camp if it had been moved to a different location, But neither Ibn al-Sheikh al-Libi nor Abu Zubaydah pursued the matter further. They continued to live in Afghanistan keeping a low profile and we know little of their activities after the closure of Khalden. Leaked US intelligence information suggests that Ibn Sheikh ran a guesthouse in Kabul in 2000 and 2001.[34] This is partly corroborated by Abu Zubaydah's diaries. Abu Zubaydah moved to Afghanistan in mid-2000 and continued to be involved with the Arab community. He is vague detailing his activities however, fearing his diaries may sometime end up in the wrong hands – which they ultimately did.[35] Abu Zubaydah and Ibn al-Sheikh both joined in the campaign to defend Afghanistan from the US-led invasion in 2001, working alongside al-Qaida's men, but this was not uncommon as many other "independent" Arabs did the same. The truth about Abu Zubaydah's connection to al-Qaida will probably never be fully known.

From 2000, the Taliban sought to regulate the activity of Arab training camps in Afghanistan. Al-Qaida went furthest in complying with the demands of the Taliban – moving the al-Faruq camp to the deserts outside Kandahar, establishing a central registration office for new recruits, and

---

[32] GZ-010016, "Recommendation for Continued Detention Under DoD Control (CD) for Guantanamo Detainee, ISN US9GZ-010016DP [Abu Zubaydah]," Department of Defense (Joint Task Force Guantanamo), November 11, 2008.

[33] Hamid and Farrall, *The Arabs at war in Afghanistan,* 259–260; Author's interview with Noman Benotman in Oslo, Norway, September 2011.

[34] LY-000557, "Update Recommendation to Transfer to the Control of Another Country for Continued Detention (TRCD) for Guantanamo Detainee, ISN: US9LY-000557DP [Abu Sufian Ibrahim Ahmed Hamouda]," Department of Defense (Joint Task Force Guantanamo), April 22, 2005; LY-000194, "Recommendation for Continued Detention Under DoD Control (CD) for Guantanamo Detainee, ISN: US9LY-000194DP [Muhammad Abdallah Mansur Al-Rimi]," Department of Defense (Joint Task Force Guantanamo), March 8, 2006.

[35] Abu Zubaydah, *The Abu Zubaydah Diaries Vol. 4,* 92.

maintaining an internal security organization to arrest and interrogate suspected spies. These changes came as al-Qaida was about to expand its organization and bring in hundreds of new recruits from the Arabian Peninsula. Ultimately, the Taliban's policies toward the Arab camps were of great benefit to al-Qaida. They allowed al-Qaida to gain a dominant position among the Arabs, and ensured that al-Qaida could continue and expand its training project in Kandahar. Al-Qaida's frontline participation with the Taliban, which is the topic of the next chapter, further strengthened al-Qaida's efforts at building a resilient organization in Afghanistan.

7

Frontline Participation

From 1996 until 2001, the Taliban's main priority was to take control over Afghanistan's territory. The Taliban's enemy was a loose coalition of anti-Taliban forces led by the former mujahidin leader Burhanuddin Rabbani and his commander Ahmed Shah Massoud. Al-Qaida's role in the Taliban's war against Massoud is often acknowledged yet rarely studied in detail. What was al-Qaida's motivations for fighting on the Taliban's frontlines, and what was the nature and extent of their participation at the front?

EARLY PARTICIPATION

1997 was a hard year for the Taliban. The militia's attempt to capture the northern Afghan city of Mazar-e-Sharif in May had failed miserably. The Uzbek warlord Abdul Malik, who had defected from Dostum to join the Taliban, swiftly defected again to Massoud, just as the Taliban was taking control over the city. Hundreds, if not thousands of Taliban troops were massacred by Abdul Malik's forces.[1]

In 1997, Taliban also experienced major setbacks on the frontline north of Kabul. During the Mazar-e-Sharif debacle, Massoud attacked Taliban positions, recaptured the strategically important town of Jabal Siraj, and pushed the frontline some fifty kilometers further south (see Map 4). It was in the aftermath of these events that an Arab commander at the Kabul front reported back to the al-Qaida leadership in Kandahar:

[1] Rashid, *Taliban*, 57–59.

Retreating from the two fronts has greatly shaken up the situation in those places: In Bagram, it has become every man for himself. And in Murad Beg, the brothers have split up into three groups. May God keep them so they can regroup and establish sentry duties.[2]

The letter, which is dated August 17, 1997, is the first clear indication that al-Qaida has started to give direct, military support to the Taliban. The letter details the monthly budget for the "front," which includes salaries for a bulldozer operator, two truck drivers, two pickup drivers, two cooks, and two security guards.[3] The existence of a budget indicates that al-Qaida at the time was financing and supporting an Arab unit that was fighting for the Taliban south of Bagram. Other internal documents from the time point in the same direction. At one point, probably in 1997, Bin Laden even sent "his personal car" to be used by the Arabs on the front.[4]

Al-Qaida's budget at the time was moderate. The Arabs who served at the frontline had a modest arsenal of military equipment. An inventory list written probably in 1998 shows the Arabs owned a number of personal weapons like Kalashnikovs, and a few squad weapons like heavy machine guns, mortars, and anti-aircraft guns. They also owned a few radios and binoculars.[5] However, there is scant indication that the Arabs owned Stingers or other prestigious weaponry.[6] The Arabs in 1997 had no weapons that differed drastically from the Taliban's arsenal made up of Soviet and Chinese leftovers from the Afghan-Soviet war. And although some of the Arabs were trained on heavy weapons like tanks and artillery, they owned few such weapons themselves, and frequently had to borrow these from the Taliban.[7]

The Arabs who served at the frontline received orders and support from the al-Qaida leadership in Kandahar. Not only did al-Qaida provide financial support to the fighters. High-ranking al-Qaida leaders

[2] AQ-MSLF-D-001-151, "Letter sent to Abu Hafs around 17/8/97, contains payment list, names and other information related to camps that belong to this organization," August 17, 1997, Conflict Records Resource Center, Washington, DC.

[3] Ibid.

[4] "A letter to sheikh Abu Hafs," undated and unsigned [probably written in or before November 1997], in AFGP-2002–003677, "Ciphers and status of Bin Laden's security," Combating Terrorism Center, West Point, NY.

[5] AQ-MSLF-D-000-824, "Weapons listing belonging to Al-Qaida and other organizations," March 1998, Conflict Records Resource Center, Washington, DC.

[6] With the exception of Mustafa Hamid, who wrote in his memoirs that al-Qaida in 1998 had "four Stingers bought from Jalalabad." Hamid, *mashru' tajikistan*, 60.

[7] See, for example, AQ-SHPD-D-000-039, "A letter from Abd al-Hadi al-Ansari to Abu Hafs," 26 November 1998, Conflict Records Resource Center, Washington, DC.

were directly involved in operational planning and decision making. This is evident from the many reports sent from the frontline to Abu Hafs al-Masri, chief of al-Qaida Military Committee. The reports detail operations, personnel situation and future battle plans. Several of these reports were written by Abd al-Hadi al-Iraqi, who was present on the Kabul frontline from mid-1997.[8] In October 1998 he was promoted to be the general commander of the frontline, a position he held until the collapse of the Taliban regime in late 2001.

Abd al-Hadi, whose real name is Nashwan Abd al-Razzaq Abd al-Baqi, played a crucial role in defining and developing al-Qaida's role on the Taliban's front. Abd al-Hadi was a former major in the Iraqi Army who came to Afghanistan to join the mujahidin around 1992. He briefly fought with Hekmatyar's Arabs in the Afghan civil war, before leaving the group and settling in Khost. Here, he joined Mustafa Hamid's Tajikistan project and most certainly came to know Abu Ata' al-Sharqi, who was al-Qaida's representative in Jihad Wal. It is not clear when or why Abd al-Hadi decided to join al-Qaida, but it was probably after May 1996 when Bin Laden returned to Afghanistan from Sudan.[9]

Al-Qaida appears to have prioritized sending fighters to the frontline. The Arabs who served on the Taliban's frontline in 1997–1998 included several second-tier al-Qaida leaders – that is, Arabs who became member of al-Qaida in 1988–1992 and who served as trainers or frontline commanders in that early period. They include Abu Ata' al-Sharqi, Abu Ziyad al-Mosuli, Abd al-Salam al-Hadrami, Abu Tamim, and Abu al-Hassan al-Masri. Abu Ata' and Abu Tamim stayed in Jihad Wal during the civil war, while the others went to Somalia and Sudan with the rest of the al-Qaida leadership. Several of them served in the East African training mission, a team of al-Qaida trainers who were sent to Ogaden in Somalia to establish a training camp for local Islamist guerrillas (see Table 7.1).

Others who were given leading roles on the front in 1997–1998 appear to have been "independent" jihadists who did not join al-Qaida until after Bin Laden returned to Afghanistan in May 1996. Some of them were veterans from the war in Bosnia, whereas others had stayed in Afghanistan during the Afghan civil war. Abd al-Hadi al-Iraqi belonged in this category.

---

[8] Abd al-Hadi's first report is dated 8 November 1997, but he is referred to in another report from August 1997. Abd al-Hadi himself wrote in a letter dated December 2000 that he had been present on the frontline "for the past four years." AQ-MSLF-D-001-151; AQ-MCOP-D-000-917, "A letter from Abd al Hadi al-Ansari to Hasan al Ishmawi (1/2)," December 24, 2000, Conflict Records Resource Center, Washington, DC.

[9] Hamid and Farrall, *The Arabs at war in Afghanistan*, 223.

TABLE 7.1 *Arabs who held leading positions on the Kabul front in 1997–1998*

Name	Position 1992–96	Appeared on Kabul front	Position on Kabul front
Abu Ziyad al-Mosuli	2nd tier AQ Somalia	1997	Leader of observation post
Abu Tamim	2nd tier AQ Afghanistan	1997	Leader of BM (rocket launcher) group
Abd al-Hadi al-Urduni (Abu Turab)	Independent Chechnya	1997	Leader of grinov (heavy machine gun) group
Al-Zubayr al-Yemeni (al-Sharqi)	Independent Chechnya	1997	Leader of tank group
Abd al-Hadi al-Iraqi	Independent Afghanistan	1997	General commander (Oct 1998–Dec 2001)
Abu Ata' al-Sharqi	2nd tier AQ Afghanistan	1998	Commander at Murad Beg (? – Oct 1998)
Umar Sayf al-Filistini	Hekmatyar Afghanistan	1998	Deputy commander (? – Aug 1999)
Abd al-Salam al-Hadrami	2nd tier AQ Somalia	1998	Frontline commander
Abu Tariq al-Tunisi	?	1998	Leader of heavy weapons
Abu al-Hassan al-Masri	2nd tier AQ Somalia	1998	Leader of frontline administration

Note: The overview is based on the following sources: AFGP-2002–003677; AQ-SHPD-D-000-039; AQ-MCOP-D-000-916/917; AQ-SHPD-D-000-089; AQ-POAK-D-000-017, "A daily activity report about Taliban battles," May 4, 1999, Conflict Records Resource Center, Washington, DC.; al-Hindukushi, *mudhakkarati min kabul ila baghdad*; Harun, *al-harb ala al-islam*; Hamid, *al-matar 90*.

It is striking that a number of frontline positions were occupied by second-tier al-Qaida members. It suggests that frontline fighting with the Taliban was al-Qaida's next "military project" after the training mission in Somalia had ended.

What were al-Qaida's motivations for getting involved on the Taliban's front? Initially, the motivation was in line with al-Qaida's general philosophy of supporting other Islamist guerrillas. Bin Laden met Mullah Omar for the first time in March 1997. During the meeting, he offered assistance to the Taliban in the form of infrastructure projects – he also offered to put "all his resources" to the Taliban's disposal to help them

in their war against the Northern Alliance.[10] Al-Qaida's establishment
of fighting units on the Kabul front in subsequent months may have
been a direct result of this meeting. Indeed, in mid-1997 the newspapers
reported that Bin Laden had sent a group of Arab fighters to the frontline
north of Kabul to strengthen the Taliban.[11]

It has been argued that Bin Laden's military and material assistance to
the Taliban was a crucial factor in the Taliban's decision to protect Bin
Laden in Afghanistan.[12] But the issue is more complicated. As illustrated
in Chapter 4, the Taliban's policies toward Bin Laden were shaped by
an ideological tug-of-war within the Taliban itself, and by fears among
the leadership that expelling Bin Laden may lead to internal dissent and
loss of religious legitimacy. Besides, the Taliban were not dependent on
Bin Laden's fighters. In 1997, for example, Jalaluddin Haqqani reportedly sent "thousands" of fighters to strengthen the Kabul frontline.[13]
Bin Laden's contributions initially amounted to no more than a handful.
Although al-Qaida sent some of their most experienced commanders to
the Taliban's frontline, it was still a drop in the ocean. Al-Qaida's offer of
assistance to the Taliban was clearly more important to al-Qaida than it
was to the Taliban.

As we have seen, al-Qaida's participation on the Taliban's front in
1997 was not an isolated incident. It may have been inspired by the sim-
ultaneous commitment of the Khost-based militants, such as Haqqani, to
whom they had historical ties. But there were also other, more fundamental reasons that Bin Laden offered fighters to the Taliban. On August 17,
1997, an al-Qaida commander at the front reported back to Abu Hafs:

God willing, the program that we have instituted will encourage the Afghans to
work and to advance forward. It will also hopefully raise their morale.[14]

Al-Qaida's support to the Taliban, in the hopes it would "raise their morale," resembles Bin Laden's original rationale for establishing al-Ma'sada,
and subsequently al-Qaida, in the late 1980s. Al-Qaida was supposed

[10] Zaydan, "*fi zill bawadir tahawwul fi al-siyasa al-pakistaniyya.*"
[11] Ahmad Zaydan, "*qafilat 'landcruiser' sawda' tu'abbir ma'a marwahiyyatayn al-hudud al-pakistaniyya–al-afghaniyya: 350 min rijal bin [ladin] li-yuqatilun fi shimal kabul,*" *al-Hayat,* July 14, 1997.
[12] See, for example, Mojdeh, *Afghanistan wa panj sal,* 163–64.
[13] Ahmad Zaydan, "*'taliban' tastanjid bi-tulabihi wa hizb yunus. al-umam al-muttahida tu'akkid qatal shi'a fi kabul,*" *al-Hayat,* June 1, 1997; Ahmad Zaydan, "*anba' an ma'arik fi dawahi qa'idat baghram shimal al-asima al-afghaniyya. ta'ira majhula taghir ala qawa'id muqatili haqqani fi kabul,*" *al-Hayat,* June 16, 1997.
[14] AQ-MSLF-D-001-151.

to be an elite Muslim fighting unit that would be an example to and an inspiration to other Muslim guerrillas. It is likely that al-Qaida members still viewed themselves this way, and that it was part of their motivation for joining the Taliban's frontline.

The Arabs on the Kabul frontline tried indeed to lead by example – at least according to their own internal reporting. For example, during a Taliban retreat in 1999 the Arabs stayed behind to ambush Massoud's forces, hoping it would encourage the Taliban back on the offensive. "Yet after that ambush, I did not see a group of Taliban that was willing to fight first," recalled Abd al-Hadi.[15] The Taliban's lack of fighting will was a recurrent topic in Arab reports from the front. As one commander lamented in 1997, "Up to this point, I don't have any ideas other than that the Taliban have lost their will to sacrifice … if only they had some semblance of how the Prophet behaved!"[16] In spite of these periodical disappointments, the Arabs continued to participate on the Taliban's frontlines until the fall of the Taliban in late 2001.

Al-Qaida also used the frontline for instrumental purposes. The frontlines served as a training and vetting ground for potential al-Qaida members, and was used to strengthening al-Qaida's own organization. The dual rationale of supporting Islamist guerrillas, and strengthening al-Qaida's own organization, is best expressed in a letter from Abd al-Hadi from November 26, 1998. Abd al-Hadi asks Abu Hafs to confirm the role of the Arabs on the Kabul frontline:

Because as far as I know, so far these tasks are:

First – to participate with the Taliban in the defense of Kabul and in the defense of the holy matters of Islam and the Muslims.

Second – An open door to train the brethren who are new, and to check their credibility and their preparedness.[17]

Over time, and especially after al-Qaida started to expand their organization in 2000 and 2001, frontline service became integrated in al-Qaida's training curriculum. By 2001, al-Qaida's recruitment policies specified that new recruits who wanted to join al-Qaida had to first complete two months frontline service with the Taliban.[18] However, when al-Qaida first joined the Taliban's frontlines in mid-1997, al-Qaida had not yet started

[15] AQ-MCOP-D-000-916/917.
[16] AFGP-2002–003677.
[17] AQ-SHPD-D-000-039, "A letter from Abd al-Hadi al-Ansari to Abu Hafs," November 26, 1998, Conflict Records Resource Center, Washington, DC.
[18] AQ-TRED-D-000-996.

offering organized training courses for new recruits. It seems, therefore, that their reasons in the beginning were mainly idealistic.

The question of whether al-Qaida's motivation for fighting with the Taliban was altruistic or self-serving is essentially obsolete. The two goals are not mutually exclusive, and for the Arabs, it was a win-win situation. Frontline participation helped recruit and educate new cadre for al-Qaida, which made the organization more resilient over time. Frontline participation was also meaningful in its own right, as it resonated with the very ideas on which al-Qaida was founded. But what was al-Qaida's actual contribution to the Taliban's war?

THE MILITARY ROLE OF AL-QAIDA

Being the general commander of the Arabs was not an easy task. In December 2000, during the last nights of Ramadan, Abd al-Hadi poured out his frustrations in a letter to a friend named Hassan. The problem was not so much the Taliban – they had a different fighting culture, after all. The best the Arabs could do was to give guidance and advice. But the Arabs in his own unit should have known better, and he himself should have handled matters differently. But what happened? He ended up disobeying the Taliban's orders in order to please his Arab subordinates. It was just unforgivable. He had failed as a commander. He signed the letter with "Abd al-Hadi al-Ansari, *al-amir al-mutaqa'id jabran*" [The Emir who was forced to resign].[19]

In spite of the melodramatic tone, there are no other indications that Abd al-Hadi quit his job, or was fired in this period or later. On the contrary, in spring 2001 he was promoted to be Deputy Commander in the Taliban's "Foreign Brigade," a military unit recently established to encompass all foreigners fighting for the Taliban.[20] Abd al-Hadi's blunder may have led to a minor punishment or reprimand of some kind. This method was rather typical for the Taliban. Mullah Dadullah, the flamboyant Taliban commander from Helmand, was once accused of ethnic cleansing in the Hazarajat – a Shia Muslim region in Central Afghanistan, inhabited by ethnic Hazaras – and was subsequently fired by Mullah Omar. But he soon returned to the frontline. By spring 2001,

---

[19] AQ-MCOP-D-000-916, "A letter from Abd al Hadi al-Ansari to Hasan al Ishmawi (2/2)," December 24, 2000. Conflict Records Resource Center, Washington, DC; AQ-MCO-D-000-917.

[20] al-Suri, *da'wat al-muqawama*, 787.

Abd al-Hadi's sins were also forgotten, and the position of al-Qaida on the Taliban's frontlines was stronger than ever.

It is widely acknowledged that Arabs participated in the Taliban's war against Massoud. But there is yet no coherent account of what they actually *did* at the front. Were the Arabs integrated with the Taliban or did they fight in their own units? Was their participation merely symbolic, or did they manage to make a real difference in the war? The rest of this section aims to answer these questions. To put the role of the Arabs in context it is necessary to start with a broad outline of the frontline north of Kabul and the military situation of the Taliban in mid-1997.

Arabs in 1997 were mainly active on two sections of the frontline north of Kabul, the "Bagram front" and the "Old Road front" (see Map 4). The Bagram front refers to the mountainous area south and southeast of the well-fortified Bagram airbase. The Old Road is the beginning of the traditional route from Kabul across the Salang Pass to Northern Afghanistan. The Old Road stretches from Kabul across the Shomali plain and up to Jabal Siraj some 90 kilometers further north. Jabal Siraj is a critical junction where the road branches west to Bamyan, north to the Salang Pass, south-east to Sarobi and northeast to the Panjshir Valley, the stronghold of Ahmed Shah Massoud.

During most of Taliban's reign, Massoud was in control of Jabal Siraj. The Old Road front fluctuated between Ghuldara Road in the south and the town of Charikar in the north. During a large summer campaign in mid-1999 the Taliban was able to briefly conquer the Massoud-controlled towns of Charikar and Jabal Siraj, but these successes were short-lived.

Arabs at the Old Road front were initially stationed at a hilltop known as Murad Beg, which is situated close to Kabul and comprised a second line of defense. In 1997, the actual frontline was situated at Ghuldara Road some five kilometers to the north of Murad Beg. In 1999, the frontline was pushed further north, to the outskirts of Charikar. Murad Beg was eventually turned into a training facility. Al-Qaida built the first temporary training camp there in late 1999. In 2001, al-Qaida used Murad Beg as a supplement to the al-Faruq camp in Kandahar.

Both Bagram and Murad Beg, where Arabs were stationed in 1997 were strategically important positions for the Taliban. This suggests that from early on, Arabs were well integrated in the Taliban's war effort. However, they were not used to confront Massoud's forces directly. They mostly worked in a defensive and supporting role – manning heavy weapons positions and working in logistics. The logistics role of the Arabs is elaborated on in a report from the frontline, written by Abd al-Hadi al-Iraqi, in November 1997:

[We] very much need another car at the Bagram front. Because of the many trips we have to make with the black car, it is quickly wearing down ... We have no other way to bring ammunition into Bagram. We have to make this trip every couple of days for water and whatever else the Taliban at the rear of the front needs.[21]

The car issue is mentioned in several of the reports that were sent from the Kabul front to the al-Qaida leadership in this period. The issue is even brought up in a meeting between the Arabs and Mullah Mohammed Rabbani, the highest representative of the Taliban in Kabul city. After the meeting, Abd al-Hadi reported to Abu Hafs:

I asked [Rabbani] for the paper for the car or for a car. He told me that he heard you already sent us two cars. I denied this ... I told him how the Sheikh [Osama Bin Laden] sent us his personal car, which is now on the front lines. He said to me – and it appeared he did not believe what I said – that he would talk to you about this car situation.[22]

The preoccupation with cars on such a high organizational level is rather peculiar – but it reflects the fact that the Taliban at the time was not a modern state, but still very much a rebel-led government. In any case it supports the interpretation that the Arabs in 1997–1998 had a logistics role, rather than a combat role at the Taliban's fronts.

In addition to working in logistics the Arabs were manning static defensive positions at Murad Beg, and Bagram. There are few battle reports available from the early period, but in an undated report from probably fall 1997 the author describes the latest achievements of the Arabs:

With praise to God, we have destroyed one of the enemy's cars on the way to Murad Beg using an 82 mm mortar, and we destroyed another car on the way to Bagram using a tank. Also, in Bagram we scored a direct hit on two enemy tanks, and now we are trying to hit the third tank which is in front of our position after they withdrew the fourth tank.[23]

Putting various reports together, it appears the Arabs in 1997 had a group of around ten fighters at Bagram and seven or eight people at Murad Beg.[24] In contrast, newspaper reports from the same period suggested Bin

---

[21] AQ-MSLF-D-001-424, "A letter from 'Abd al-Hadi al-Ansari to Sheikh Taysir," November 8, 1997, Conflict Records Research Center, Washington, DC.
[22] AFGP-2002-003677.
[23] Ibid.
[24] Based on the number and type of weapons at Bagram quoted in AFGP-2002-003677; and AQ-MSLF-D-001-151; see also AQ-SHPD-D-000-039.

Laden had sent "350 fighters" to the front.[25] Some of them were killed or taken prisoner during Massoud's advance in May 1997, and others quit shortly after, but it is still an exaggeration by all standards. It seems to confirm the popular rule of thumb that Afghan number estimates are closer to the truth if divided by ten.[26]

Internal al-Qaida documents confirm that Arabs had problems finding qualified personnel for the front. "Presently, there is a supply of weapons here, but there aren't any trained men to use them" said one report from August 1997.[27] In a report from November the same year, Abd al-Hadi discusses withdrawing the Arabs from Murad Beg and concentrating all the forces in Bagram. He says, if the Arabs and Harakat ul-Jihad ul-Islami (HUJI) put their forces together they can form "an appropriate sized group (its number is expected to be around 20 brothers)."[28]

The reason for the suggested move is not personnel shortages per se, but problems in cooperating with Harakat ul-Ansar (HUA), a group of Pakistani fighters who were sharing responsibility for the Murad Beg positions with the Arabs. Abd al-Hadi's letter provides some insight into the rather petty day-to-day challenges of cooperating with other militant groups,

For instance they will ask, who is the leader? Why are only the Arabs commanders? Why do they fire more than us? Why don't they give us an opportunity? ... etc ... these are words spoken by some of the new members of Harakat ul-Ansar, whom we didn't know before.[29]

In the same letter, Abd al-Hadi adds what seems an update to the matter: "As you may know, there has now been a little improvement in the Harakat ul-Ansar situation; we have reached some level of understanding."[30]

In the end, the Arabs did not move from Murad Beg to Bagram. Instead the opposite happened. The Arabs in November 1998 handed their positions at Bagram over to a local Taliban group, in order to concentrate fully at Murad Beg. The reasons for the withdrawal are not clear, but Abd al-Hadi's report suggests it was a decision made by the Arabs themselves, and rather regretfully:

---

[25] Zaydan, "*qafilat 'landcruiser' sawda'*."
[26] See, for example, Robert Grenier, *88 days to Kandahar: A CIA diary* (New York: Simon & Schuster, 2015): 339.
[27] AQ-MSLF-D-001-151.
[28] AQ-MSLF-D-001-424.
[29] Ibid.
[30] Ibid.

With great pain, and deep sorrow, the Bagram Center was handed over to the Taliban (Mullah Ibrahim group), as we have talked to Mullah Abd al-Razzaq, the Deputy Minister of Defense, about this matter and he approved that. The final commissioning, along with the withdrawal of the brothers, was completed on November 21, 1998.[31]

There may be many reasons for the withdrawal. Perhaps it was due to personnel shortages, combined with several seminal events happening in the fall of 1998: the start of al-Qaida's terrorist campaign against the United States, the destruction of al-Qaida's training camps in Khost, and the death of the experienced commander Abu Ata' al-Sharqi on the Kabul front. But the move may also have been due to some petty reason, such as disagreements with local commanders. Anyway, from late 1998, al-Qaida concentrated their forces on one section of the frontline only: Murad Beg, the "gateway to Kabul."[32]

Murad Beg refers here to a series of hilltops close to Kabul and overlooking the Old Road. The fighting position at Murad Beg was developed in the aftermath of the big Taliban retreat in May 1997. After the retreat, the frontline between Taliban and Massoud was situated at Ghuldara road junction, some thirty-five kilometers north of Kabul city. Murad Beg was five kilometers behind this frontline, to function as a second line of defense for Kabul city. The Arabs at Murad Beg were not fighting Massoud directly, but were involved in supportive activities such as logistics and manning heavy weapons positions. Al-Qaida would hold these positions until after the battles of Charikar in August 1999, when the frontline again was moved to the north.

Al-Qaida was not the only group responsible for Murad Beg. They shared the responsibility with at least two other foreign groups – Harakat ul-Ansar, which occupied the hilltop closest to the Old Road, and "the Bengalis," which is likely a reference to Harakat ul-Jihad ul-Islami's Bangladesh branch. The Bengalis occupied some hills to the east of the Arabs.[33]

During 1998 and into the spring of 1999, Abd al-Hadi developed the Arab positions at the Murad Beg frontline. They establish a series of positions for ambush, observation, and supportive weapons. The Arabs had more heavy weapons here than they had when abandoning Bagram

---

[31] AQ-SHPD-D-000-039.

[32] al-Hindukushi, *mudhakkarati min kabul ila baghdad*, 108.

[33] AQ-POAK-D-000-018, "Daily military report by Abd al Hadi al Ansari with details on a battle between the Taliban and the enemy on the front north of Kabul," May 8, 1999. Conflict Records Resource Center, Washington, DC.

in 1998. The arsenal included mostly Soviet-made mortars, cannons, single- and multibarrel rocket launchers and a tank.[34]

Murad Beg was set up as a second line of defense that would be activated should Massoud break through the Taliban's frontline at Ghuldara. This never actually happened. The Taliban's frontline at Ghuldara was attacked directly on one occasion, on May 3, 1999, but Taliban managed to repel the attack. During that event, the Arabs were subject to artillery shelling, and according to the reports, small groups of enemy fighters who sought to infiltrate their positions.[35]

Between shellings and the occasional infiltration attempt, life at the Murad Beg – like so many wars – comprised of waiting. A volunteer who used the nickname Abu al-Shaqra' al-Hindukushi, who came to Afghanistan in 1999, published a detailed memoir of his experiences at the front. It gives a glimpse into the daily life of the Arabs at Murad Beg. The location is referred to here as Jabal Sabir (Sabir Mountain).

Days went by and I acclimatized to the new atmosphere at Jabal Sabir, which was not as difficult as I had expected. My relationship with all the brothers got stronger … In the daytime we took Sharia lessons from one of the brothers who studied [religion] or military lessons from Abd al-Hadi al-Iraqi, the overall commander. In the nighttime we took turns doing guard duty.[36]

In August 1999, the Taliban carried out the "Charikar offensive" – a large offensive against Massoud in which the Arabs participated. It was a big happening, according to Fadil Harun who worked for the al-Qaida leadership in Kandahar at the time. He resented that he was not allowed to take part in the battle himself. "Everyone was there, even Sheikh Osama."[37] Bin Laden was probably not physically present on the frontline, but according to Abd al-Hadi, gave direct orders to the Arabs during the battle. The orders were transmitted to the fighters via radio from Sayf al-Adl.[38]

On August 2, Taliban captured Charikar and Bagram, and pursued Massoud's forces all the way back into the Panjshir valley. But the success was short-lived. After a few days Massoud counterattacked and Taliban withdrew to their previous frontlines close to Kabul. Then, a few weeks

---

[34] AQ-MSLF-D-000-037, "A letter in the form of a logistics and operations status report sent to Usama Bin Laden," October 28, 1998, Conflict Records Resource Center, Washington, DC.
[35] AQ-POAK-D-000-017.
[36] al-Hindukushi, *mudhakkarati min kabul ila baghdad,* book 8.
[37] Harun, *al-harb ala al-islam,* 387.
[38] AQ-MCOP-D-000-916/917.

later, the Taliban attacked again and managed to move the Old Road frontline to Qarabagh, close to Bagram airbase.[39] All in all, the Charikar offensive was a major victory for the Taliban.

The Arabs led by Abd al-Hadi al-Iraqi played mostly a supportive role during the offensive. As a preparation for the attack, the Taliban started clearing the minefields around Bagram airbase. According to al-Hindukushi, a team of five Arabs was sent by Abd al-Hadi to take part in the mine-clearing operation.[40] The Arabs likely had the necessary skills to do so, acquired from the Arab training camps in the late 1980s and early 1990s. Abd al-Hadi himself was said to have attended a "combat engineer course" taught in one of al-Qaida's Jihad Wal camps back in 1992.[41]

In addition to the mine-clearing, the Arabs at Murad Beg seem to have functioned as a backup force to the Taliban that stayed in the rear during the main offensive. Abd al-Hadi recalled,

After the Taliban arrived at Charikar, Sadr Saib [Taliban commander in charge of the rear line] made a request to me and Abdul Salam. He said, "It would be better for you all to stay in Dosarak and to not venture outside of it. You should form a reserve line."[42]

At that time, some of the Arabs had already gone to Charikar to be closer to the frontline. It is not clear who these Arabs were, but Abd al-Hadi described them as a group that had previously split off from the Arabs at Murad Beg. At this time in 1999, various Arab militant groups were establishing themselves in Afghanistan – many of them, such as Abu Mus'ab al-Suri's group, preferred to work independently with the Taliban rather than being under al-Qaida command.

During the Charikar offensive, fissures became apparent within Abd al-Hadi's group. Not all the Arabs were happy with the role assigned to them by the Taliban. They did not want to form a reserve line at Dosarak – they wanted to go to the front and combat Massoud's forces directly. As one of the Arabs told Abd al-Hadi,

Enough is enough. I want to go to the front; the Taliban are in Jabal Siraj, and our brothers are in Charikar. I wish to go to the front and stay there. I am sorry, but I will not go back one step and this is my resignation.[43]

---

[39] *Afghan Islamic Press*, August 2–12, 1999.
[40] al-Hindukushi, *mudhakkarati min kabul ila baghdad,* book 8.
[41] Harun, *al-harb ala al-islam,* 128–129.
[42] AQ-MCOP-D-000-916/917.
[43] Ibid.

Abd al-Hadi could understand their sentiments, but he was committed to following the orders of the Taliban. But discipline in his ranks was falling apart. Even his deputy commander, Abd al-Salam al-Hadrami, suggested to Abd al-Hadi they should just disobey the Taliban and go to the front. When not even his deputy was on his side, what could Abd al-Hadi do? In the end he decided that they should all go to Charikar instead of forming the reserve line. The Arabs never made it to Charikar – at that point Massoud counterattacked and routed the Taliban forces from Charikar all the way back to their old frontlines.[44]

These events were the backdrop to Abd al-Hadi's sentimental letter to his friend Hassan in December 2000, which Abd al-Hadi signed with "the Emir who was forced to resign." In the grand scheme of things, the event was likely a minor one – one of the many bickerings over authority and leadership that had existed since the start of the Afghan-Arab movement in the 1980s. These bickerings were sparkled with the cultural prejudice that existed among the different Arab nations. Abd al-Hadi found it rather typical that his personal conflicts in 1999 had included Gulf Arabs, for as he lamented: "How could an Iraqi give orders to the honorable men from Hejaz and the wise men from the country of wisdom [Yemen]! This is a joke, yet it is a heavy one."[45]

Both Abd al-Hadi and Abd al-Salam continued to serve in leading positions on the Taliban's frontlines after 1999. From now on, Arabs expanded their military footprint in Afghanistan, which culminated in the establishment of a "Foreign Brigade" under the Taliban's Department of Defense in the spring of 2001. The Foreign Brigade was not an all-Arab unit but was meant to encompass all foreign fighters in Afghanistan including Pakistani and Uzbek groups. Parallel to this development, al-Qaida started using the Taliban frontline more systematically to train and test cadre for their own organization.

EXPANSION AND UNITY

After the battles of Charikar in August 1999, which ended with victory for the Taliban, Abd al-Hadi was certain that the frontline would never again return to Murad Beg.[46] He was right. During 2000 and 2001, the

---

[44] AQ-MCOP-D-000-916/917.
[45] Abu Mus'ab al-Suri displayed a similar prejudice toward Gulf Arabs, according to al-Suri biographer Brynjar Lia. AQ-MCOP-D-000-916/917; and Lia, *Architect of global jihad*, 279–80.
[46] AQ-MCOP-D-000-916/917.

Old Road front between Taliban and Massoud continued to be situated in the Qarabagh area, some kilometers south of Charikar. Here, the occasional clashes between Taliban and Massoud continued. At the same time, Taliban started building up forces in northern Afghanistan, in the provinces of Takhar and Baghlan, to gradually encircle Massoud and Rabbani's remaining strongholds in the Panjshir and Badakhshan. By now, Taliban controlled about 90 percent of Afghanistan's territory.

From mid-1999 to early 2001 there is a gap in al-Qaida's operational reporting. Other sources suggest that after 1999, the Arabs established a new "frontline" in an area called Dosarak, and the Murad Beg area was turned into a training and administrative site. Al-Hindukushi was present at the time the Arabs established the new frontline:

After a few days we settled in Dosarak area. We established our center there, to the right of the main road [Old Road]. The Pakistanis established their center to the left of the road. In this way we could ensure the protection of the road while the Afghan brothers advance. The house we used as a center was a rear area for our trenches, which were situated 150 meters in front of it.[47]

The Arabs at Dosarak seem to have fulfilled the same military role as the Arabs previously at Murad Beg. The purpose of the Arab position was to observe the Old Road and to hinder Massoud's forces from advancing, should they break through the Taliban's first frontline further north.

The number of Arabs present at the frontlines must have increased after 1999, due to the influx of new recruits to al-Qaida's training camps. In 1997, there were some twenty al-Qaida fighters on the Taliban's frontline. In early 2001, the number was reportedly "between 80 and 120," according to an informed source.[48] However, there was no drastic increase in the number of combat positions manned by Arabs. In 2001 the Arabs manned a secondary frontline position called the "Omar Sayf Center." It was on the Old Road, and is likely identical to the center they established at Dosarak after the Charikar offensive. The name was likely a tribute to Omar Sayf al-Filistini, who was killed in the second phase of that offensive. In addition, Arabs established a presence at the Bagram frontline, which they had abandoned in November 1998. The third large concentration of Arabs north of Kabul was at Murad Beg, where al-Qaida had established the Malik Training camp in late 2000 as a supplement to

---

[47] al-Hindukushi, *mudhakkarati min kabul ila baghdad,* book 8.
[48] Hamid and Farrall, *The Arabs at war in Afghanistan.*

al-Faruq camp in Kandahar. Arabs also worked in rear positions closer to Kabul carrying out administrative and logistical tasks.[49]

Abd al-Hadi al-Iraqi wanted the Arabs to play a more offensive role in the Taliban's war. This is evident from a letter he wrote in June 2000 to an unknown receiver. In the letter, he discusses how the Arabs could improve their performance on the Taliban's frontlines, based on his "four years of experience" on the Kabul front.[50] In Abd al-Hadi's view, the participation of the Arabs must still seek to fulfill two purposes – to assist the Taliban, and to use the frontline as a training ground for al-Qaida's own members. However, at that time, the Arabs were not getting enough experience in conducting offensive operations. He does not elaborate on the reasons for this, but notes that al-Qaida's own training programs had so far created "inflation" in certain skills such as defensive operations and heavy weapons, whereas other skills such as offensive operations, were lacking.

At the end of the letter, Abd al-Hadi lists a number of suggestions on how to improve the current situation. The last point is the most specific: "Putting in place clear policies to join the Taliban on the front."[51] Elaborating the issue, he says the Arabs should take part in the Taliban's offensive operations, as well as in the defensive ones. He notes the challenges of working in defensive positions:

1. Not having enough good weapons.
2. Not enough ammunition with the Taliban, and lack of ammunition in the markets.
3. The difficulty of arranging it with the Taliban, because they consider the heavy weapons and its ammunition one of the matters they must control completely.
4. Lack of patience among the brothers to stay with the artillery in the rear for a long time.

The last point, that the Arabs "lacked patience" to stay in the rear, was a well-known phenomenon by now and was probably one of the main reasons that Arabs disobeyed the orders of the Taliban during the Charikar offensive. Although Arab foot soldiers generally just wanted action, Abd al-Hadi saw organizational benefits of creating offensive battle units – this would motivate recruits and give them useful battlefield skills.

---

[49] Mentioned in various U.S. Department of Defense documents. See, for example: SA-000199; YM-000837; SA-000196.
[50] AFGP-2002-000091.
[51] Ibid.

The only problem was the Taliban's "fighting style," which relied on sudden withdrawals – as seen in the battle of Charikar in 1999. This could lead to potentially dangerous situations. In the worst case, the Arabs would be abandoned in the middle of the battle and end up being massacred or imprisoned by Massoud's forces. But Abd al-Hadi had a number of solutions at hand – basically, the Arabs had to be self-sufficient during battle by setting up their own emergency response force, medical unit, and artillery support.[52]

As al-Qaida was contemplating to get a more active role at Taliban's front, the number of foreign fighters coming to Afghanistan was increasing. The number of foreign militant organizations in Afghanistan also multiplied. The largest organizations were the Pakistani groups HUA and HUJI, and the Uzbek group Islamic Movement of Uzbekistan (IMU), led by two veterans from the Tajik civil war, Tahir Yuldashev and Juma Namangani. There was also an Uighur group named East Turkestan Islamic Movement (ETIM), led by Hassan Mahsum.

There were several Arab groups, but al-Qaida was by far the largest and most organized. Al-Qaida was the Arab group that most actively participated on the Taliban's frontline. According to Mustafa Hamid, al-Qaida in early 2001 had "around 80 to 120 people on [Taliban's] front, the Libyans had 11 and Abu Mus'ab al-Suri had between 10 and 20. The other Arab groups had only a handful of people each on the front."[53] The Central Asians and Pakistanis had 300 to 400 fighters on the Taliban's frontline, according to conservative estimates.[54]

The increase in the number of groups fighting for the Taliban created a need for better organization. This was perhaps the main motivation for Mullah Omar's establishment of a "Foreign Brigade" in spring 2001. The brigade, which was also referred to as Brigade 21, the 22nd Division, or al-liwa (Arabic for Brigade) was a military unit established by Mullah Omar around March 2001. It was organized under the Taliban's Ministry of Defense and the purpose was to gather all foreign fighters in Afghanistan under one command.

Mullah Omar appointed Juma Namangani, the military commander of IMU, as the supreme commander of the brigade. Bin Laden and al-Qaida

52 AFGP-2002-000091.
53 Hamid and Farrall, The Arabs at war in Afghanistan, 275–276.
54 Ibid.; "Islamic Movement of Uzbekistan (IMU) letter detailing the establishment of the IMU's Bukhari Camp," July 20, 2001, Combating Terrorism Center, West Point, NY. The latter document confirms that on July 20, 2001, IMU had 200 families in Afghanistan (presumably the families of IMU fighters) that needed housing.

gave their support to the project, as did the ETIM, the EIJ, the Libyans and Abu Mus'ab al-Suri.[55] Namangani appointed Abd al-Hadi al-Iraqi and a Pakistani commander to be his deputies. The Arab and Pakistani groups on the frontline probably kept their original chain of command – Arabs who fought on the Taliban's frontline in mid-2001 said that Abd al-Hadi al-Iraqi was their top commander.

The formation of the Foreign Brigade may have been a result of the increased role played by central Asian militants in Afghanistan, especially from February 2001 when a number of Tajik militants were expelled from Tajikistan and subsequently joined the IMU. In the long term, the IMU envisioned using northern Afghanistan to launch a war in central Asia.[56] Several of the Arabs, including Abu Mus'ab al-Suri and Mustafa Hamid, were proponents of this strategy as well. Needless to say, the issue would have created major controversies within the Taliban who were ever torn between the conflicting aims of consolidating their nascent Islamic State and supporting the plight of oppressed Muslims elsewhere. By convincing IMU to join the fight on the Taliban's frontlines, the Taliban put off the issue of *jihad* in Central Asia.

Another motivation for forming the brigade, mentioned by several independent sources, was that Mullah Omar was tired of the bickering between the various foreign militants in Afghanistan about who should be their leader.[57] Even if al-Qaida did not get the leading role, Bin Laden supported the brigade. Al-Qaida was generally defiant to the Taliban's orders, and was in favor of efforts to unify the ranks of the Muslims.

After the brigade was established, the Arabs expanded their presence to northern Afghanistan in connection with a general build-up of Taliban forces in Kunduz and Takhar. The Kabul frontline in this period was relatively calm. The Taliban's strategy at the time was to first capture the northern provinces of Takhar and Badakhshan – if they succeeded, Massoud's stronghold in the Panjshir valley would be completely surrounded.

As the Taliban were building up for a large offensive in the north, the Arabs moved the Omar Sayf center from the Old Road front to the

---

[55] Hamid and Farrall, *The Arabs at war in Afghanistan*, 273–278. Alternative accounts of the Foreign Brigade's establishment can be found in al-Suri, *da'wat al-muqawama*, 787; and Исломий Амирликнинг кулаши [The Fall of the Islamic Emirate]. Islamic Movement of Uzbekistan homepage, accessed September 26, 2014, on file with author.
[56] Исломий Амирликнинг кулаши.
[57] Mojdeh, *Afghanistan wa panj sal*; Hamid and Farrall, *The Arabs at war in Afghanistan*, 273–278.

Khwaja Ghar front in Takhar.[58] The Arabs continued to man positions at the Bagram front. This is confirmed by Arabs who were present at the Kabul front in 2001: As the Taliban started building up for a large offensive in the north in spring 2001, Arabs were "sent to either Bagram or Takhar."[59] John Walker Lindh, known as the "American Taliban," was among the foreign volunteers who was sent to the Takhar frontline. In other words, the Arabs did not open up new fronts, they simply moved their fighters from one front to the other. Abd al-Salam al-Hadrami, the Yemeni deputy of Abd al-Hadi, moved to the Takhar front in this period and was the overall commander for the Arabs there.

Arabs who went to Takhar, fought together with Uzbeks and Pakistanis in the framework of Juma Namangani's Foreign Brigade. The brigade by this time was responsible for a section of the Khwaja Ghar frontline. It was well organized with front and backline positions, heavy weapons support, resting and supply areas, and a medical clinic staffed with Russian-trained doctors.[60]

Little is known about the relationship between Abd al-Hadi al Iraqi and Juma Namangani. According to one source, Abd al-Hadi initially was upset with the decision to appoint Juma Namangani as overall commander, and threatened to withdraw his force from the front. However, he complied after Bin Laden ordered him to do so.[61] Juma Namangani was a former Soviet Paratrooper who, ironically, had fought in the Afghan-Soviet war on the side of the Russians. Afterwards he switched sides and fought with the Islamists in the Tajik civil war, before establishing the IMU together with Tahir Yuldashev. It is likely that "Juma bey" as he was called, had an offensive fighting style, resembling that of regular armies – unlike the Taliban, who were sensitive to taking losses and who tended to "run away from battle," as Abd al-Hadi once put it. It suggests Arabs from now on, had the opportunity to play a more independent and offensive role in the war, as Abd al-Hadi had envisioned in mid-2000.

Mustafa Hamid suggested that Bin Laden in spring 2001 did not give priority to fighting at the Taliban's frontlines.[62] However, other sources disagree. Bin Laden continued to encourage the other Arab groups in Afghanistan to fight for the Taliban. He publically swore allegiance to

---

[58] AQ-MISC-D-000-972.
[59] SA-000199.
[60] Исломий Амирликнинг кулаши.
[61] Hamid and Farrall, *The Arabs at war in Afghanistan*, 278.
[62] Ibid.

Mullah Omar. And Al-Qaida used some of their top military planners to prepare for a spectacular operation far behind Taliban's enemy lines: The assassination of the Taliban's arch-enemy, Ahmed Shah Massoud.

SPECIAL OPERATIONS

Vahid Mojdeh, a former official in the Taliban's Foreign Ministry, remembered the two Arab-speaking journalists who had arrived in Kandahar. He was surprised that their camera equipment was hopelessly outdated. "Why are they bringing such an old-fashioned camera," he had thought to himself.[63] Only later did he understand why. The camera was used to hide the bomb that killed Ahmed Shah Massoud, leader of the Northern Alliance.

The assassination of Ahmed Shah Massoud on September 9, 2001 has sometimes been described as a "preparation" for the September 11 attacks and the subsequent US-led invasion of Afghanistan. Massoud's murder was supposed to pave the way for the Taliban's final defeat of the Northern Alliance, thereby removing the only local ally the United States could rely on during an invasion. Others have suggested that al-Qaida staged Massoud's murder to please Mullah Omar so that he would be more willing to accept the 9/11 attacks.

Both these claims are based on the premise that al-Qaida at the time was only concerned with their international terrorist campaign against the United States. In reality, al-Qaida was pursuing multiple agendas in Afghanistan including organization building and support to the Taliban's state-building project. Against this backdrop, it is probably more accurate to view the Massoud murder as a special operation behind enemy lines, carried out to give the Taliban a strategic advantage in the war.

US intelligence sources say that the Massoud murder was planned by Sayf al-Adl, whereas Egyptian explosives expert Abdul Rahman al-Muhajir helped construct the bomb. Furthermore, there was a group of midlevel operatives involved in the planning. They included Mohammed Zahran, a Saudi, and Gharib al-Sana'ani, a Yemeni. Both of them were frontline commanders north of Kabul. Mohammed Zahran was in charge of an observation post overlooking Bagram. Gharib al-Sana'ani was a deputy to frontline commander Abd al-Salam al-Hadrami. A third member of the group was Talha al-Jaza'iri, who was associated with Abu

[63] Author's interview, Kabul, 2009.

Jaffar al-Jaza'iri at the Algerian House in Jalalabad. French authorities have connected Abu Jaffar to the Massoud murder.[64]

The three of them were allegedly trained by Abu Jihad al-Masri, who became general commander of the Kabul front, and afterward, at least one of them (Zahran) attended a course for special operatives, given by Abdul Rahman al-Muhajir, al-Qaida's top explosives expert in Kandahar. The course specialized in surveillance and assassinations. US intelligence also suggests Gharib al-Sana'ani received extensive "special training" at a guesthouse in Kandahar. It suggests that al-Qaida was building up a "Special Operations" capacity by tapping off resources from al-Qaida's international operations experiences, and that they used it against the Northern Alliance.[65]

US intelligence information states that Zahran's group was involved in several operations behind enemy lines north of Kabul. One of them was the assassination of a Massoud commander at Bagram, called "Baba Jumba," in July 2001. The account cannot be confirmed from open sources – newspapers contain no reporting about the remote-controlled truck bomb blast, which allegedly took place outside Baba Jumba's house and killed twelve people including the commander.[66]

Nevertheless, training manuals found in Afghanistan after 2001 suggest that al-Qaida was training for these types of operations behind enemy lines. Al-Qaida's ambition was to carry out Special Forces-type operations and to be a strategic capacity of the Taliban. The murder of Ahmed Shah Massoud was indeed an operation of strategic significance – not in the context of 9/11 but in the context of the Taliban's war against Massoud.

Over time, al-Qaida's frontline participation with the Taliban became an integrated part of al-Qaida's own training and education program. The existence of active frontlines in Afghanistan served al-Qaida's own interests perfectly. The frontlines attracted recruits and they served as testing and training grounds for future al-Qaida cadre. Al-Qaida's international terrorist operations could not possibly attract, absorb, and test prospective members of al-Qaida the same way as the frontlines did. In other words, al-Qaida was dependent on having access to a frontline in order to build a resilient organization. Resilience would be essential for an organization that was by now entrenched in war with the world's greatest superpower.

[64] SA-000713, "Detainee Assessment Brief ICO Guantanamo Detainee, ISN US9SA-000713DP [Mohammed Muti-Zahran]," Department of Defense (Joint Task Force Guantanamo), July 4, 2008.
[65] Ibid.
[66] Ibid.

8

International Terrorism

In 1998–2001, al-Qaida staged a series of international terrorist attacks against the United States. The twin suicide bombings of the US Embassies in Kenya and Tanzania on August 7, 1998 killed 224 civilians. The suicide attack on the US warship USS Cole in Yemen killed 17 US sailors. The hijacking and subsequent downing of four passenger airplanes in New York, Washington, DC, and Pennsylvania on September 11, 2001 killed close to 3,000 civilians. So far, this book has described al-Qaida as a vanguard and an elite Muslim army but no doubt, al-Qaida will be remembered for their spectacular, mass-casualty terrorist attacks. This chapter seeks to place al-Qaida's international terrorist campaign in context of its other activities in Afghanistan. How was the international terrorist campaign organized and what was its strategic purpose?

THE EAST AFRICA OPERATION

On August 7, 1998 at 10:30 A.M., a Saudi suicide bomber, Jihad Ali Azzam, detonated a truck bomb outside the US Embassy in Nairobi, Kenya. 213 people were killed including 12 Americans. Almost simultaneously at 10:39 A.M., an Egyptian suicide bomber, Hamden Khalif Allah, detonated a truck bomb outside the US Embassy in Dar-es-Salaam, Tanzania. Eleven people were killed including one American. Fewer people were killed in Tanzania because the US Embassy there was located in a less crowded area, and a water truck parked in front of the Embassy absorbed much of the explosion.[1]

---

[1] Becky Champagne, ed., "Anatomy of a terrorist attack: An in-depth investigation into the 1998 bombings of the U.S. Embassies in Kenya and Tanzania," Briefing paper, Matthew B. Ridgway Center, University of Pittsburgh, 2005.

The East Africa Operation was carried out by two separate execution teams; one in Kenya, and one in Tanzania. In Kenya the execution team comprised Azzam, the suicide bomber; Mohamed al-Owhali, who rode the truck to the explosion site and exited shortly before the explosion; and Fadil Harun, who led the suicide truck to the Embassy in a separate vehicle, and who cleaned up the cover apartment after the attack. Azzam was killed in the explosion. Al-Owhali was arrested by Kenyan authorities and extradited to the United States. Harun escaped to Afghanistan and continued to work for al-Qaida until he was killed in 2009.

Harun, as described in previous chapters, was a Black African from the Comoros, who joined al-Qaida around 1991. He fought with al-Qaida's guerilla units in Gardez and Nangarhar in 1991–1992. He worked in the administration of Jihad Wal camp in Khost. He was with Bin Laden in Sudan from 1993–1996. After Bin Laden moved back to Afghanistan in 1996, Harun stayed behind as part of al-Qaida's East Africa network.

Azzam, the suicide bomber, was a Saudi who had joined al-Qaida in 1996 or 1997. He was from Mecca and his real name was Jihad Muhammad Ali al-Harazi. He was the cousin of Abd al-Rahim al-Nashiri – who later became the mastermind of the *USS Cole* bombing in Aden, Yemen in 2000.[2] Al-Owhali, possibly designated as a second suicide bomber, was a British-born Saudi who went to train in Khalden in 1996, and who fought on the Taliban's frontlines in 1997 before he was recruited to the East Africa plot.[3] In late 1997 or early 1998 they both received mission-specific training in Afghanistan, learning how to conduct clandestine operations in urban environments, before being sent to Kenya on June 19 and August 1, 1998, respectively.[4]

When Azzam arrived in Nairobi in June 1998, he was met at the airport by Fadil Harun. Harun did not know Azzam from before. "He is from the generation of the second Afghanistan period, that is, the Taliban period," Harun recalled. "They do not know me, and I do not know them."[5] The same was true for al-Owhali. Azzam and al-Owhali were young Saudis recruited into al-Qaida after bin Laden's return to Afghanistan in 1996.

---

[2] Moreover, Azzam was allegedly a "friend" of two other Meccans, Khalid al-Midhar and Nawaf al-Hazmi, who fought in Bosnia in 1995 before going to Afghanistan to receive training, and who ultimately became two of the nineteen 9/11 hijackers. *The 9/11 Commission report*, 155.

[3] *USA v. Osama bin Laden et al*, Trial transcript p. 1518.

[4] Champagne, "Anatomy of a terrorist attack," 59.

[5] Harun, *al-harb ala al-islam*, 317.

Some sources say they were handpicked by Bin Laden, but this is hard to verify. What seems certain, is that Bin Laden in this period actively tried to increase the number of Saudi and Yemeni recruits in al-Qaida. Bin Laden approached Gulf Arabs already in Afghanistan, such as the "Northern Group," a group of Arabs who had tried to join the Tajik civil war in 1996. Al-Qaida also approached Gulf Arabs who came to train in Khalden. As stated earlier, Khalden at the time was the only training camp in Afghanistan that offered basic training to recruits regardless of group affiliation. It had strong facilitation networks in Europe and the Middle East, and attracted Gulf Arabs who wanted to fight classical *jihad* in Bosnia, Chechnya, or elsewhere.

All of this suggests that al-Qaida's first international operatives, Azzam and al-Owhali, were recruited among Gulf Arabs who came to Afghanistan to train for classical *jihad* in 1996–1997. After being acquainted with al-Qaida and its anti-American agenda, they volunteered to carry out suicide missions abroad. They received specialized training in al-Qaida camps in Khost, and were sent to Kenya shortly before the attacks were to be carried out.

The three operatives in Kenya received support from senior al-Qaida members. Fadil Harun was in charge of the Kenya cell. Above him in command was Abu Muhammad al-Masri (aka Abdullah Ahmed Abdullah, aka "Saleh") who was in charge of al-Qaida's East Africa network. The East Africa network was a group of al-Qaida members who stayed behind in East Africa, mainly Kenya, after Bin Laden relocated to Afghanistan in May 1996. Abu Muhammad al-Masri became in charge of the network after Abu Ubaydah al-Banshiri, second in command of al-Qaida, drowned in a ferry accident on Lake Victoria on May 23, 1996. Abu Muhammad al-Masri has been described as "one of Zawahiri's men" and the chief bomb maker in the 1998 plot, but this is likely a conflation of several individuals involved in the plot.[6] Abu Muhammad al-Masri was among the original members who joined al-Qaida in 1988–1989. He was married to the daughter of an Egyptian Islamic Jihad official, but otherwise there are few indications that he was an EIJ member himself.[7] He may have taken basic explosives courses in Afghanistan – standard education for al-Qaida cadre on his level – but he was not the chief bomb maker,

---

[6] Wright, *The looming tower*, 270.
[7] "*masadir amirikiyya tatahaddath an ittisalat bayn abu muhammad al-masri wa sayf al-adl wa khaliyyat al-riyad*," *al-Sharq al-Awsat*, May 17, 2003, http://archive.aawsat.com/details.asp?article=171251&issueno=8936#.VwNuZPmLRaQ; Harun, *al-harb ala al-islam*, 94.

because this was another Egyptian, Abu Abd al-Rahman, who was sent from Afghanistan to Kenya for the purpose. Fadil Harun described Abu Muhammad as having high religious credentials – he had studied under the famous Salafi sheikh Nasr al-Din al-Albani. In the early 1990s he had been in charge of the Jihad Wal portion of al-Qaida's training camps in Khost.[8] After the death of al-Banshiri in 1995, and the resignation of another high-ranking al-Qaida official around the same time, he rose to become number three in al-Qaida.

Other senior al-Qaida members who supported the Kenya cell directly were Abu Abd al-Rahman al-Muhajir, an al-Qaida explosives expert, and Mohamed Sadiq Odeh, a Palestinian al-Qaida member. Abu Abd al-Rahman al-Muhajir traveled from Afghanistan to Kenya in mid-1998 to help construct the bomb used in the attack. He finished his work the day before the bombings, on August 6, 1998, and left Kenya along with the rest of the al-Qaida members in the region not directly involved in executing the attacks. Mohamed Odeh was part of al-Qaida's East Africa network and was already based in Kenya at the time of the bombings.[9] It seems he was not a vital part of the preparations cell, as he was not involved in the final stages of attack preparations. However, he received massive attention after the attacks because he was one of four individuals who were arrested and convicted in the United States in connection with the bombings. His testimony in the case was crucial because it linked Osama bin Laden and al-Qaida directly to the attacks.

The attack cell in Dar-es-Salaam had a similar set-up as the attack cell in Nairobi, with separate teams for preparation and execution. The suicide bomber, Hamden Khalif al-Awad (aka Ahmed al-Almani) was a member of the Egyptian Islamic Jihad who had taken an explosives course with Abu Abd al-Rahman al-Muhajir in the early 1990s. He had previously been involved in EIJ's attempt to assassinate the Egyptian President Hosni Mubarak in Addis Abeba, Ethiopia, in June 1995. Thus, he had long experience with international terrorism. It is unclear if he was formally a member of al-Qaida. Fadil Harun said that the EIJ had "allowed him to carry out operations with us [al-Qaida]."[10] He arrived in Tanzania

---

[8] Harun, *al-harb ala al-islam*, 120.

[9] Mohamed Odeh became a member of al-Qaida in March 1992, received advanced training in al-Qaida's Khost camps in 1992–1993 and was part of al-Qaida's training mission in Somalia in 1993. See Mohamed Odeh's testimony to the FBI, http://americanjihadists.com/1998-08-31-FBI-FD302-Odeh-all.pdf.

[10] Harun, *al-harb ala al-islam*, 317.

a week or so before the attacks. He was assisted by the Tanzanian Khalfan Khamis Muhammad who rode the truck to the bomb site, got out before it exploded, and cleaned up the safe house before fleeing the country. Like the Kenya cell, the Tanzania cell took orders from Abu Muhammad al-Masri and received technical support from Abu Abd al-Rahman who had flown in from Afghanistan for the occasion.

There are many more details to the East Africa Operations that have been omitted from this brief review. The point here is, first, to remind the reader that the East Africa bombings in August 1998 were definitely organized by al-Qaida. The operation was ordered by Abu Hafs al-Masri, al-Qaida's number two, and organized locally by Abu Muhammad al-Masri, al-Qaida's number three. Bin Laden's direct role in the attack is unclear. Some accounts indicate bin Laden was personally involved in planning the bomb plot as he had been interested in attacking the US Embassy in Kenya from the early 1990s.[11] Others, like Fadil Harun, say that planning was conducted by himself and Abu Muhammad al-Masri, and that bin Laden was informed of the timing and targets only a few days in advance. According to Harun, Abu Hafs had originally asked Abu Muhammad al-Masri to target US warships in the port of Mombasa. But when it became clear that the US Navy would not turn up in Mombasa in 1998, Abu Muhammad and Fadil Harun decided on targeting a US embassy. They also made the decision to target not just one, but two embassies simultaneously.[12] The truth of Bin Laden's involvement in operative aspects of the attacks remains unclear, even today. This is an important observation in itself, as will be further discussed later.

The second point is that al-Qaida was not dependent on their Taliban sanctuary in Afghanistan to carry out these attacks. The composition of the operative cells in Kenya and Tanzania suggests the attacks were organized mainly outside Afghanistan, by al-Qaida's East African branch. The organizational expertise and resources required to carry out the attacks were mainly developed during al-Qaida's first Afghanistan phase

[11] This account is based on the testimony of Ali Mohamed, the American-Egyptian former US Army instructor who became member of Egyptian Islamic Jihad. Ali Mohamed was tasked with conducting surveillance of the US embassy, among other targets. According to Mohamed, "Bin Laden looked at the picture of the American Embassy [in Nairobi] and pointed to where a truck could go as a suicide bomber." The testimony was given as part of a plea deal with the US government in the year 2000. It is possible that Mohamed exaggerated his own and Bin Laden's role in the 1998 bombings. Wright, *The looming tower*, 198.

[12] Harun, *al-harb ala al-islam*, 300–329.

in 1988–1992. In this period, al-Qaida ran training camps in Khost, and al-Qaida was co-located with Egyptian Islamic Jihad (EIJ) and al-Jama'a al-Islamiyya (JI). Both groups had long experience in urban and international terrorist operations, and it is likely that their experiences were transferred to al-Qaida. EIJ contributed directly to the attack in Dar-es-Salaam by allowing one of their experienced operatives, Ahmed al-Almani, to be part of the attack cell.

Al-Qaida used the Afghanistan sanctuary to recruit and train two Saudi suicide operatives, Azzam and al-Owhali. They were the only members of the plot who were recruited after 1996. Azzam and al-Owhali trained in Khalden and al-Qaida's training camps in Jihad Wal. They may have fought in Arab units on the Taliban's frontline north of Kabul in 1997, like many other Arabs who came to Afghanistan in this period looking for a place to wage *jihad*. After being recruited, Azzam and al-Owhali were probably trained in terrorist tactics in al-Qaida's training camps in Afghanistan. However, in this period, these camps and their access points – the porous border between the Tribal Areas of Afghanistan, and Khost – were hardly a matter of priority for the Taliban. As we recall from Chapter 6, in 1997 the Taliban was experiencing major military setbacks in Northern Afghanistan and on the frontline north of Kabul.[13] In sum, the East Africa bombings had an extremely small footprint in Afghanistan.

The East African Operation had several implications for al-Qaida in Afghanistan. The most immediate effect was the destruction of al-Qaida's training camp infrastructure in Khost on August 20, 1998. However, the US missile strikes failed to kill any high-ranking al-Qaida leaders and had no major disruptive effects on al-Qaida's training project. Al-Qaida soon moved their training camps to temporary locations, before settling in Kandahar in the spring of 2000. Instead of disrupting al-Qaida's activities in Afghanistan, the US missile strikes had the opposite effect of making bin Laden an instant celebrity, both locally and internationally. This, in turn, made it harder for the Taliban to expel him.

The East Africa bombings was the first international terrorist attack with confirmed links to al-Qaida. Yet, the Taliban in Afghanistan refused to believe that Osama bin Laden had anything to do with the bombings. This is understandable. The bombings were organized and carried

---

[13] See, for example, the account of American journalist John Miller who interviewed Bin Laden in Khost in 1998. Miller, Stone, and Mitchell, *The cell*, 176–192.

out by a small group of trusted individuals within al-Qaida. Bin Laden used middlemen based outside Afghanistan to coordinate the attacks, presumably to hide his own role in the operation. Although traditional terrorism is aimed at generating maximum publicity, placing the perpetrators and their political agenda at center stage, al-Qaida acted somewhat differently. The 1998 attacks appear to be a mixture of terrorism and covert operation, aimed at protecting bin Laden's status as a guest with the Taliban.

The 1998 attacks and their aftermath no doubt boosted al-Qaida's confidence. The US missile strikes on August 20 had failed to kill Bin Laden and the Taliban was disinterested in exploring the matter further. The Taliban took an uncompromising stance on Bin Laden, refusing to expel him in spite of international pressure and sanctions. This was a gesture of large symbolic significance. Islamists in the region no doubt remembered how the Pakistani government had expelled Arab mujahidin to face torture in their home countries in the 1990s, and how they had expelled Ramzi Yousef, a Muslim, to the "infidel" United States, in 1995. Bin Laden himself no doubt remembered how he had been betrayed and expelled by the Sudanese regime in 1996, after investing heavily in the country.

Feeling confident, al-Qaida in 1999 embarked on a period of re-organization and expansion. After the East Africa bombings, al-Qaida's East Africa network was dismantled and the remaining operatives moved to Afghanistan. They included Abu Muhammad al-Masri, number three in al-Qaida after Abu Hafs, and Fadil Harun, who was appointed as Abu Hafs' secretary. Abu Abd al-Rahman, the Egyptian who built the bombs used in 1998, continued working in al-Qaida as a bomb engineer and explosives instructor. This ensured that al-Qaida's experiences during the East African attack were transferred to the next generation of al-Qaida cadre.

In late 1999 al-Qaida organized a cadre course – a clear indication that the organization was in the process of expansion. Veterans from the East Africa operation were represented among the instructors. Abu Muhammad al-Masri gave a lecture entitled "Palestine and world politics," Fadil Harun lectured on the East Africa operation, and Abu Abd al-Rahman gave explosives lessons. The course finished just in time for the inauguration of al-Qaida's new flagship project – the new al-Faruq training camp in Kandahar. By now al-Qaida had gradually changed its role in Afghanistan, from secret organization to services office for incoming volunteers.

Bin Laden's confidence and optimism is reflected in a speech to the
al-Qaida leadership in September 2000:

[After the 1998 operation] we succeeded in mobilizing the masses ... We expect
huge waves [of recruits] within few months. Treat the matter as if we are an
Islamic government in exile, we moved from the phase of potentiality to the phase
of expansion and preparedness and large responsibilities.[14]

In August and September 2000 alone, more than 120 new recruits arrived
in Kandahar to train in al-Qaida's camps. Bin Laden had reason to be
optimistic. His sanctuary with the Taliban was also safe for the time
being. In November 1999, the Taliban had again refused to expel Bin
Laden to the United States, even when threatened with UN sanctions.
Time was ripe for a new covert operation against the United States.

THE USS COLE ATTACK

"Dear Sheikh ... Why were the strikes against the Americans delayed?
Will they be executed soon? And what will our role be?"[15] There seemed
to be no end to the questions asked by recruits in al-Qaida's training
camps.[16] During June and July 2000, the question of why Bin Laden had
delayed "the martyrdom operation" on the Americans was asked on at
least three different occasions.[17] We do not know Bin Laden's answer. But
we know that an al-Qaida cell in Yemen had already tried, and failed, to
attack the US warship *USS The Sullivans* on January 3, 2000.[18] It was
going to be al-Qaida's second operation against the Americans and the
first, major attack on American targets on the Arabian Peninsula.[19] It is
quite likely that Bin Laden had hinted to eager followers in Afghanistan
that something big was in the making. He would certainly do this later.
"It is no secret that we are planning to strike America and NATO," he
boasted in June 2001, less than three months before the 9/11 attacks.[20]

---

[14] AFGP-2002-801138, "Various admin documents and questions," 99.
[15] Ibid., 60.
[16] AFGP-2002-801138 recorded 291 different questions asked in the period from June
2000 to March 2001.
[17] AFGP-2002-801138, 144, 153, 160.
[18] *Terrorism 2000/2001*, undated report, Federal Bureau of Investigation, U.S. Department
of Justice.
[19] I assume here that al-Qaida was not involved in the previous terrorist attacks against
American targets on the Arabian Peninsula, despite claims to the contrary. This view is
supported in Hegghammer, "Deconstructing the myth about al-Qa`ida and Khobar."
[20] Bin Laden, *bushrayat lil-shaykh usama.*

The suicide operation against *USS The Sullivans* failed for rather mundane reasons: The operatives miscalculated the tide and the boat loaded with explosives got stuck in the sand. But the blunder passed in silence. The al-Qaida cell was able to recover the boat and on October 3, 2001 they made a second attempt at the *USS Cole*, which at the time was anchored in the port of Aden. This time, they succeeded. The explosion ripped a large hole in the ship's hull and killed seventeen US sailors.[21] More importantly, the attack caused the US Navy to stop refueling in the Port of Aden. It seemed that al-Qaida's strategy of attacking US targets abroad was starting to work.

The *USS Cole* operation was carried out by a network of Saudi and Yemeni operatives led by the Saudi Abd al-Rahim al-Nashiri. Al-Nashiri was a veteran jihadist who was radicalized in the early 1990s and fought in Tajikistan, Chechnya and Afghanistan. He was a cousin of Azzam, the suicide bomber who carried out the attack on the US Embassy in Nairobi. Al-Nashiri claims he joined al-Qaida in 1998 after Azzam was killed. Bin Laden subsequently tasked him to carry out terrorist attacks on the Arabian Peninsula.[22] Nashiri planned the failed attack on *USS The Sullivans* in January 2000, the attack on the *USS Cole* in October 2000 and the attack on a French oil tanker, *MV Limburg*, in 2002, in addition to several plots that never materialized.

The Yemeni al-Qaida member Walid bin Attash (aka Khallad) was initially an important part of al-Nashiri's network. Bin Attash was radicalized in the first half of the 1990s, trained in Afghanistan, and attempted to join the *jihad* in Tajikistan. He joined al-Qaida in 1996, shortly after Bin Laden returned from Sudan. He then fought on the Taliban's frontlines where he lost a leg in 1997.[23] He was pulled out of the operational cell in Yemen after briefly being arrested by Yemeni authorities, then released. He continued to function as an external communications link between al-Nashiri and Bin Laden in Afghanistan.[24]

---

[21] "The investigation into the attack on the U.S.S. Cole," Report of the House Armed Services Committee Staff, May 2001.

[22] *The 9/11 Commission report*, 152–153; SA-010015, "Combatant Status Review Tribunal Input and Recommendation for Continued Detention Under DoD Control (CD) for Guantanamo Detainee, ISN: US9SA-010015DP [Abd al-Rahim al-Nashiri]," Department of Defense (Joint Task Force Guantanamo), December 8, 2006.

[23] YM-010014, "Combatant Status Review Tribunal Input and Recommendation for Continued Detention Under DoD Control (CD) for Guantanamo Detainee, ISN: US9YM-010014DP [Walid bin Attash]," Department of Defense (Joint Task Force Guantanamo), December 8, 2006.

[24] Ali Soufan, *The black banners: The inside story of 9/11 and the war against al-Qaeda* (New York: W.W. Norton & Co., 2011): 261–262.

There were other facilitators in Yemen, including Jamal al-Badawi. He rented apartments and bought the boat used in the attack. He fought in Bosnia in the 1990s and then went to Afghanistan and trained in Jihad Wal. He was based in Yemen when al-Qaida decided to start planning for the USS Cole attack.[25]

Two suicide operatives were initially selected for the operation: The Yemenites Taha al-Ahdal and Salman al-Adani. After the attack on the USS *The Sullivans* failed they both died in unrelated events. Al-Ahdal got killed on the frontline in Afghanistan and al-Adani drowned in an accident in Yemen. They were replaced by two other Yemenites, Hassan al-Khamiri and Ibrahim al-Thawr (aka Nibras). There are indications that at least three of the four operatives had fought in Bosnia in the mid-1990s.[26] After the Bosnian war ended in 1995, Arab volunteers typically went home, or sought out other active frontlines, such as in Tajikistan and Chechnya, or went to acquire training in Khost, Afghanistan. The four suicide operatives appear to have followed this pattern, eventually being recruited by Bin Laden in Afghanistan in 1996 or later. One of the USS *Cole* bombers, Al-Khamiri, had allegedly risen in al-Qaida's ranks to become Emir of al-Faruq in Khost at the time of the 1998 missile strikes.[27]

Another member of al-Nashiri's network is worth mentioning. Ahmed al-Darbi, a Saudi from Ta'if, became part of al-Nashiri's network after the USS *Cole* bombing.[28] He was recruited in Saudi Arabia in 1996, went to the Khalden camp to train, and after the three-month Basic Course he was selected to meet with Bin Laden in Jalalabad. Bin Laden sent him for "two to three months" advanced training in Jihad Wal in early 1997. Afterward, he fought on the Taliban's frontline north of Kabul, served in Bin Laden's bodyguard force, and worked as a trainer in al-Farouq camp, while it was located outside Kabul. All these assignments were typical assignments for up-and-coming al-Qaida cadre. Sometime after the USS

[25] YM-0001457, "Detainee Assessment Brief ICO Guantanamo Detainee, ISN PK9YM-0001457DP [Abdu Ali Sharqawi, aka Riyadh the Facilitator]," Department of Defense (Joint Task Force Guantanamo), July 7, 2008; Soufan, *The black banners*, 260.

[26] SA-000669, "Response to the Designated Civilian Official (DCO) Decision to Transfer Guantanamo Detainee, Al Zuhayri, Ahmad Zayid Salim, ISN US9SA-000669DP," Department of Defense (Joint Task Force Guantanamo), December 29, 2008; Soufan, *The black banners*, 239.

[27] Soufan, *The black banners*, 152.

[28] SA-000768, "Recommendation to Retain under DoD Control (DoD) for Guantanamo Detainee, ISN: US9SA-000768 [Ahmed al-Darbi]," Department of Defense (Joint Task Force Guantanamo), October 1, 2004.

Cole attack in October 2000, he started working for al-Nashiri. He was directly involved in organizing a plot to target oil tankers in the Strait of Hormuz.[29]

The *USS Cole* bombing was carried out by a new generation Saudi and Yemenite al-Qaida members who were radicalized in the first half of the 1990s, and who joined al-Qaida in 1996 or later. Al-Nashiri, the leader of the plot, appears to have been the most experienced of the lot, as he was among the oldest (35 years old at the time of the bombing) and fought in Tajikistan at the very beginning of the Tajik civil war in 1992–1993. The others got their first jihadist experiences in Bosnia, and later in Afghanistan under the Taliban. In 1996–1998, Saudis and Yemenis who came to Afghanistan were actively targeted for recruitment by Osama Bin Laden. The *USS Cole* attack was, in a sense, a result of this recruitment effort.

The majority of operatives for the *USS Cole* attack were recruited and trained in Afghanistan – in Bin Laden's Jalalabad residence and in al-Qaida's training camps in Khost. According to one source, al-Qaida's chief explosives expert, Abu Abd al-Rahman al-Muhajir, gave explosives training to al-Nashiri, the plot leader, while the latter was in Afghanistan.[30] Al-Muhajir did not travel to Yemen to build the bomb – as he had done in the East Africa operation – presumably because he was wanted in the 1998 Embassy bombings, and al-Qaida did not want to risk his arrest. However, operatives involved in the *USS Cole* plot travelled freely between Yemen and Afghanistan on forged passports.

After the *USS Cole* attack, there were no US missile strikes on Afghanistan. US authorities suspected that Bin Laden was behind the attack but were not able to prove it with certainty. Key members of al-Nashiri's network, including al-Nashiri and Bin Attash, fled to Afghanistan prior to the attack and only peripheral members were arrested in Yemen. According to the *9/11 Commission Report*, President Clinton decided to not carry out retaliatory strikes, due to the lack of incriminating evidence against Bin Laden. This evidence did not surface until after 2002, when key operatives, including al-Nashiri, were arrested and transferred to the US detention facility at Guantánamo Bay, Cuba.[31]

---

[29] SA-000768.

[30] Soufan, *The black banners*, 264.

[31] Al-Nashiri was arrested in the UAE in November 2002, while Bin Attash was arrested in Karachi, Pakistan in April 2003. They were both sent to the American detention facility at Guantánamo Bay, Cuba.

The lack of a US response further increased the confidence of al-Qaida. In Afghanistan, bin Laden openly praised the *USS Cole* attack. Two of al-Qaida's guesthouses in Kandahar were named after the suicide operatives: The Nibras guesthouse was the main point of entry for new recruits coming to Afghanistan to train in al-Faruq. The Hassan guesthouse was for trained fighters.[32] In February 2001, Bin Laden recited a poem praising the *USS Cole* attack at the wedding of his son Hamza. However, in line with al-Qaida's covert strategy, he was careful not to claim direct responsibility for the attack. Again, the Taliban saw no reason to question Bin Laden about his role in the attacks.

The *USS Cole* attack illustrates how Afghanistan had started playing a more important role as launch pad for al-Qaida's international operations. Most of the *USS Cole* operatives were recruited and trained in Afghanistan in 1996 or later. They were classical jihadists who were looking for opportunities after the Bosnian war ended in 1995. They came to Afghanistan to train or to fight in Tajikistan, and ended up being recruited by Bin Laden. It was not mainly Bin Laden or al-Qaida that attracted these recruits to Afghanistan, but the combination of long-running training camps in Khost, such as Khalden, and active jihadist struggle in Tajikistan.

Another, crucial role played by Afghanistan in both 1998 and 2000 is that it functioned as a safe refuge for operatives who survived al-Qaida's international terrorist plots. This lessened the chance that they might be captured and Bin Laden's role in the plot compromised. It also meant that their expertise and experiences could be transferred to new al-Qaida members. Abu Abd al-Rahman al-Muhajir, the bomb maker in Nairobi and Dar-es-Salam, continued to run bomb-making courses at the Kandahar Airport complex in Afghanistan. Al-Nashiri continued to plot ambitious, sea-borne terrorist attacks for al-Qaida, including the bombing of a French oil tanker, *MV Limburg*, off the coast of Yemen, in 2002. Walid bin Attash, the guy who was briefly arrested in Yemen and subsequently pulled out of the *USS Cole* operation, also continued to be involved in international terrorist planning – including al-Qaida's next, big operation: The 9/11 attacks.[33]

---

[32] See, for example, YM-000689, "Recommendation for Continued Detention Under DoD Control (CD) for Guantanamo Detainee, ISN US9YM-000689DP [Mohammed al-Hatabi]," Department of Defense (Joint Task Force Guantanamo), May 12, 2008.

[33] YM-010014.

THE 9/11 ATTACKS

The course of events on September 11, 2001 are presumably well known. There is hardly a terrorist attack in history that has been more studied and analyzed than the 9/11 attacks.[34] This overview will not go through the timeline or details of the attacks, but concentrates on the attack perpetrators and their links with Afghanistan.

In terms of recruitment, the 9/11 hijackers can roughly be divided into three groups: The "initial selectees" included two Saudis, Khalid al-Midhar and Nawaf al-Hazmi, who were supposed to obtain pilot training but who eventually became muscle hijackers. They were from the same generation al-Qaida members as East Africa operatives Azzam and al-Owhali, and most of the *USS Cole* bombers. They became radicalized in the first half of the 1990s and fought classical *jihad* in Bosnia, before joining Bin Laden in Afghanistan, probably in 1996–1997. They were appointed to be part of the 9/11 plot in spring 1999, when Bin Laden, Abu Hafs and Khalid Sheikh Muhammad started planning for the 9/11 attacks.[35]

The second group of recruits was the "Hamburg cell," comprised of four Arab students in Hamburg: Mohammed Atta from Egypt, Ramzi bin al-Shibh from Yemen, Marwan al-Shehhi from the Emirates, and Ziad Jarrah from Lebanon. They were originally motivated to go to Chechnya to fight, but ended up going to Afghanistan in late 1999. Here, they were approached and recruited by Bin Laden. Three of the four Hamburg cell members became pilots for the 9/11 attack. The fourth, Ramzi bin al-Shibh, failed to get a visa to the United States and instead became the cell's external coordinator.

The third group of recruits were the rest of the muscle hijackers who were recruited in Afghanistan between mid-2000 and April 2001. They were part of a large contingent of recruits who came to Afghanistan after al-Qaida had established its new training camp structure in Kandahar. By mid-2000, this training camp structure appears to have been fully operational, with basic training in the al-Faruq camp outside Kandahar, specialized training at Kandahar Airport, and various sites in Kabul, and systems for registration and evaluation of recruits.

---

[34] For a thorough overview of 9/11, see, in particular, *The 9/11 Commission report*; and Yosri Fouda and Nick Fielding, *Masterminds of terror: The truth behind the most devastating terrorist attack the world has ever seen* (Edinburgh: Mainstream Publishing, 2003).

[35] *The 9/11 Commission report*, 155.

There is one 9/11 perpetrator not mentioned here – the fourth pilot, Saudi-born Hani Hanjour. He was in Afghanistan in the late 1980s to support mujahidin in the Afghan-Soviet war. Later, he moved to the United States, started pilot training in 1996, and finally obtained a commercial certificate in 1999. In spring 2000 he went to Afghanistan to train in al-Farouq, and this is when he was recruited to the 9/11 plot. Hanjour likely replaced one of the original pilot hijackers. At least three other al-Qaida operatives – the "initial selectees" Midhar and Hazmi, and the "Hamburg cell" member Binalshibh – had originally been appointed as pilots but failed along the way. Hanjour, with his pilot's license and long experience living in the United States was the perfect candidate to fill the slot.

The 9/11 hijackers differed from the recruits to the East Africa operation and the *USS Cole* attack, in that only two of them actually had a previous "career" in al-Qaida (see Table 8.1). The "original selectees," Midhar and Hamza, had been in al-Qaida since 1996–1997 and presumably, served in various positions including frontline service with the Taliban. The rest got recruited shortly after their arrival to Afghanistan, and they were generally kept separate from the rest of al-Qaida's cadre. Cell leader Mohammed Atta and the rest of the Hamburg cell were recruited shortly after arriving in Afghanistan in late 1999, and spent most of their time afterward preparing for 9/11. Some of the "muscle hijackers" received basic training in al-Faruq in late 2000, but it is unclear if this happened before or after their selection. After their selection they were told to go home and obtain US visas, then to return to Afghanistan for mission-specific training. This training was given by a private instructor in al-Qaida's Airport Complex in late 2000 to early 2001. Afterward, they were shipped to the United States.[36] In other words the hijackers were kept separate from the rest of al-Qaida's organizational structure in Afghanistan. This makes sense, because of the need to keep the operation secret. It also illustrates how al-Qaida had become more professional in planning international terrorist attacks with a small footprint in Afghanistan.

Al-Qaida's international terrorist attacks in 1998–2001 were secretive operations. Only a few senior al-Qaida members were involved in the planning process. The operations were coordinated by Abu Hafs al-Masri, al-Qaida's military chief, or Osama bin Laden himself. They appointed a chief for the operation: Abu Muhammad al-Masri for East Africa, al-Nashiri for *USS Cole* and Khalid Sheikh Muhammad for 9/11. The international terrorist campaign itself was compartmentalized – to

---

[36] *The 9/11 Commission report*, 234–236.

TABLE 8.1 *Participants in al-Qaida's international terrorist campaign, 1998–2001*

Name	Nationality	Role	Joined AQ
East Africa Operation 1998			
Abu Muhammad al-Masri	Egypt	Leader of Operation	1988–1989
Abu Abd al-Rahman	Egypt	Chief bomb-maker	1988–1989
Nairobi cell			
Fadil Harun	Comoros	Cell leader/ facilitator	1991
Jihad M. Ali al-Harazi (Azzam)	Saudi Arabia	Suicide operative	1996–1997
Mohammed al-Owhali	Saudi Arabia	Suicide operative	1996–1997
Dar es-Salaam cell			
Khalfan Khamis Muhammad	Tanzania	Facilitator	Unknown
Hamden Khalif al-Awad	Egypt	Suicide operative	EIJ
USS Cole attack 2000			
Abd al-Rahim al-Nashiri	Saudi Arabia	Leader of operation	1998
Walid bin Attash (Khallad)	Yemen	Facilitator	1996
Jamal Muhammad al-Badawi	Yemen	Facilitator	1996–1999
Taha al-Ahdal	Yemen	Suicide operative	1996–1999
Salman al-Adani	Yemen	Suicide operative	1996–1999
Hassan al-Khamiri	Yemen	Suicide operative	1996–1998
Ibrahim al-Thawr (Nibras)	Yemen	Suicide operative	1996–1999
Ahmed al-Darbi	Saudi Arabia	Facilitator	1996–1997
9/11 attacks 2001			
Khalid Sheikh Muhammad	Kuwait	Coordinator abroad	1999
Ramzi bin al-Shibh	Yemen	Coordinator abroad	1999
American Airlines 11			
Mohammed Atta	Egypt	Cell leader, Pilot hijacker	1999
Abdulaziz al-Omari	Saudi Arabia	Muscle hijacker	2000–2001
Wail al-Shehri	Saudi Arabia	Muscle hijacker	2000–2001
Walid al-Shehri	Saudi Arabia	Muscle hijacker	2000–2001
Satam al-Suqami	Saudi Arabia	Muscle hijacker	2000–2001
United Airlines 175			
Marwan al-Shehhi	UAE	Pilot hijacker	1999
Fayez Banihammad	UAE	Muscle hijacker	2000–2001
Mohannad al-Shehri	Saudi Arabia	Muscle hijacker	2000–2001
Hamza al-Ghamidi	Saudi Arabia	Muscle hijacker	2000–2001
Ahmed al-Ghamidi	Saudi Arabia	Muscle hijacker	2000–2001

(continued)

TABLE 8.1 *(Continued)*

Name	Nationality	Role	Joined AQ
American Airlines 77			
Hani Hanjour	Saudi Arabia	Pilot hijacker	2000
Khalid al-Midhar	Saudi Arabia	Muscle hijacker	2000–2001
Majid Moqed	Saudi Arabia	Muscle hijacker	2000–2001
Nawaf al-Hazmi	Saudi Arabia	Muscle hijacker	2000–2001
Salem al-Hazmi	Saudi Arabia	Muscle hijacker	2000–2001
United Airlines 93			
Ziyad Jarrah	Lebanon	Pilot hijacker	1999
Ahmed al-Haznawi	Saudi Arabia	Muscle hijacker	2000–2001
Ahmed al-Nami	Saudi Arabia	Muscle hijacker	2000–2001
Saeed al-Ghamdi	Saudi Arabia	Muscle hijacker	2000–2001

the extent that al-Nashiri probably did not know about Khalid Sheikh Muhammad's attack plotting, and vice-versa. Bin Laden or Abu Hafs usually selected suicide operatives and gave them training in Afghanistan when appropriate. The exception, it seems, is the *USS Cole* attack in which al-Nashiri may have selected the suicide operatives without Bin Laden's approval.[37] Abu Hafs also appointed key personnel to give technical assistance whenever appropriate. In the 1998 attack, the chief bomb-maker, al-Muhajir, traveled outside Afghanistan to give assistance. After 1998, when al-Qaida tightened its security, mission-specific training was given inside Afghanistan, usually at al-Qaida's special facility at Kandahar Airport.

Over time, al-Qaida leadership increasingly relied on "outsiders" to plan and carry out international attacks. By "outsiders" I mean militants who were not part of al-Qaida's cadre development program. As detailed in Chapter 5, the cadre would follow specific training courses and serve in various positions on the frontline, as guesthouse managers, or in al-Qaida's guard force. They would eventually fill senior positions in the organization. The international terrorist campaign was organized separately, by a small elite within the organization and relied on newly arrived recruits to execute the operation. If we study al-Qaida's terrorist campaign in isolation, we see a highly professional network with international reach and adeptness at operational security. But when we see it in relation with al-Qaida's other activities in Afghanistan, we see the contours of a dual strategy.

---

[37] *The 9/11 Commission report*, 191.

9

Al-Qaida's Dual Strategy

Al-Qaida was involved in a range of activities in Afghanistan not immediately connected to international terrorism. Some of these activities were designed to support the Taliban and other militant groups. The duty to support other Muslims was at the core of al-Qaida's philosophy as described in its foundation documents from 1988. However, it was not a strategic priority.

The main argument presented here is that after Bin Laden's return to Afghanistan in 1996, al-Qaida followed a dual strategy. While a small part of al-Qaida was involved in staging international terrorist attacks, the larger part was involved in building a resilient organization. The strategy was designed not just for the short-term goal of expelling the United States from the Middle East, but for the long-term goal of ousting local Arab governments and replacing them with Islamic ones. In the following sections, I review al-Qaida's activities in Afghanistan over time and explain how the dual strategy developed and why. I end with a discussion of the strategic rationale behind 9/11.

THE EARLY PERIOD (1988–1996)

Al-Qaida's foundation charter from 1988 stated that "cadre preparation" and "spreading the sentiment of *jihad*" should be the core tasks of the organization.[1] The core tasks are well reflected in al-Qaida's activities in Afghanistan in 1988–1992. In this period, al-Qaida established its first training camps in Khost and Nangarhar. The purpose of the camps was

[1] Berger, *Benevolence International*, 345.

to train Arab guerrilla units to fight on the frontlines in Afghanistan. Most of these units fought in the war against the Afghan Communist regime in 1989–1992. All major Islamist resistance parties in Afghanistan viewed the Afghan Najibullah regime as an extension of the Soviet occupation of Afghanistan. Fighting Najibullah was therefore seen as a legitimate *jihad*.

In the camps, al-Qaida developed a relatively professional training methodology. This was likely due to Bin Laden's targeted recruitment of former Egyptian Army officers such as Abu Hafs al-Masri, into the organization. Al-Qaida had high ambitions and high standards for its training. Ambitions were so high that in al-Qaida's very first training course in 1989, only three of about fifty recruits passed the course. Al-Qaida later adjusted the requirements, illustrating how al-Qaida was a learning organization. Meanwhile al-Qaida spread "the sentiment of *jihad*" among Afghan mujahidin, mainly by promoting a culture of martyrdom and self-sacrifice.

After the start of the Afghan civil war in 1992, al-Qaida stopped participating on the frontlines in Afghanistan. The reason was that al-Qaida, like the majority of the Afghan-Arab community in Peshawar, saw fighting in the Afghan civil war as a *fitna* (civil strife) rather than legitimate *jihad*. Al-Qaida continued to use Afghanistan for training, but without sending fighters to frontlines. In this period al-Qaida arranged the first known "cadre course" – a course dedicated to educating midlevel leaders for al-Qaida's organization. Then al-Qaida embarked upon a new project. Bin Laden moved to Sudan to support the nascent Islamic regime of Hassan al-Turabi, while al-Qaida's military committee sent a group of senior cadre to Somalia to train Islamist guerrillas there.

Al-Qaida kept a small contingent in Afghanistan to maintain al-Qaida's training camps, but this was challenging for two reasons. First, Pakistani authorities started to intensify their security crackdowns on Arabs in Peshawar and put in place an extradition treaty with Egypt. This meant that al-Qaida's cadre lost their freedom of movement. Secondly, the camps inside Afghanistan experienced pressure from Afghan mujahidin groups who wanted al-Qaida's weapons and ammunition for the civil war. As a result most of al-Qaida moved to East Africa and prioritized the training mission in Somalia.

During 1992–1996, al-Qaida spent most of its military resources in Somalia to train local Islamist guerrillas there. Thus al-Qaida's cadre training continued, but on a local level. At the same time, Bin Laden invested heavily in the Sudan – partly in an effort to support the nascent

Islamic state of Hassan al-Turabi. Al-Qaida as an organization was not involved in fighting in this period but Bin Laden probably provided financial and moral support to other groups. Veterans of the Afghan-Arab movement were involved in various conflicts especially in Algeria and Bosnia. Two jihadi groups – the Armed Islamic Group (GIA) and Egyptian Islamic Jihad (EIJ) – started to use international terrorism as part of their strategy. Al-Qaida would soon follow suit, but not until after Bin Laden's return to Afghanistan in 1996.

LAUNCHING THE NEW WAR (1996–1998)

In 1996, Bin Laden was expelled from Sudan. He returned to Nangarhar in Eastern Afghanistan as there were few other options available at the time. Afghanistan was still at civil war, but Nangarhar at the time was relatively peaceful. Bin Laden enjoyed the protection of a local commander, Engineer Mahmoud, whom he knew well from the Afghan-Soviet war. In addition, al-Qaida still had access to a cluster of training camps in Khost. The training camps were under the protection of the local government there, which was connected to the Zadran tribe of Jalaluddin Haqqani. At the time of Bin Laden's return to Afghanistan, the Khost government had already joined the Taliban. In practice this made little difference, because the Taliban left it up to the local government to run the affairs in the province.

Shortly after his return to Afghanistan, Bin Laden declared war on US troops in Saudi Arabia. Bin Laden's anti-American sentiment had been building up over time, in part caused by the stationing of US forces in Saudi Arabia after the first Gulf War in 1991, and in part due to his own failed attempts at "reforming" the Saudi Arabian regime. His expulsion from Sudan in 1996, which was caused in part by US pressure on the Sudan, appears to have been the last straw. Shortly after Bin Laden's return to Afghanistan he activated al-Qaida's training camps in Khost and started targeting Saudis and Yemenis for recruitment. At this time, Bin Laden had not yet entered into a formal alliance with the Taliban, but enjoyed the protection of local tribal leaders on Afghanistan's periphery. Bin Laden was determined to fight the war against the United States, even if he did not yet enjoy formal sanctuary with the Taliban.

Initially it appears that Bin Laden envisioned a "guerrilla war" against US troops in Saudi Arabia. In practice this would mean a campaign of terrorist attacks carried out by a clandestine organization trained in Afghanistan, then sent back to Saudi Arabia. There were two major challenges. First, Bin Laden did not have a large following in Saudi Arabia. He had around a hundred followers in Afghanistan, but almost none of them were Saudis. If al-Qaida was going to start a guerrilla campaign in Saudi Arabia, they literally had to start from scratch.

The second challenge was that Bin Laden's call for *jihad* did not resonate well with dominant perceptions of militant *jihad* at the time – neither on the Peninsula nor elsewhere. Militant *jihad* in the 1990s took two main forms. First, there was the view that *jihad* against "apostate rulers" was more important than *jihad* against foreign invaders. This view was promoted by, among others, the influential Jordanian ideologue Abu Muhammad al-Maqdisi.[2] It was operationalized by large revolutionary movements, such as the Armed Islamic Group (GIA) in Algeria, and Egyptian Islamic Jihad and al-Jama'a al-Islamiyya in Egypt, in the 1990s. By calling for attacks on the Americans, Bin Laden argued for prioritizing the original infidels before the apostate rulers. This was hard to accept for militants who had grown up looking to revolutionary Islamists as their heroes. Besides, there were authoritative Islamic sources – including the Quran itself – arguing that "near enemies" should be prioritized.[3]

Then, there was the view that fighting the foreign invader should take precedence over fighting apostate rulers. Abdullah Azzam was the proponent of this view, which has been coined classical *jihad*.[4] The classical *jihad* was operationalized by the Afghan-Arab movement who fought the Soviet invasion of Afghanistan in the 1980s, and by foreign fighters in Bosnia and Chechnya in the 1990s. To make his arguments resonate with Azzam's views, Bin Laden framed the Americans as "foreign occupiers" by referring to the presence of American military troops in Saudi Arabia. But this also meant that he had to declare the Saudi regime as apostates, because it was the Saudi regime that had invited US troops into the country. The argumentation itself was not new. The so-called *Sahwa* ("Awakening") movement had declared the presence of US troops in Saudi Arabia illegal already back in 1991. But the Sahwa was generally not interested in armed *jihad*. Bin Laden's attempt to tap into the grievances of the Sahwa thus resonated with a radical fringe of the movement only. As for the classical jihadists, they generally viewed the Saudi regime as legitimate – the regime had even sponsored and assisted classical *jihad* in Afghanistan, Bosnia, and elsewhere.

---

[2] Joas Wagemakers, *A quietist jihadi: The ideology and influence of Abu Muhammad al-Maqdisi* (New York: Cambridge University Press, 2012): 70–71.

[3] Wagemakers, *A quietist jihadi*, 70–71.

[4] Hegghammer, *Jihad in Saudi Arabia*, 7.

Bin Laden's 1996 *Declaration of jihad* on the United States thus fell between two chairs. It did not resonate with revolutionary Islamists who believed that near enemies should be prioritized. It did not resonate with the classical jihadists who believed the Saudi royal family to be legitimate Islamic rulers, and who therefore preferred fighting abroad. Al-Qaida needed to demonstrate the power of their own narrative. They needed to convince the Muslims that their agenda was sound and that it was feasible. Only then would Bin Laden be able to attract the number of recruits needed to build up a clandestine organization in the Arabian Peninsula – or elsewhere, for that matter. But how should they do it when al-Qaida did not yet have an operational network in the Peninsula?

Al-Qaida activated its strongest military asset at the time – a dormant network of experienced operatives in East Africa – and tasked them with carrying out an attack on American targets in the region. This is how international terrorism became part of al-Qaida's strategy. The concept was not really new. Al-Qaida simply returned to the core task of spreading the sentiment of *jihad* by carrying out professional, yet daring attacks and promoting a culture of martyrdom and self-sacrifice.

Al-Qaida may have reasoned at this stage that international terrorism was a more effective way of harming the United States than guerrilla attacks against US targets inside the Peninsula. They may also have reasoned that international terrorist attacks would kill fewer innocent Muslims than attacks inside a Muslim country. But ultimately, the choice was taken as a result of many contributing factors, not least, the need to launch al-Qaida's agenda during a time when few would be interested in – or could not even fathom – that there could be alternative ways of waging *jihad*.

The East Africa operation cannot be understood in the context of military strategy alone. Al-Qaida had not yet built an organization in Afghanistan at the time of the attack and they spent their most precious military asset – the East Africa network – on one single attack. Al-Qaida's networks in East Africa were dismantled after the attack and remaining members relocated to Afghanistan. Al-Qaida then had to spend time building up a new attack capacity. Why not build the organization first, and then carry out a more intensive attack campaign? This supports the interpretation that the main purpose of the East Africa operation was propaganda.

Like almost all terrorist attacks, the East Africa operation was shaped by coincidences and human mistakes. The attack in Nairobi killed a large number of Kenyan Muslims, which was probably not part of the original plan. A few al-Qaida operatives, including the senior al-Qaida member Mohammed Siddiq Odeh, got arrested after the attack and handed over to the United States. At the time of the attacks, al-Qaida also lacked a clear propaganda strategy: No one filmed the operations and none of the suicide bombers recorded their testament prior to the attack. But in the end, even the failures seemed somehow to work to al-Qaida's advantage. The large number of casualties in the Nairobi bombing ensured that that the attacks generated huge media attention. The testimony of Mohammed Odeh and other arrested suspects made sure that Bin Laden was indicted in the case, and thus, he became an instant celebrity. The United States even sent cruise missiles to Afghanistan to try and kill him. The Taliban, for their part, refused to expel Bin Laden from their country, arguing he was their "guest." Luckily for al-Qaida, the Taliban did not suspect – or did not want to know about – Bin Laden's direct role in the attacks. Bin Laden was ensured continued protection in Afghanistan under the Taliban.

By 1998, al-Qaida had successfully launched its war on the United States and from now on they would focus on two activities in Afghanistan: Organization-building and continuation of the international terrorist campaign. The two activities were mutually reinforcing: The international terrorist campaign strengthened al-Qaida's image, boosted their credibility, and helped draw recruits to Afghanistan. The organization-building made it easier to select and train suicide operatives for the international terrorist campaign. The period from 1999–2001 was a period of huge expansion, thanks in part to al-Qaida's alliance with the Taliban regime.

EXPANSION UNDER THE TALIBAN (1999–2001)

Osama bin Laden entered into a formal alliance with the Taliban in the spring of 1997, when he met with Mullah Omar in Kandahar and agreed to carry out reconstruction projects and to send fighters to the Taliban's frontline. The Taliban's conquest of Afghanistan in 1996 had been an unexpected turn of events for al-Qaida, but by mid-1997, al-Qaida's leadership seemed convinced that the Taliban's state-building project was a project worth supporting. When al-Qaida decided to expand their organization in 1998, their alliance with the Taliban turned out to be fruitful.

Al-Qaida's decision to build an organization under the Taliban did face certain challenges. First, the Taliban put restrictions on Bin Laden's propaganda campaign. This meant that Bin Laden could not openly take responsibility for terrorist attacks or call on people to come to

Afghanistan to train. In the end, this did not seem to hamper al-Qaida's ability at drawing recruits to Afghanistan. Over time, al-Qaida developed a network of professional recruiters in the Gulf and enlisted charismatic Saudi scholars to talk warmly about Taliban and al-Qaida. These efforts contributed directly to recruitment from the Arabian Peninsula to al-Qaida's camps in 1999–2001.[5]

Another challenge was that al-Qaida's frontline participation with the Taliban was controversial. The Taliban was not fighting a foreign occupier, but the Tajik commander Ahmed Shah Massoud, who was a fellow Muslim and a hero from the Afghan-Soviet war. Many of the recruits coming to Afghanistan were reluctant to believe that fighting Massoud was a legitimate *jihad*. To minimize these controversies, al-Qaida propped up the Taliban's Islamic Emirate as a true Islamic state, with Mullah Omar its legitimate leader. Bin Laden's political support to the Taliban, including his public oath of allegiance in 2001, may be seen as part of this effort.

Despite these minor challenges, al-Qaida's alliance with the Taliban had enormous benefits for al-Qaida's organization-building project. Al-Qaida enjoyed freedom of movement within Afghanistan. They were allowed to run training camps in Kandahar and Kabul. The Taliban's frontline gave opportunity to test and train cadre for al-Qaida's organization. It was easy for recruits to enter and exit Afghanistan, both through official and unofficial border-crossings.[6]

Crucially, al-Qaida believed that frontlines would continue to exist in the region, even after the Taliban conquered all of Afghanistan. Abu Hafs in 1997 seemed convinced that the Taliban would be willing to extend the *jihad* to Central Asia after Afghanistan was won. The Taliban's extension of support to the Islamic Movement of Uzbekistan (IMU) in 1999 was another hint in that direction. We do not know if the Taliban would actually have pursued such a strategy, if they had remained in power. There were certainly elements within Taliban's leadership who would have opposed an expansionist policy. But this is beside the point. Al-Qaida adjusted their strategies to their own perceived reality. In their view, the Taliban state had the potential to become a launch pad for Islamic revolution elsewhere, not least, in the neighboring countries with suppressed Muslim populations, such as Central Asia. All of this made the Taliban state the perfect location for al-Qaida's organization-building project.

[5] Based on statements of Guantánamo detainees, who emphasised the role of professional recruiters.
[6] Harun, *al-harb ala al-islam.*

Meanwhile, al-Qaida's planning for international terrorist attacks continued unabated. Planning for the USS *Cole* attack started in late 1998 and planning for 9/11 started in early 1999. The terrorist campaign followed a familiar pattern of gradual escalation in both ambition and violence. The activities ran parallel to, but organizationally separate from, al-Qaida's efforts at building a resilient organization in Afghanistan.

By mid-2000, al-Qaida had opened their flagship training facility, al-Faruq in Kandahar. They had succeeded in setting up a recruitment and facilitation network in the Arabian Peninsula. They had expanded into a "services office" in Afghanistan, organizing the influx of recruits and offering training and support to other militant groups, even those that did not explicitly support Bin Laden's far-enemy strategy. And Bin Laden experienced the continued support of the Taliban regime – especially in late 1999, when the Taliban decided to protect Bin Laden even when faced with UN sanctions. In mid-2000 al-Qaida was a confident organization – even thinking of itself as a "government in exile."[7]

Al-Qaida's confidence was boosted when the United States failed to respond to the USS *Cole* attack in October 2000. Al-Qaida was prepared that the United States might carry out a new set of missile strikes against al-Qaida's camps, similar to what they had done in 1998. But nothing happened. The USS *Cole* attack provoked no US response at all. This probably contributed to convincing Bin Laden that his strategy was working and that the United States was becoming weaker by the day.

THE STRATEGY BEHIND 9/11

There are two dominant views on the strategic rationale behind 9/11: One camp argues that the purpose of 9/11 was to drag the United States into a costly guerrilla war in Afghanistan. The other camp argues that the purpose of 9/11 was to make the United States crumble and withdraw into self-imposed isolation. The two views are irreconcilable: The first view describes 9/11 as a strategic success for al-Qaida, whereas the second describes it as a strategic failure. I argue that both views represent thoughts and desires of Bin Laden at the time of 9/11: Bin Laden believed – though he was not certain – that the United States would collapse as a result of 9/11. Bin Laden was willing to – though it was not his first choice – to meet Americans in face-to-face combat in Afghanistan.

[7] In AFGP-2002–801138, 99.

However, none of the views presented earlier give an accurate description of al-Qaida's pre-9/11 strategy.

To understand al-Qaida's strategic behavior it is necessary first of all, to realize that al-Qaida's strategies were never fixed. They were constantly adjusted to make use of opportunities that arose. Up until 9/11, Bin Laden did not know how devastating the attacks would be, or how the United States would react to them. This view is supported in contemporary primary sources. In a videotaped conversation between Bin Laden and a Saudi Shaykh visiting Afghanistan on November 7, 2001, Bin Laden stated,

... we calculated in advance the number of casualties from the enemy, who would be killed based on the position of the [World Trade Center] tower. We calculated that the floors that would be hit would be three or four floors. I was the most optimistic of them all ... I was thinking that the fire from the gas in the plane would melt the iron structure of the building and collapse the area where the plane hit and all the floors above it only. This is all that we had hoped for.[8]

Furthermore, Bin Laden believed that no matter how the United States chose to react to 9/11, the reaction would serve al-Qaida's goals. In a letter to Mullah Omar dated October 3, 2001, only four days before the US-led bombing campaign on Afghanistan, Bin Laden outlined his argument in detail:

1) If [America] remains silent and fails to respond to the jihadi operations, it will lose prestige internationally. This will in turn force America to withdraw its forces from abroad and to concentrate on domestic matters ... It will be transformed from a superpower to a third-rate power, like Russia.

2) If [America] carries out a [military] campaign against Afghanistan, it will carry a heavy economic burden for an extended period of time. This will in turn ... cause it to suffer the same destiny as the USSR: Withdrawal from Afghanistan, fragmentation, and self-imposed isolation.[9]

---

[8] Osama bin Laden, "Transcript of Usama bin Laden video tape," text of conversation between Osama bin Laden and Shaykh Khaled al-Harbi in Afghanistan on November 7, 2001, translated by George Michael and Kassem M. Wahba on December 13, 2001. Unpublished, courtesy Norwegian Government official (anonymized).

[9] Osama bin Laden, "*ila ali al-qadr amir al-mu'minin al-mulla muhammad 'umar mujahid hafidhahu allah* [letter to Mullah Omar from Osama bin Laden dated October 3, 2001]," unpublished, courtesy former Taliban official (anonymized).

The strategic rationale behind 9/11 must be understood in light of al-Qaida's own perception of their struggle. In June 2001, Bin Laden described al-Qaida's struggle as a three-phased process. First, to expel the Americans from the Middle East. Second, to oust the local Arab governments. And third, to establish Islamic governments in their place. In 2001 al-Qaida was still in the first phase of the struggle. The goal of this phase was to expel the Americans from the Middle East, primarily through a strategy of international terrorism. But al-Qaida's pre-9/11 strategy was not just designed for the short-term goal of expelling the United States from the Middle East, but for the long-term goal of ousting local Arab governments and replacing them with Islamic ones. This is why al-Qaida followed a dual strategy in Afghanistan: organization building and international terrorism.

No matter the outcome of 9/11, al-Qaida needed a resilient organization in Afghanistan. If the United States collapsed after 9/11 – which is likely what Bin Laden hoped for – al-Qaida would be ready to move to the second phase of their plan: A campaign of revolutionary violence in the Middle East. If the United States invaded Afghanistan, al-Qaida would continue with the first phase of the plan, but with a different military strategy that involved guerrilla warfare on Afghan soil. Afghanistan thus played a central part in al-Qaida's war-fighting strategy prior to 9/11: as a launch pad for Islamic revolution or, alternatively, as a graveyard for al-Qaida's enemies.

AL-QAIDA'S DILEMMA

Bin Laden did not intend the United States to invade Afghanistan in 2001 and destroy the Taliban regime, but he was willing to accept the risk that it might happen. It may seem like an idiosyncrasy. Practically everyone who knew Bin Laden describe him as a pious Muslim who dedicated his life to establishing Islamic rule on earth. Yet, he was willing to bring about the destruction of the Taliban's Islamic state – one that he himself had helped nurture – for the sake of pursuing what must be viewed as a modern strategy of international terrorism.

Bin Laden himself did not see it that way. He argued that the Prophet Muhammed's first action after becoming a Muslim was to wage *jihad* to spread Islam. Thus, *jihad* was a more important duty than everything else in Islam including prayer, fasting, alms, and pilgrimage. Bin Laden's Salafi background shines through in his argumentation. Salafis believe it is important to go back to the very fundamentals of Islam to find guidance for correct behavior. Bin Laden claimed that by putting *jihad* above everything else, he was simply following the example of the Prophet. But in reality, it allowed him to put aside core tenets of Islam for the sake of waging a modern campaign of international terrorism.

Was 9/11, then, a result of Bin Laden's "religious fanaticism" or modern political grievances? The answer is neither. 9/11 was the result of Bin Laden's self-perception and belief in the superiority of his own strategy. The self-perception said that al-Qaida was the vanguard of the Islamic revolution. The strategy said that war against the United States was an absolutely necessary step toward Islamic revolutions in the Middle East.

Just like in Jaji in 1987, Bin Laden again stepped up to take the battle that no one else dared to take – even at the peril of himself, and those around him.

Epilogue

"I have been betrayed," said Ahmad Saʻid Khadr, the Egyptian-Canadian veteran of the mujahidin movement and long-time acquaintance of Osama bin Laden.[1] It was September 12, 2001, and it would soon become impossible to be an Arab in Afghanistan. The United States – still in shock after the devastating terrorist attacks on New York and Washington the day before – was about to start a manhunt for anyone even remotely connected to Bin Laden's organization. Khadr was an Arab living in Afghanistan, which by itself could be reason enough to become a suspect. But his case was gloomier. He had met Bin Laden on several occasions and his Kabul-based charity – the Health and Education Project International – was suspected of involvement in transferring money on behalf of al-Qaida. On October 10, 2001, the United States elevated Khadr to a "prime suspect" in the September 11 terrorist attacks.

In reality, it is unlikely that Khadr had advance knowledge of the 9/11 attacks, let alone that he assisted in planning them. Nevertheless he became one of many of the Arab casualties in the US-led War on Terror. Like many Arabs in Afghanistan at the time, Khadr initially joined the campaign to defend the Taliban regime against the US-led invasion in October–December 2001. Then he went into hiding in the Tribal Areas of Pakistan and was killed in 2003 in a shootout with Pakistani security forces.[2]

---

[1] Author's interview with eyewitness source (anonymized).
[2] Abu Ubayda al-Maqdisi, *shuhada fi zaman al-ghurba* (N.p.: Al-Fajr Media Center, 2008): 178.

Al-Qaida itself suffered heavy losses in the US-led military campaign on Afghanistan. They lost the sanctuary they had enjoyed under the Taliban. They lost their training camp infrastructure and the unique freedom of movement that only a state-sponsored sanctuary could offer. They lost their most talented military commander, Abu Hafs al-Masri, who was killed in an air strike in November 2001.

Al-Qaida must also have lost confidence. The Arab fighters who gathered to fight the Americans in Tora Bora and in Kandahar Airport in December 2001 did not stand a chance against the superior US airpower. Bin Laden's pessimism at the height of the Tora Bora campaign shines through in the will he wrote during the battle, and in radio conversations intercepted by the United States. "I'm sorry for getting you involved in this battle, if you can no longer resist, you may surrender with my blessing," was allegedly Bin Laden's last words to his fighters.[3]

But Bin Laden escaped the US military campaign and so did a number of high-ranking cadre, including Ayman al-Zawahiri, Sayf al-Adl, Abu Muhammad al-Masri, and Abd al-Hadi al-Iraqi. Al-Qaida's leadership at this point dispersed into three areas: Sayf al-Adl led a group who fled to Iran and who were put under various forms of house arrest from 2002. This group included Mustafa Hamid, the Egyptian journalist-turned jihadist who was always close to al-Qaida leadership but who never joined al-Qaida; Abu Muhammad al-Masri who staged the East Africa operation and who later became administrator of al-Qaida's camps and fronts in Afghanistan; and several of Bin Laden's family members.

A second group hid in the Pakistani Tribal Areas, primarily in South and North Waziristan. They included Abd al-Hadi al-Iraqi and Hamza al-Ghamidi, who had been high-ranking frontline commanders for al-Qaida in Afghanistan. They continued to support the Taliban's guerrilla war in Afghanistan along with several non-al-Qaida members, such as Abu al-Layth al-Libi, a Libyan jihadist who had abandoned the nationalist struggle in Libya and dedicated himself to fighting on the Taliban's frontlines. The group also included members of al-Qaida's new international operations branch – al-Qaida members who planned international terrorist operations after 2001, including the London bombings on July 7, 2005.

A third group were the city dwellers – al-Qaida operatives who hid in large Pakistani cities such as Karachi and Rawalpindi, and in lesser-known, smaller cities such as Abbottabad. Here we find the remains of al-Qaida's

---

[3] Dalton Fury, *Kill Bin Laden: a Delta Force Commander's account of the hunt for the world's most wanted man* (New York: St. Martin's Press, 2008): 233–34.

old international operations network, which was heavily targeted by Pakistani security forces after 2001. Ramzi bin al-Shibh, coordinator for 9/11 was arrested in Karachi in 2002. Walid bin Attash, facilitator in both *USS Cole* and 9/11 was arrested in Karachi in 2003. Khalid Sheikh Muhammad, mastermind of 9/11, was captured in Rawalpindi in 2003. In this group we also find some high-ranking leaders. Osama bin Laden was located and killed by a team of CIA operatives in Abbottabad in May 2011. As for Ayman al-Zawahiri, who took over leadership of al-Qaida after Bin Laden's death, his current whereabouts are unknown.

From these three locations – Iran, Waziristan, and large Pakistani cities – al-Qaida continued to operate as an organization after 2001. To outline al-Qaida's activities after 2001 is beyond the scope of this book. Let me just end with some preliminary thoughts about al-Qaida's post-2001 strategy.

After losing their sanctuary in Afghanistan, al-Qaida was forced to alter their strategy. Instead of building an organization on the fringe of the Muslim world, they started supporting Islamist guerrillas in the center. After 2001, al-Qaida established local branches in the Middle East and North Africa including al-Qaida in Iraq (AQI), al-Qaida on the Arabian Peninsula (AQAP) and al-Qaida in the Islamic Maghreb (AQIM). Al-Qaida did not build the organizations from scratch, but tapped into existing insurgent movements and allowed them to use al-Qaida's brand name.

At the same time, al-Qaida continued its international terrorist campaign – not in a covert manner from a state-sponsored sanctuary (i.e. Taliban-run Afghanistan), but from Muslim tribal areas outside state control such as Waziristan and later, from tribal areas of Yemen. The dual strategy of organization-building and international terrorism remained, but the various activities got geographically separated. As a result, violence that was carried out in al-Qaida's name frequently spun out of control and gave al-Qaida a bad reputation. The leader of al-Qaida in Iraq, Abu Mus'ab al-Zarqawi is a case in point. Al-Zarqawi spent time in al-Qaida's training camps in late 1999, but he was not an al-Qaida member, and he was never educated within al-Qaida's cadre development program. In sum, there is little doubt that the US-led invasion of Afghanistan in 2001 had negative effects on the organizational cohesion of al-Qaida.

Would al-Qaida be able to reestablish their sanctuary in Afghanistan, should the Taliban come back to power? This scenario was the reason that the United States went to war with the Taliban in the first place, and why they invested millions of dollars in a counterinsurgency campaign in

Afghanistan. The question of what would happen to al-Qaida if Taliban came back to power has been asked many times. But the question is obsolete, because the world has moved on since 2001.

First, the war against terror has changed. The drone has become an accepted weapon. Drone technology has made it harder for al-Qaida to maintain physical sanctuaries. The drone technology pushes al-Qaida further underground, and further out into the tribal periphery. Drones do not differ between tribal sanctuaries and Taliban-controlled territory.

Second, the Taliban has changed. The Taliban was always divided on whether to host Bin Laden or not. Mullah Omar – often described as the main proponent of hosting Bin Laden – passed away in 2013 and the leadership is in the process of being transferred to a next generation. In any case, different personal and tribal dynamics shape the decisions of the Taliban. We still know little of how these dynamics worked during the Taliban regime and we know even less about how they work today.

Third, al-Qaida's near enemies have changed. The enemy that al-Qaida was countering in 1996–2001 – the Middle Eastern dictators – have been ousted in a series of popular revolutions known as the 'Arab Spring'. Some countries are run by new dictators, much in the same fashion as before. Others have collapsed into civil war, creating new opportunities and challenges for the jihadist movement.

Finally, al-Qaida's organization has changed. Osama bin Laden is dead. Ayman al-Zawahiri has taken over as leader. A number of al-Qaida's cadre have been killed or captured. Others have defected to rival groups like the Islamic State. Al-Qaida is weakened, but it does not mean they are irrelevant. Al-Qaida has most certainly adapted its strategy to fit to the new realities, as it did so many times in the past. So the question we should ask now is not whether al-Qaida will ever be able to return to Afghanistan but what their next strategy is going to be.

Select Bibliography

ARABIC PRIMARY SOURCES

Abu Qudama, Salih al-Hami. *fursan al-farida al-gha'iba: al-zarqawi wa al-jihad al-afghan.* Place and publisher unknown, 2007. Accessed via *Jihadi Document Repository*, University of Oslo on February 24, 2016. www.hf.uio.no/ikos/english/research/jihadi-document-repository/

al-Adl, Sayf. *tajrubati ma'a abi mus'ab al-zarqawi.* Undated, Minbar al-Tawhid wal-Jihad. Accessed October 12, 2011. www.tawhed.ws/pr?i=6477

"'al-afghan-al-arab' ikhtaffu am tahawwalu ila 'taliban arab'? taliban wa kabul: ma'rakat taqsim afghanistan." *al-Hayat,* September 30, 1996.

"akthtar min ra'i: mustaqbal al-afghan al-arab ba'da hazimat taliban." *al-Jazeera,* November 23, 2001. Accessed February 25, 2016. www.aljazeera.net/

"al-amil al-mazduj 'ramzi' lil-hayat: rattabna liqa' lil-zawahiri ma'a khattab fa-i'taqalatu al-shurta al-daghestaniyya ... wa-rashwa bi-40 alf dular i'adatahu ila afghanistan." *al-Hayat,* March 9, 2014. Accessed February 25, 2016. www.alhayat.com/Articles/977568

"ba'dama ablaghahu za'im al-haraka 'istiya'ihi' min tasrihatihi. bin ladin wa'ada 'taliban' bi-waqf al-tahdid min afghanistan." *al-Hayat,* August 25, 1998.

Bin Laden, Osama. "i'lan al-jihad ala al-amrikyyin al-muhtallin li-bilad al-haramayn." *al-Quds al-Arabi,* August 23, 1996.

"bayan al-jabha al-islamiyya al-alamiyya li-jihad al-yahud wa al-salibiyyin." *al-Quds al-Arabi,* February 23, 1998.

bushrayat lil-shaykh usama. Speech given in Afghanistan, around June 19, 2001. Published by al-Sahab, July 2014. *FFI's Jihadi Video Database,* Kjeller, Norway, video no. 855.

"ila ali al-qadr amir al-mu'minin al-mulla muhammad umar mujahid hafid-hahu allah." October 3, 2001. Unpublished, courtesy former Taliban official (anonymized).

"khutbat id al-fitr 1420 h." al-Sahab, January 2000. Transcribed by Nukhbat al-I'lam al-Jihadi.

al-Dakhil, Turki. *"tarhib irani bi-qarar al-sa'udiyya talab rahil al-qa'im bi al-a'mal al-afghani."* al-Hayat, September 24, 1998.

Diraz, Isam. *usama bin ladin yarwi ma'arik ma'sadat al-ansar al-arab bi-afghanistan.* First edition. Cairo: Al-Manar al-Jadid, 1991.

Hamid, Mustafa. *khiyana ala al-tariq.* Place and publisher unknown, date unknown. Accessed via *Jihadi Document Repository*, University of Oslo, on February 12, 2016. www.hf.uio.no/ikos/english/research/jihadi-document-repository/

al-hamaqa al-kubra. Place and publisher unknown, date unknown. Accessed via *Jihadi Document Repository*, University of Oslo, on February 12, 2016. www.hf.uio.no/ikos/english/research/jihadi-document-repository/

al-matar 90. Place and publisher unknown, date unknown. Accessed via *Jihadi Document Repository*, University of Oslo, on March 11, 2016. www.hf.uio .no/ikos/english/research/jihadi-document-repository/

fatah khost. Place and publisher unknown, date unknown. Accessed via *Jihadi Document Repository*, University of Oslo, on February 12, 2016. www .hf.uio.no/ikos/english/research/jihadi-document-repository/

mashru' tajikistan. Place and publisher unknown, date unknown. Accessed via *Jihadi Document Repository*, University of Oslo, on February 12, 2016. www.hf.uio.no/ikos/english/research/jihadi-document-repository/

"bin ladin wa harakat taliban: sina'at al-harb wa al-hazima." Mafa al-Siyasi – Adab al-Matarid, May 3, 2010. Accessed November 5, 2010. www.mafa .asia/ar/temp.php?K_Mafa=10521&id1=7&detail=38&cnl=0&t_p=1

Harun, Fadil [Fadil Abdallah Muhammad]. *al-harb ala al-islam: qissat fadil harun.* Vol. 1. Place and publisher unknown, 2009.

al-Hindukushi, Abu al-Shukara. *mudhakkarati min kabul ila baghdad, al-juz 1–9.* Place and publisher unknown, 2007. Accessed via *Archive* on February 5, 2016. https://archive.org/details/@alhindkoshi

"ibn ladin yahudd al-pakistaniyyin ala da'm harakat 'taliban'." al-Hayat, November 19, 1998.

Isma'il, Jamal Abd al-Latif. *bin ladin wa al-jazira wa ... ana.* Place unknown: Dar al-Huriya, 2001.

Ittihad Ulama Afghanistan. *"al-fatwa bi-sha'n ikhraj usama bin ladin."* 3 Sha'ban 1420 [November 11, 1999]. In *al-mizan li-harakat taliban* by Yusuf al-Uyayri. Place unknown: Markaz al-Dirasat wa al-Buhuth al-Islamiyya, 2001, 76–77. Accessed via *Jihadi Document Repository* on March 4, 2016. www .hf.uio.no/ikos/english/research/jihadi-document-repository/

"kunt jaran li-abu mus'ab al-zarqawi." Shabakat Ana al-Muslim, June 27, 2006. Accessed March 8, 2016. www.muslm.org/vb/showthread .php?167769

"ma'a al-shuhada'." Al-Jihad 77 (April/May 1991): 46–47.

al-Maqdisi, Abu Ubayda. *shuhada' fi zaman al-ghurba.* Place unknown: Al-Fajr Media Center, 2008. Accessed via al-Ikhlas on February 4, 2008. www .alekhlaas.net/

*mawsu'at al-jihad, al-juzz al-awwal: al-amn wal-istikhbarat.*2nd electronic edition. Afghanistan: Maktab al-Khidamat, 1424 H. [2003].

Muhammad, Basil. *al-ansar al-arab fi afghanistan.* 2nd edition. Riyadh: Lajnat al-Birr al-Islamiyya, 1991.

Muhammad, Fadil Abdallah. See Harun, Fadil.

Munib, Abu al-Harith. *"al-shaykh haqqani fi hadith ma'a manba' al-jihad."* *Manba' al-Jihad* 2, no. 18, 18–20.

Munib, Wazir Ahmad. *"al-shaykh yunus khalis li-manba' al-jihad."* *Manba' al-Jihad* 2, no. 18, 22–24.

Omar, Mullah Muhammad. *"radd amir al-mu'minin ala risala."* 3 Sha'ban 1420 [November 11, 1999]. In *al-mizan li-harakat taliban* by Yusuf al-Uyayri. Place unknown: Markaz al-Dirasat wa al-Buhuth al-Islamiyya, 2001, 77–78. Accessed via *Jihadi Document Repository*, University of Oslo, March 4, 2016. www.hf.uio.no/ikos/english/research/jihadi-document-repository/

"al-safir al-afghani fi al-qahira: ibn ladin mawjud fi mantiqat taliban." al-Hayat, February 20, 1999.

Salah, Muhammad. *"'al-jabha al-islamiyya al-alamiyya': tahdhirat jadida lil-amirikyyin. albright tutalib 'taliban' bi-taslim usama bin ladin."* al-Hayat, August 19, 1998.

"taliban tanfi anba' an itlaq rusas ma'a hurrasihi. afghanistan: ibn ladin yu'awid al-zuhur qariban." al-Hayat, May 3, 1999.

waqa'i' sanawat al-jihad: rihlat al-afghan al-arab. Cairo: Khulud lil-Nashar, 2001.

Salim, Muhammad. *"al-yawm tahrir al-muslimin wa ghadan iqamat al-khilafa al-islamiyya."* al-Jihad, no. 119 (March 1995): 20.

Sandarusi, Hassan and Muhammad Salah. *"tazahurat fi duwal arabiyya wa islamiyya. rusia wa al-sin wa al-yapan tantaqidu al-ijra' al-amiriki. britanya wa faransa tu'ayyidan...,"* al-Hayat, August 22, 1998.

"al-sa'udiyya taqta' ilaqatiha al-diblumasiyya ma'a taliban li-istimrariha fi istikhdam aradiha li-iwa' al-irhabiyyin." al-Sharq al-Awsat, September 26, 2001. Accessed March 12, 2011, www.aawsat.com/details.asp?section=4&article=58797&issueno=8338

al-Shu'aybi, Hamud bin Uqla. *"su'al an shara'iyyit hukumat al-taliban."* 02/09/1421 H. [November 28, 2000]. Accessed September 17, 2015. www.aloglaa.com/?section=subject&SubjectID=180

al-Suri, Abu Mus'ab. *afghanistan wa al-taliban wa ma'rakat al-islam al-yawm.* Kabul: Markaz al-Ghuraba' lil-Dirasat al-Islamiyya, 1998.

"muqabala ma'a sahifat al-ra'i al-amm al-kuwaytiyya." Transcript of Abu Mus'ab al-Suri's interview with journalist Majid al-Ali in Kabul, Afghanistan, 18 March 1999. Unpublished, courtesy Brynjar Lia.

da'wat al-muqawama al-islamiyya al-alamiyya. Place and publisher unknown, 2004. Accessed via *Jihadi Document Repository*, University of Oslo, March 4, 2016. www.hf.uio.no/ikos/english/research/jihadi-document-repository/

Tawil, Camille. *"al-suba'i lil-hayat: iran salamat majmu'a min al-masriyyin wa 12 a'ila min 'al-jama'a' adat tawwa'an."* al-Hayat, December 13, 2003.

"washington ta'udd qarar ittiham diddahu li-idfa' siffa qanuniyya ala mulahaqatihi. 'taliban' tarfud ardan amirikiyyan li-'hiwar' bi-sha'n usama bin ladin." al-Hayat, August 26, 1998.

Zaydan, Ahmad. *"ala amal tahqiq shurut al-i'tiraf al-dawli ba'd ibti'adiha an ibn ladin. taliban tuharrim al-mukhaddarat wa tatlaf mahasilaha."* al-Hayat, February 20, 1999.

"al-haraka a'tat al-aman li-ma la yaqill an 400 arabi wa rahabat bi-wujudihim. bin laden wa 'al-afghan al-arab' fi manatiq saytarat taliban." al-Hayat, October 5, 1996.

"al-ulama' al-afghan yabhathun fi mas'alat ibn ladin." al-Hayat, September 23, 1998.

"anba' an ma'arik fi dawahi qa'idat baghram shimal al-asima al-afghaniyya. ta'ira majhula taghir ala qawa'id muqatili haqqani fi kabul." al-Hayat, June 16, 1997.

"bin ladin yubayi'u za'im taliban." al-Jazeera, April 10, 2001.

"fi zill bawadir tahawwul fi al-siyasa al-pakistaniyya al-da'ima lil-haraka. bin ladin yuttafiq ma'a za'im 'taliban' ala tanfidh mashari' fi al-janub." al-Hayat, March 6, 1997.

"muhadathatahu shamilat al-irhab wa al-mukhaddarat wa huquq al-mar'a … wa mudifu bin ladin qallalu min ahamiyyat tahdidatihi. richardson fi afghanistan aqna'a 'taliban' bi-hudna li-bad' al-hiwar." al-Hayat, April 18, 1998.

"qafilat «landcruiser» sawda' tu'abbir ma'a marwahiyyatayn al-hudud al-pakistaniyya–al-afghaniyya: 350 min rijal bin [ladin] li-yuqatilun fi shimal kabul." al-Hayat, July 14, 1997.

"shukuk fi muwafaqat amirika … wa al-iraq wa al-shishan wajhatan muhtamilatan. ibn ladin yuwafiq ala mughadarat afghanistan shart an tatakattam taliban ala makanihi." al-Hayat, October 30, 1999.

"'taliban' ahatat al-liqa' bi-ajwa' min al-takattum. ibn ladin istaqbal wafdan min ulama' al-yaman." al-Hayat, November 30, 1998.

"'taliban' ajilat fi naqlihi wa hadharatu min hajamat. bin ladin fi qandahar ba'idan an al-sahafa wa hirsan ala amnihi." al-Hayat, April 8, 1997.

"'taliban' tastanjid bi-tulabihi wa hizb yunus. al-umam al-muttahida tu'akkid qatal shi'a fi kabul." al-Hayat, June 1, 1997.

Zaydan, Ahmad and Turki al-Dakhil. *"mas'ud yuballigh 'al-hayat' asr askariyyin pakistaniyyin fi shimal kabul. tawaqqu' darba amirikiyya jadida li-'taliban' bi-sabab ibn ladin."* al-Hayat, October 21, 1998.

al-Zawahiri, Ayman. *fursan tahta rayat al-nabi.* First edition. Place unknown: Minbar al-Tawhid wal-Jihad, 2001. Accessed via *Jihadology* on February 5, 2016. https://azelin.files.wordpress.com/2010/11/ayman-al-zawahiri-knights-under-the-prophets-banner-first-edition.pdf

fursan tahta rayat al-nabi. 2nd edition. Place unknown: al-Sahab, 2010. Accessed via *Jihadology* on February 5, 2016. https://azelin.files.wordpress.com/2010/11/ayman-al-zawahiri-knights-under-the-prophets-banner-second-edition.pdf

al-tabri'a: risala fi tabri'at ummat al-qalam wa al-sayf min munqissat tuhmat al-khawa wa al-da'f . Place and publisher unknown, 2008. Accessed via *Jihadi Document Repository,* University of Oslo, March 4, 2016. www.hf.uio.no/ikos/english/research/jihadi-document-repository/

ENGLISH PRIMARY SOURCES

"A terrorist's testimony [Ahmed Ressam's testimony before the Federal District Court of the Southern District of New York, July 2001]." *PBS Frontline*, undated. Accessed December 17, 2010. www.pbs.org/wgbh/pages/frontline/shows/trail/inside/testimony.html

Abu Zubaydah. *The Abu Zubaydah Diaries, vol. 1–6*. Translated to English by the Federal Bureau of Investigation, US Department of Justice. Published by *al-Jazeera*, December 3, 2013. Accessed May 21, 2015. http://america.aljazeera.com/multimedia/2013/11/original-documentstheabuzubaydahdiaries.html

"Afghan factions alliance to have no effect on Nangrahar govt." *Business Recorder*, May 19, 1996.

"Afghan rebel gains against Soviets reported by U.S. aide." *Washington Post*, July 6, 1987. Accessed via *Los Angeles Times* on February 10, 2016. http://articles.latimes.com/1987-07-06/news/mn-1274_1_soviet-troops

"Afghan Ulema declare death for Arab warlord." Dawn archive, June 21, 1996.

"America must give up its irrational attitude. An interview with Minister of Information of the Islamic Emirate of Afghanistan, Maulavi Qudratullah." *Taleban Home Page, New York Office*, July 19, 2000. Accessed via *Internet Archive*, http://web.archive.org/web/20010205154600/www.taleban.com/interviews.htm

Berger, J. M. Editor. *Beatings and Bureaucracy: The Founding Memos of Al Qaeda*. N.p.: Intelwire Press, 2012.

Benevolence International: Court documents concerning an al Qaeda-linked charity front based in Chicago, Ill. N.p.: Intelwire Press, 2006.

Ali Mohamed: Documents, transcripts and analysis regarding al Qaeda's most dangerous sleeper agent. N.p.: Intelwire Press, 2006.

Bin Laden, Osama. "Transcript of Usama bin Laden video tape." Text of conversation between Osama bin Laden and Shaykh Khaled al-Harbi in Afghanistan on November 7, 2001. Translated by George Michael and Kassem M. Wahba on December 13, 2001. Unpublished. Courtesy Norwegian Government.

"Concern at reactivation of Afghan militant camps." *The News*, November 22, 1996.

Cullison, Alan. "Inside al-Qaeda's hard drive: Budget squabbles, baby pictures, office rivalries – and the path to 9/11." *The Atlantic Monthly*, September 2004.

Cullison, Alan and Andrew Higgins, "Once-stormy terror alliance was solidified by cruise missiles." *Wall Street Journal*, August 2, 2002.

"Eng. Hekmatyar proposes a united Islamic force for the Muslim world." *The Mujahideen* 4, no. 3 (September/October 1990): 8.

Farivar, Masood. *Confessions of a Mullah warrior*. New York: Atlantic, 2009.

Fisk, Robert. "Muslim leader warns of a new assault on US forces." *The Independent*, March 22, 1997.

"The man who wants to wage holy war against the Americans." *The Independent*, March 22, 1997.

Grenier, Robert. *88 days to Kandahar: a CIA diary*. New York: Simon & Schuster, 2015.

Hamid, Mustafa. *The history of the Arab Afghans from the time of their arrival in Afghanistan until their departure with the Taliban.* Serialized in *al-Sharq al-Awsat*, December 8–14, 2004. Translated to English by Foreign Broadcast Information Service (FBIS).

Hamid, Mustafa and Leah Farrall. *The Arabs at war in Afghanistan.* London: Hurst, 2015.

al-Hammadi, Khalid. "Al-Qa'ida from within, as narrated by Abu-Jandal (Nasir al-Bahri)." Part 1-10. Originally published in Arabic in *al-Quds al-Arabi* March 20 – April 4, 2005. Translated to English by Foreign Broadcast Information Service (FBIS).

Hegghammer, Thomas. *Dokumantasjon om al-Qaida: Intervjuer, kommunikéer og andre primærkilder, 1990–2002* [Documentation on al-Qaida: Interviews, communiqués and other primary sources, 1990–2002]. Kjeller: Norwegian Defence Research Estabslishment (FFI), 2002.

    Al-Qaida statements 2003–2004: A compilation of translated texts by Osama bin Laden and Ayman al-Zawahiri. Kjeller: FFI, 2005.

Hikmatyar, Gulbuddin. *Secret plans, open faces: From the withdrawal of Russians to the fall of the coalition government.* Transl. by Sher Zaman Taizi. Peshawar: Area Study Centre, 2004.

Hirschkorn, Phil, and Peter Bergen. "Rare photos reveal Osama bin Laden's Afghan hideout." *CNN*, March 11, 2015.

"I am not afraid of death [Jamal Isma'il's interview with Osama bin Laden on 22 December 22, 1998]." *Newsweek*, January 11, 1999.

Imran, Mohammad Ali. "Afghan Ulema declare death for Arab warlord." *The Muslim*, June 21, 1996.

"Iran opens consulate in Jalalabad." *The Muslim*, June 10, 1996.

Iqbal, Anwar. "Bin Laden forms a new Jihadi group." *United Press International*, June 26, 2001.

"Jalalabad reaps economic reward of local peace." *The Muslim*, July 10, 1996.

Khan, Behroz. "Saudi Arabia seeking deportation of bin-Laden from Afghanistan." *The News*, March 3, 1997.

Khan, Ismail. "Arab group threatens war against 'evil West, Muslim proteges'." *The News*, May 14, 1996.

"Little comfort for families of Mujahideen." *Pakistan Times*, July 12, 1996.

Miller, John, Michael Stone and Chris Mitchell. *The cell: inside the 9/11 plot and why the FBI and CIA failed to stop it.* New York: Hyperion, 2002.

Murshed, S. Iftikhar. *Afghanistan: The Taliban years.* London: Bennett and Bloom, 2006.

Nasiri, Omar. *Inside the Jihad: My life with Al Qaeda.* New York: Basic Books, 2006.

"New Afghan line-up." *The News*, May 15, 1996.

"Radical Arabs use Pakistan as base for Holy War." *New York Times*, April 8, 1993.

Sasson, Jean, Najwa bin Laden and Omar bin Laden. *Growing up Bin Laden: Osama's wife and son take us inside their secret world.* Oxford: Oneworld, 2009.

Schroen, Gary C. *First in: An insider's account of how the CIA spearheaded the war on terror in Afghanistan.* New York: Presidio Press, 2005.

Shaikh, Shakil. "Taliban to hand over 150 terrorists to Pakistan." *The News,* October 6, 1999.

The Destruction of the American Destroyer USS Cole. Al-Sahab, 2001. Arabic with English subtitles. Accessed via *FFI's Jihadi Video Database,* Kjeller, Norway. Videos no. 647 and 648.

al-Suri, Abu Mus'ab and Abu Khalid al-Suri. "Noble brother Abu-Abdallah [Letter to Osama bin Laden dated July 17, 1998]." Unpublished, courtesy Brynjar Lia, Andrew Higgins, and Alan Cullison.

"Transcript of Usama bin Laden video tape." US Department of Defense, December 13, 2001. Accessed May 19, 2011. www.defense.gov/news/Dec2001/ d20011213ubl.pdf

Yusufzai, Rahimullah. "The best story of my carreer." *Newsline,* January 10, 2010.

Zaeef, Abdul Salam. *My life with the Taliban.* London: Hurst, 2010.

PRIMARY SOURCES IN OTHER LANGUAGES

Исломий Амирликнинг кулаши *[The Fall of the Islamic Emirate; Uzbek].* Islamic Movement of Uzbekistan homepage, accessed September 26, 2014. On file with author.

El Aroud, Malika. *Les soldats de lumière [Soldiers of Light; French],* Dépôt légal: D/2003/9625/2, Imprimé en Belgique. Electronic version.

Mojdeh, Vahid. *Afghanistan wa panj sal sultah taliban [Afghanistan under five years of Taliban sovereignty; Persian].* 2nd ed. Tehran: Nashreney, 1382 h. Translated from Persian by Sepideh Khalili and Saeed Ganji. Unpublished, 2003.

Mutawakil, Wakil Ahmad. *Afghanistan aw Taliban [Afghanistan and the Taliban; Persian].* Place and publisher unknown, 1384 h. [2005]. Excerpts of the book are translated by Naeem Saddeqi (unpublished, 2011).

Omar, Mullah Mohammad. *Qawanin mulla omar: Majmua qawanin taliban dar afghanistan [The Laws of Mullah Omar: Collection of the Taliban's Laws in Afghanistan; Persian].* Tehran: Negah Amroz, 1381 h. Translated by Faezeh Robinson (unpublished, 2011).

Saqib, Allama Arshad Hassan. "Delightful facts." Translated from Urdu by Noshad Mehsud. *Al-Arshad,* vol. and date unknown, 50–57. Accessed via *PIPS Compendium 1.*

Von Follath, Erich and Stefan Aust. "Und dann schrie Mullah Omar [And then screamed Mullah Omar; German]. *Der Spiegel* 11, 2004: 118–122.

ARCHIVES CONSULTED

"Bin Laden's Bookshelf." *Office of the Director of the National Intelligence,* Washington, DC. www.dni.gov

"The Harmony Program." *Combating Terrorism Center,* West Point, NY. Accessed online. www.ctc.usma.edu/programs-resources/harmony-program (January 29, 2016).

"Al-Qaeda and Associated Movements Collection." *The Conflict Records Resource Center*. National Defense University, Washington, DC.

"The Guantanamo Files." *Wikileaks*. Accessed online. http://wikileaks.ch/gitmo/ (July 31, 2012).

"The September 11th Sourcebooks," *The National Security Archive*. Accessed online. www.gwu.edu/~nsarchiv/NSAEBB/sept11/ (February 24, 2011).

Pak Institute of Peace Studies (PIPS), Islamabad, Pakistan. Sources referred to here as *PIPS Compendium 1 and 2*.

FFI's Jihadi Video Database. Norwegian Defence Research Establishment (FFI), Kjeller, Norway.

Dawn archive, 1993-2001 (including newspaper clippings from *Business Recorder, The News, The Muslim, Pakistan Times* and *United Press International*). Karachi, Pakistan.

Al-Hayat electronic archives, 1994–2001.

Afghan Islamic Press Online, 1992–2001.

Al-Quds al-Arabi electronic archives, 1998–2001.

CAPTURED DOCUMENTS

"06 Ramadan." November 11, 2002. From "Bin Laden's Bookshelf, Declassified Material – May 20, 2015." *Office of the Director of the National Intelligence*, Washington, DC.

AFGP-2002-000091. "Notes from Abd al-Hadi." Undated. *Combating Terrorism Center*, West Point, NY.

AFGP-2002-000100. "This document contains a flyer addressed to all Arab immigrants. The flyer lists the Islamic Emirate officials' names that would assist the Arab immigrants in entering the Emirate." Undated. FMSO/Internet Archive. Accessed March 9, 2016. www.docexdocs.com/internetarchive/AFGP-2002-000100.pdf

AFGP-2002-000112. "Al-Qa'ida staff count public appointments." Undated. *Combating Terrorism Center*, West Point, NY.

AFGP-2002-001111, "Letters to Abu Khabab." Undated [ca. 1999]. *Combating Terrorism Center*, West Point, NY.

AFGP-2002–003677, "Ciphers and status of bin Laden's security." Undated *Combating Terrorism Center*, West Point, NY.

AFGP-2002–800321. "Information from the Military Committee Al-Mujahideen Affairs Office." Court filing, *Alsabri v. Obama*, United States District Court, District of Columbia, 2011. Accessed March 7, 2016. www.docexdocs.com/gtmo/AFGP-2002-800321-Original.pdf

AFGP-2002–801138. "Various admin documents and questions." Undated [circa June 3–Sept 22, 2000]. *Combating Terrorism Center*, West Point, NY.

"Al Adl letter." June 13, 2002. *Combating Terrorism Center* West Point, NY.

AQ-MCOP-D-000-041, "Letter from Abu Massab to Abu Khabab; An invitation to Sheikh Abu-Mussab al-Suri and Sheikh 'Isa al-Masri to attend a meeting, from the administration of the military camp of the strangers of Qargha Division." Undated [before September 19, 1999]. Conflict Records Resource Center, Washington, DC.

AQ-MCOP-D-000-916, "A letter from Abd al Hadi al-Ansari to Hasan al Ishmawi (2/2)," December 24, 2000. Conflict Records Resource Center, Washington, DC.

AQ-MCOP-D-000-917, "A letter from Abd al Hadi al-Ansari to Hasan al Ishmawi (1/2)," December 24, 2000. Conflict Records Resource Center, Washington, DC.

AQ-MCOP-D-000-922, "Personal letter regarding training and other issues from Abu Ataa al Sharqi to Abu Hafs." May 1, 1997, Conflict Records Resource Center, Washington, DC.

AQ-MCOP-D-001-149. "Al-Qaida letters." Undated [circa 1997]. Conflict Records Resource Center, Washington, DC.

AQ-MCOP-D-001-159. "The third report to Sudan," March 21, 1994, Conflict Records Resource Center, Washington, DC.

AQ-MISC-D-001-033, "Letter to Abu Khabab from Abu al-Bara'a," undated, Conflict Records Resource Center, Washington, DC.

AQ-MISC-D-001-034, "Recommendation letters to Abu Khabab to attend training at the toxin session and requests for aluminium powder and other materials for the toxin training, training requests for other brothers, and letters of other matters." February 27, 2000, Conflict Records Resource Center, Washington, DC.

AQ-MISC-D-001-264, "Abu Musab al-Suri's datebook from Afghanistan in 1999 with names and some addresses of al-Qaeda members, Taliban officials and others; mentions al-Qaeda guest house at Qargha." Undated [circa January 2000–March 2000], Conflict Records Resource Center, Washington, DC.

AQ-MSLF-D-000-037. "A letter in the form of a logistics and operations status report sent to Usama bin Laden," October 28, 1998. Conflict Records Resource Center, Washington, DC.

AQ-MSLF-D-000-824. "Weapons listing belonging to al-Qaida and other organizations," March 1998. Conflict Records Resource Center, Washington, DC.

AQ-MSLF-D-001-151, "Letter sent to Abu Hafs around 17/8/97, contains payment list, names and other information related to camps that belong to this organization." August 17, 1997. Conflict Records Resource Center, Washington, DC.

AQ-MSLF-D-001-422, "Top secret letter from Ahmed bin 'Abd al-Aziz to Abu Alfaraj, the subjects: The meeting of Chief of Staffs for the Security and Military Committees." December 7, 1998, Conflict Records Resource Center, Washington, DC.

AQ-MSLF-D-001-424, "A letter from 'Abd al-Hadi al-Ansari to Sheikh Taysir," November 8, 1997, Conflict Records Research Center, Washington, DC.

AQ-MSLF-D-001-509, "A letter by Abd al-Aziz to Abu Hafs inquiring about the condition of Osama Bin Laden following the publication of several news reports about the Taliban's intention to hand him over to the Saudi Government," April 23, 1997, Conflict Records Resource Center, Washington, DC.

AQ-PMPR-D-001-421. "Letter from Ahmad bin 'Abd al-'Aziz to 'Abd al-Hadi in regards to a meeting of the general staff of the Security and Military

Committee." December 7, 1998, Conflict Records Resource Center, Washington, DC.

AQ-PMPR-D-001-554. "Two letters to Osama bin Laden, one from Mowlawi Mohammed Yunis of the Islamic Party of Afghanistan and one from H. Ibn al-Sheikh," April 1, 1997, Conflict Records Resource Center, Washington, DC.

AQ-PMPR-D-001-837. "Al-Qa'eda recruitment and new personnel forms." April 25, 2001, Conflict Records Resource Center, Washington, DC.

AQ-POAK-D-000-017. "A daily activity report about Taliban battles." May 4, 1999. Conflict Records Resource Center, Washington, DC.

AQ-POAK-D-000-018. "Daily military report by Abd al Hadi al Ansari with details on a battle between the Taliban and the enemy on the front north of Kabul," May 8, 1999. Conflict Records Resource Center, Washington, DC.

AQ-SHPD-D-000-039. A letter from Abd al-Hadi al-Ansari to Abu Hafs, November 26, 1998. Conflict Records Resource Center, Washington, DC.

AQ-SHPD-D-000-089. "A letter sent from the leader of a military group called Abou Atta el Charki to his training chief Abou Hafsse," September 4, 1994, Conflict Records Resource Center, Washington, DC.

AQ-SHPD-D-000-809, "Loose pages of a book about Usama bin Laden," 1419 h [April 1998–April 1999]. Conflict Records Resource Center, Washington, DC.

AQ-SHPD-D-001-285, "Document contains al-Qaeda review of the 9/11 attacks on the United States one year later," undated (circa September 2002), Conflict Records Research Center, Washington, DC.

AQ-SHTP-D-000-103. "Letter to Abu Khalid from Abu Hafs Al-Masri about cooperation of Taliban, Al Qaida and Pakistan." Date unknown [circa March 1997–June 1997]. Conflict Records Resource Center, Washington, DC.

AQ-TBGD-D-000-003. "13 clauses concerning immigration policies for Taliban-era Afghanistan." Undated [circa January–March 2000], Conflict Records Resource Center, Washington, DC.

AQ-TBGD-D-001-153. "Report on camps," date unknown, Conflict Records Resource Center, Washington, DC.

AQ-TRED-D-000-924. "Report by Abu 'Ataa' Al-Sharqi evaluating training programs between Al-Qaida and Tajik mujahideen with recommendations for improvements," January 13, 1994, Conflict Records Resource Center, Washington, DC.

AQ-TRED-D-000-996. "Description of several courses in al-Qaeda training program for new recruits." Undated [ca. 1998–2001]. Conflict Records Resource Center, Washington, DC.

AQ-TRED-D-001-406. "Various topics pertaining to al-Qaida operations and possibly al Farouq from personnel, weapons, equipment, training etc." Undated. Conflict Records Resource Center, Washington, DC.

"Islamic Movement of Uzbekistan (IMU) letter detailing the establishment of the IMU's Bukhari Camp." July 20, 2001. Combating Terrorism Center, West Point, NY.

"To our respected Shaykhs." From "Bin Laden's Bookshelf, Declassified Material – March 1, 2016." Office of the Director of the National Intelligence, Washington, DC.

US DEPARTMENT OF DEFENSE

AF-000782. "Recommendation for Continued Detention Under DoD Control (CD) for Guantanamo Detainee, US9AF-000782DP [Awal Gul]." Department of Defense (Joint Task Force Guantanamo), February 15, 2008.

GZ-010016. "Recommendation for Continued Detention Under DoD Control (CD) for Guantanamo Detainee, ISN US9GZ-010016DP [Abu Zubaydah]." Department of Defense (Joint Task Force Guantanamo), November 11, 2008.

KU-00028. "Recommendation for Continued Detention Under DoD Control (CD) for Guantanamo Detainee, ISN: US9KU-000228DP [Abdullah Kamel Abdullah]." Department of Defense (Joint Task Force Guantanamo), December 27, 2005.

LY-000194. "Recommendation for Continued Detention Under DoD Control (CD) for Guantanamo Detainee, ISN: US9LY-000194DP [Muhammad Abdallah Mansur Al-Rimi]." Department of Defense (Joint Task Force Guantanamo), March 8, 2006.

LY-000557. "Update Recommendation to Transfer to the Control of Another Country for Continued Detention (TRCD) for Guantanamo Detainee, ISN: US9LY-000557DP [Abu Sufian Ibrahim Ahmed Hamouda]." Department of Defense (Joint Task Force Guantanamo), April 22, 2005.

LY-000708. "Recommendation for Continued Detention Under DoD Control (CD) for Guantanamo Detainee, ISN US9LY-000708DP [Ismael Ali Bakush]." Department of Defense (Joint Task Force Guantanamo), January 22, 2008.

MO-000075. "Update Recommendation to Transfer to the Control of Another Country for Continued Detention (TRCD) for Guantanamo Detainee, ISN: US9MO-000075D [Lahassimi Najib]." Department of Defense (Joint Task Force Guantanamo), June 3, 2005.

MO-000244. "Recommendation for Continued Detention Under DoD Control (CD) for Guantanamo Detainee, ISN US9MO-000244DP [Abdulatif Nasser, aka Abu al-Harith]." Department of Defense (Joint Task Force Guantanamo), October 22, 2008.

SA-000063. "Recommendation for Continued Detention Under DoD Control (CD) for Guantanamo Detainee, US9SA-000063DP [Maad al-Qahtani]." Department of Defense (Joint Task Force Guantanamo), February 15, 2008.

SA-000196. Recommendation for Continued Detention Under DoD Control (CD) for Guantanamo Detainee, ISN US9SA-000196DP [Musa al-Amri]." Department of Defense (Joint Task Force Guantanamo), March 31, 2007.

SA-000199. Recommendation for Continued Detention Under DoD Control (CD) for Guantanamo Detainee, ISN: US9SA-000199DP [Jabd Al Rahman Maath

Thafir Al Umari]." Department of Defense (Joint Task Force Guantanamo), May 5, 2006.

SA-000669. "Response to the Designated Civilian Official (DCO) Decision to Transfer Guantanamo Detainee, AL ZUHAYRI, AHMAD ZAYID SALIM, ISN US9SA-000669DP." Department of Defense (Joint Task Force Guantanamo), December 29, 2008.

SA-000713. "Detainee Assessment Brief ICO Guantanamo Detainee, ISN US9SA-000713DP [Mohammed Muti-Zahran]." Department of Defense (Joint Task Force Guantanamo), July 4, 2008.

SA-000768. "Recommendation to Retain under DoD Control (DoD) for Guantanamo Detainee, ISN: US9SA-000768 [Ahmed al-Darbi]. Department of Defense (Joint Task Force Guantanamo), October 1, 2004.

SA-010015. "Combatant Status Review Tribunal Input and Recommendation for Continued Detention Under DoD Control (CD) for Guantanamo Detainee, ISN: US9SA-010015DP [Abd al-Rahim al-Nashiri], Department of Defense (Joint Task Force Guantanamo), December 8, 2006.

SY-000489. "Detainee Assessment Brief ICO Guantanamo Detainee, ISN US9SY-000489DP [Abd Al Rahim Abdul Raza Janko]." Department of Defense (Joint Task Force Guantanamo), June 30, 2008.

YM-0001457. "Detainee Assessment Brief ICO Guantanamo Detainee, ISN PK9YM-0001457DP [Abdu Ali Sharqawi, aka Riyadh the Facilitator]." Department of Defense (Joint Task Force Guantanamo), July 7, 2008.

YM-000242. "Recommendation for Continued Detention Under DoD Control (CD) for Guantanamo Detainee, ISN US9YM-000242DP [Khaled Ahmad]." Department of Defense (Joint Task Force Guantanamo), April 7, 2008.

YM-000689. "Recommendation for Continued Detention Under DoD Control (CD) for Guantanamo Detainee, ISN US9YM-000689DP [Mohammed al-Hatabi]. Department of Defense (Joint Task Force Guantanamo), May 12, 2008.

YM-000837. "Recommendation for Continued Detention Under DoD Control (CD) for Guantanamo Detainee, ISN US9YM-000837DP [Bashir Nasir Ali al-Marwalah]." Department of Defense (Joint Task Force Guantanamo), May 30, 2008.

YM-010014. "Combatant Status Review Tribunal Input and Recommendation for Continued Detention Under DoD Control (CD) for Guantanamo Detainee, ISN: US9YM-010014DP [Walid bin Attash]." Department of Defense (Joint Task Force Guantanamo), December 8, 2006.

US DEPARTMENT OF STATE

Department of State (Islamabad) Cable. "Afghanistan: Bin Laden reportedly in Jalalabad." October 14, 1996. Accessed March 2, 2016. https://wikileaks.org/plusd/cables/96ISLAMABAD8679_a.html

Department of State (Islamabad) Cable. "Afghanistan: Taliban asserts "Arabs" have fled training camps; bin Laden's whereabouts unknown," September

19, 1996. Accessed March 2, 2016. https://wikileaks.org/plusd/cables/96ISLAMABAD8055_a.html

Department of State (Islamabad) Cable. "Afghanistan: Taliban official confirms that Mullah Omar asked bin Laden to refrain from "anti-Saudi" activities." March 27, 1997. Accessed March 3, 2016. https://wikileaks.org/plusd/cables/97ISLAMABAD2488_a.html

Department of State (Islamabad) Cable. "Afghanistan: Tensions reportedly mount within Taliban as ties with Saudi Arabia deteriorate over bin Laden." September 28, 1998. *National Security Archive.*

Department of State (Islamabad) Cable. "Afghanistan: The enigmatic Mullah Omar and Taliban descision-making." March 28, 1997. Accessed February 29, 2016. https://wikileaks.org/plusd/cables/97ISLAMABAD2533_a.html

Department of State (Islamabad) Cable. "Osama bin Laden: Charge underscores U.S. concerns on interviews; Taliban envoy says bin Laden hoodwinked them and it will not happen again," December 30, 1998. *National Security Archive.*

Department of State (Islamabad) Cable. "Osama bin Laden: Taliban spokesman seeks new proposal for resolving bin Laden problem." November 28, 1998. *National Security Archive.*

Department of State (Islamabad) Cable. "Pakistan/Afghanistan reaction to U.S. air strikes," August 24, 1998. *National Security Archive.*

Department of State (Peshawar) Cable. "Afghanistan: Taliban agree to visits of militant training camps, admit bin Ladin is their guest," January 9, 1997. *National Security Archive.*

Department of State (Peshawar) Cable. "Afghanistan: Taliban stall in permitting Western journalists access to Osama bin Laden," November 11, 1996. Accessed February 29, 2016. https://wikileaks.org/plusd/cables/96PESHAWAR1059_a.html

Department of State (Washington) Cable. "Afghanistan: Taliban's Mullah Omar's 8/22 Contact with State Department," August 23, 1998. *National Security Archive.*

Department of State (Washington) Cable. "Afghanistan: Meeting with the Taliban," December 11, 1997. *National Security Archive.*

Department of State (Washington) Cable. "Afghanistan: Taliban convene Ulema, Iran and bin Ladin on the agenda," September 25, 1998. *National Security Archive.*

Department of State (Washington) Cable. "Afghanistan: Whereabouts of extremist supporter Osama bin Laden." September 4, 1996. Accessed February 29, 2016. https://wikileaks.org/plusd/cables/96STATE183372_a.html

Department of State (Washington) Cable. "Afghanistan: Saudi polcouns says they still want bin Laden," May 5, 1997. Accessed March 3, 2016. https://wikileaks.org/plusd/cables/97STATE83213_a.html

Department of State (Washington) Cable. "Demarche to the Taliban on terrorism," September 18, 1996. Accessed March 1, 2016. https://wikileaks.org/plusd/cables/96STATE194868_a.html

Department of State (Washington) Cable. "Message to Mullah Omar," October 1, 1998. *National Security Archive.*

State Department Report. "U.S. Engagement with the Taliban on Osama Bin Laden." July 16, 2001. *National Security Archive.*

SECONDARY SOURCES

9/11 Commission report. New York: W. W. Norton, 2004.

Al-Qaida's (mis)adventures in the Horn of Africa. West Point, NY: Combating Terrorism Center, 2007. Accessed February 25, 2016. www.ctc.usma.edu/posts/al-qaidas-misadventures-in-the-horn-of-africa.

Andreassen, Tor Arne. "Hos Talibans læremester [Visiting the Taliban's mentor]." *Aftenposten,* October 19, 2001.

Ashour, Omar. *The de-radicalization of jihadists: Transforming armed islamist movements.* London: Routledge, 2009.

Atwan, Abdel Bari. *The secret history of al-Qa'ida.* London: Saqi Books, 2006.

Bell, Kevin. *Usama bin Ladin's "Father Sheikh": Yunus Khalis and the return of al-Qai'da's leadership to Afghanistan.* West Point, NY: Combating Terrorism Center, 2013. Accessed February 29, 2016. www.ctc.usma.edu/v2/wp-content/uploads/2013/05/CTC_Yunus-Khalis-Report-Final1.pdf.

Bergen, Peter and Paul Cruickshank. "Revisiting the early Al Qaeda: An updated account of its formative years." *Studies in Conflict and Terrorism* 35, no. 1 (2012): 1–36.

Bergen, Peter. *Holy War, Inc.: Inside the secret world of Osama bin Laden,* 4th edition. London: Phoenix, 2003.

The Osama bin Laden I know: An oral history of al-Qaeda's leader. New York: Simon & Schuster, 2006.

Brown, Vahid. "The facade of allegiance: Bin Laden's dubious pledge to Mullah Omar." *CTC Sentinel* 3 (1)(2010): 1–6.

Cracks in the foundation: Leadership schisms in al-Qa'ida from 1989–2006. West Point, NY: Combating Terrorism Center, 2007.

Brown, Vahid and Don Rassler. *Fountainhead of jihad: The Haqqani nexus, 1973–2012.* London: Hurst, 2013.

Burke, Jason. *Al Qaeda: The true story of radical Islam.* London: Penguin, 2004.

Champagne, Becky. Editor. "Anatomy of a Terrorist Attack: An in-Depth Investigation Into into the 1998 Bombings of the U.S. Embassies in Kenya and Tanzania." *Briefing paper, Matthew B. Ridgway Center, University of Pittsburgh,* 2005.

Coll, Steve. *The bin Ladens: Oil, money, terrorism and the secret Saudi world.* London: Penguin, 2009.

Ghost wars: The secret history of the CIA, Afghanistan, and bin Laden, from the Soviet invasion to September 10, 2001. New York: Penguin Press, 2004.

Cragin, R. Kim. "Early History of Al-Qa'ida." *The Historical Journal* 51, (4) (2008): 1047–1067.

Crews, Robert D., and Amin Tarzi. *The Taliban and the crisis of Afghanistan.* Cambridge, MA: Harvard University Press, 2008.

Dorronsoro, Gilles. *Revolution unending: Afghanistan 1979 to the present*. London: Hurst, 2005.

Federal Bureau of Investigation, "Adnan G. El Shukrijumah." Accessed March 7, 2016. www2.fbi.gov/wanted/terrorists/terelshukrijumah.htm.

Fergusson, James. *Taliban: The unknown enemy*. Cambridge, MA: Da Capo Press, 2010.

Fouda, Yosri and Nick Fielding. *Masterminds of terror: The truth behind the most devastating terrorist attack the world has ever seen*. Edinburgh: Mainstream Publishing, 2003.

Fury, Dalton. *Kill Bin Laden: a Delta Force Commander's account of the hunt for the world's most wanted man*. New York: St. Martin's Press, 2008.

Giustozzi, Antonio. *Koran, Kalashnikov and laptop: The neo-Taliban insurgency in Afghanistan*. London: Hurst, 2007.

Gohari, M. J. *The Taliban: Ascent to power*. Karachi: Oxford University Press, 2001.

Grau, Lester W. *The bear went over the mountain: Soviet combat tactics in Afghanistan*. 2nd ed. Washington DC.: National Defense University Press, 1996.

Griffin, Michael. *Reaping the whirlwind: The Taliban movement in Afghanistan*. London: Pluto Press, 2001.

Gunaratna, Rohan. *Inside al Qaeda: Global network of terror*. New York: Berkley, 2003.

Harpviken, Kristian Berg. *Social networks and migration in wartime Afghanistan*. Basingstoke: Palgrave Macmillan, 2009.

Hegghammer, Thomas. *Jihad in Saudi Arabia: Violence and pan-Islamism since 1979*. Cambridge: Cambridge University Press, 2010.

"Deconstructing the myth about al-Qa'ida and Khobar." *CTC Sentinel* 1 (3) 20–22.

Hopkirk, Peter. *The great game: The struggle for empire in central Asia*. New York: Kodansha, 1992.

Isby, David C. "Four battles in Afghanistan." *Soldier of Fortune*, April 1988, 32–34.

Jalali, Ali Ahmad, and Lester W. Grau. *The Other Side of the Mountain: Mujahideen Tactics in the Soviet-Afghan War*. Fort Leavenworth, KA: Foreign Military Studies Office, 1995.

Jenkins, Brian M. *Countering Al Qaeda: an appreciation of the situation and suggestions for strategy*. Santa Monica, CA: RAND, 2002.

Jones, Seth G. *Counterinsurgency in Afghanistan*. Santa Monica, CA: RAND Corporation, 2008.

Kazimi, Nibras. "The Caliphate attempted." *Current Trends in Islamist Ideology* vol. 7 (2008): 5–49.

Kilcullen, David. *The Accidental Guerrilla: Fighting small wars in the midst of a big one*. London: Hurst, 2009.

Lahoud, Nelly. *Beware of Imitators: al-Qa'ida through the lens of its Confidential Secretary*. West Point, NY: Combating Terrorism Center, 2012. Accessed February 5, 2016. www.ctc.usma.edu/posts/beware-of-imitators-al-qaida-through-the-lens-of-its-confidential-secretary.

Lia, Brynjar. *Architect of global jihad: The life of al-Qaida strategist Abu Mus'ab al-Suri*. New York: Columbia University Press, 2008.

Maley, William. Editor. *Fundamentalism reborn? Afghanistan and the Taliban*. London: Hurst, 1998.

Marsden, Peter. *The Taliban: War, religion and the new order in Afghanistan*. London: Zed Books, 1998.

McCants, Will. *The ISIS apocalypse: the history, strategy, and doomsday vision of the Islamic State*. New York: St. Martin's Press, 2015.

Nojumi, Neamatollah. *The rise of the Taliban in Afghanistan: Mass mobilization, civil war, and the future of the region* New York: Palgrave, 2002.

Rashid, Ahmed. *Taliban: Militant Islam, oil and fundamentalism in Central Asia*. New Haven: Yale University Press, 2000.

Taliban: Islam, oil and the new great game in central Asia. London: Tauris, 2002.

Rubin, Barnett R. *The fragmentation of Afghanistan: State formation and collapse in the international system*, 2nd edition. New Haven: Yale University Press, 2002.

Scheuer, Michael [Anonymous]. *Through our enemies' eyes: Osama bin Laden, radical Islam, and the future of America*. Washington DC.: Brassey's, 2003.

Scheuer, Michael. *Osama bin Laden*. New York: Oxford, 2011.

"Coalition Warfare, Part II: How Zarqawi Fits into Bin Laden's World Front," *Terrorism Focus* (April 28, 2005), https://jamestown.org/program/coalition-warfare-part-ii-how-zarqawi-fits-into-bin-ladens-world-front/.

Soufan, Ali. *The Black Banners,: The inside story of 9/11 and the war against al-Qaeda*. New York: W.W. Norton & Co., 2011.

Stenersen, Anne. *Brothers in Jihad: Explaining the relationship between al-Qaida and the Taliban, 1996–2001*. PhD dissertation, University of Oslo, 2012.

"Al-Qaeda versus Najibullah: Revisiting the role of foreign fighters in the battles of Jalalabad and Khost, 1989–92." In Scott Gates, and Roy Kaushik (eds.). *War and state-building in Afghanistan: Historical and modern perspectives* (London: Bloomsbury, 2014): 131–146.

Al-Qaeda's quest for weapons of mass destruction, 1996–2008: The history behind the hype. Saarbrücken: VMD, 2008.

Stenersen, Anne and Phillip Holtmann. "The three functions of UBL's "greater pledge" to Mullah Omar (2001–2006–2014)." *Jihadology*, January 8, 2015. http://jihadology.net/2015/01/08/guest-post-the-three-functions-of-ubls-greater-pledge-to-mullah-omar-2001-2006-2014/

Tawil, Camille. *Brothers in arms: The story of al-Qa'ida and the Arab jihadists*. London: Saqi Books, 2010.

Terrorism 2000/2001. Federal Bureau of Investigation, US Department of Justice. Accessed March 12, 2016. www.fbi.gov/stats-services/publications/terror/terror00_01.pdf.

"The investigation into the attack on the U.S.S. Cole." Report of the House Armed Services Committee Staff, May 2001. Accessed March 14, 2016. www.bits.de/public/documents/US_Terrorist_Attacks/HASC-colereport0501.pdf.

"U.S. missiles pound targets in Afghanistan, Sudan." *CNN*, August 20, 1998. Accessed March 28, 2011, http://edition.cnn.com/US/9808/20/us.strikes.01/

Van Linschoten, Alex Strick, and Felix Kuehn. *An enemy we created: The myth of the Taliban/Al Qaeda merger in Afghanistan, 1970–2010.* London: Hurst, 2012.

Wagemakers, Joas. *A quietist Jihadi: the ideology and influence of Abu Muhammad al-Maqdisi.* New York: Cambridge University Press, 2012.

Weaver, Mary Anne. "The short, violent life of Abu Musab al-Zarqawi." *The Atlantic,* June 8, 2006. Accessed March 8, 2006. www.theatlantic.com/magazine/archive/2006/07/the-short-violent-life-of-abu-musab-al-zarqawi/304983/.

Weiner, Tim. "Terror suspect said to anger Afghan hosts," *New York Times,* March 4, 1999. Accessed June 7, 2010, www.nytimes.com/1999/03/04/world/terror-suspect-said-to-anger-afghan-hosts.html?pagewanted=1.

Whitaker, Raymond. "Fall of Afghan city could spell end for Kabul." *The Independent,* September 12, 1996. Accessed February 29, 2016. www.independent.co.uk/news/world/fall-of-afghan-city-could-spell-end-for-kabul-1362913.html.

Wright, Lawrence. *The looming tower: Al-Qaeda and the road to 9/11.* New York: Knopf, 2006.

Yousaf, Mohammad and Mark Adkin. *The bear trap: Afghanistan's untold story.* London: Leo Cooper, 1992.

Index